D1005680

BRAVE GIRLS 365-DAY DEVOTIONAL

OTHER BOOKS IN THE BRAVE GIRLS BRAND

Brave Girls Holy Bible

Brave Girls Bible Stories

Brave Girls: Beautiful You

Brave Girls: Better Than Perfect

Brave Girls: Faithful Friends

BRAVE GIRLS 365 DEVOTIONAL

Written by Jennifer Gerelds
and Tama Fortner

Illustrated by Aleksey and Olga Ivanov

A Division of Thomas Nelson Publishers

Brave Girls 365-Day Devotional

Published in Nashville, Tennessee, by Tommy Nelson. Tommy Nelson is an imprint of Thomas Nelson. Thomas Nelson is a registered trademark of HarperCollins Christian Publishing, Inc.

Cover design by Micah Kandros Design

Illustrations by Aleksey and Olga Ivanov

This text includes material that has been adapted from previously published works in Tommy Nelson's Brave Girls series:

Beautiful You (Nashville: Nelson, 2015)
Better Than Perfect (Nashville: Nelson, 2015)
Faithful Friends (Nashville: Nelson, 2015)
The Brave Girls Bible (Nashville: Nelson, 2015)

Tommy Nelson titles may be purchased in bulk for educational, business, fund-raising, or sales promotional use. For information, please e-mail SpecialMarkets@ThomasNelson.com.

ISBN-13: 978-0-7180-8976-4

Library of Congress Cataloging-in-Publication Data

Names: Gerelds, Jennifer, author. | Ivanov, A. (Aleksey), illustrator.
Title: Brave girls 365-day devotional / written by Jennifer Gerelds and Tama Fortner ; illustrated by Aleksey and Olga Ivanov.
Description: Nashville : Thomas Nelson, 2016. | Includes bibliographical references and index.
Identifiers: LCCN 2016006132 | ISBN 9780718089764 (hardcover : alk. paper)
Subjects: LCSH: Girls--Prayers and devotions--Juvenile literature. | Devotional calendars--Juvenile literature.
Classification: LCC BV4860 .G46 2016 | DDC 242/.62--dc23 LC record available at https://lccn.loc.gov/2016006132

Printed in China

16 17 18 19 20 LEO 6 5 4 3 2 1

Mfr: LEO / Heshan, China / September 2016 / PO #9396052

With God's power working in us, God can do much, much more than anything we can ask or think of. To Him be glory.

EPHESIANS 3:20–21

Introduction

We have this hope, so we are very brave.

2 CORINTHIANS 3:12

If you had to name the top five bravest people you know, who would make the list? Maybe your mom or dad? A pastor? A teacher? A friend?

You?

Chances are, you've probably never thought of yourself as brave. After all, it's not likely that you've rescued someone from a burning building or saved someone from drowning (you know, all those heroic acts you've seen someone do on TV that everyone calls "brave"). No, you are just you, doing your school thing, going to church, and having fun with hobbies and friends. *No real need for bravery around here*, you might think.

Well, that's what the girls in our church youth group thought at first too. Hope, Glory, Honor, Gracie, and Faith—the girls you'll meet in the next few pages—didn't see anything really spectacular about their lives. A word like *bravery* was supposed to be saved for big-time heroes, not small-town, ordinary girls, right?

So when they all began studying how God used ordinary girls in the Bible to accomplish amazing things for His kingdom, they were blown away. Story after story showed how God worked incredible wonders whenever His girls simply followed His lead. It didn't take sensational abilities or outrageous events—just simple faith from regular people trusting an extraordinary God to do miraculous things.

Our youth group girls are all super excited to tell you what God has shown them about His brave Bible girls and the really cool ways He's helping them to be brave for God at school, at home, in their sports, with their friends—pretty much everywhere. It seems God didn't just make girls brave back then. He's still at it today. And now He's calling you. Ready for some action? Be brave and turn the page. It's time to get going!

And remember: it's His love that makes us strong.

Meet the Brave Girls

Hope

Ready for a game of football? Yeah, I know I'm a girl. And girls aren't supposed to play football, right? Well, you haven't seen me with my brothers. Every Saturday afternoon we're out in the yard playing flag football with our neighbors. And if it isn't football, it's soccer or softball. We even have a volleyball net! I guess that's one advantage to living on a farm outside of town—plenty of room to play hard.

I actually have a girly side to me that likes to dress up and be pretty and all that stuff. But give me a pair of broken-in jeans, a T-shirt, and a good group of friends, and I'm happier than a homecoming queen.

I guess you could say nothing in my life is all that fancy. Farm life just isn't that way. But I have a terrific family. I'm the oldest, and my two younger brothers are twins my parents adopted from the Ukraine when they were two years old. I love those guys, even though they bother me sometimes. We all work together around the farm and around

our church. We help out with the local charity too because we can't get over how good God has been to us. And sharing His hope with others? Well, it beats football any day.

I do admit that I have a challenge I don't like to talk about: reading. I do okay in school for the most part. But when I read, the letters get mixed up, and sometimes it looks like another language to me. They call it dyslexia. I call it embarrassing. But I do my best to remember that God can help me tackle this challenge. And He's where I'm learning to put my—you guessed it—hope!

Glory

If you could be anywhere in the world right now, where would you be? I'm kind of torn. Half of me would want to be on a high mountain somewhere, enjoying a beautiful sunset. Or maybe the beach, looking out across the sparkling waters. But the other half of me would be just as wonderstruck walking down the streets of New York City with my mom and sisters, shopping for all the latest fashions! I mean, you can never have enough boots, right? Or scarves and earrings and nail polish to match?

Yes, I know it might sound weird, but there is a common thread to everything I love: beauty! I love beauty wherever I see it: in this awesome world God created, in a gorgeous dress in a store window, and in the great hugs I get from my friends. I think God's beauty is everywhere—you just have to look for it.

Lately, I've had to look a little harder. Life at home wasn't so pretty, and just last summer my parents got divorced. For a while, I got really mad at God and forgot about the good in the world. But then my friends from the youth group started writing me encouraging notes and inviting me over. Their love and friendship was, well, beautiful—and it got me noticing all the other amazing ways God shows His love to me. I've started to see how God can take even the ugly, hard things in life and turn them into something good. I'm working on forgiving my parents and praying that God will use me to encourage other girls like me. You know, God can take even the messiest of situations and use them for His glory!

Honor

My friends say that whenever and wherever there's a challenge, I'm the one to take it! Maybe that's why I always pick up stray animals and bring them home. I love to care for my furry friends and figure out how to make them better. I'm always going to the library to find new books to help me in my animal rescue mission! In fact, I love to read books in general. Last summer I started volunteering at the library so that I could help other kids learn to love books too.

But my biggest challenge lately hasn't been at the library or with my five pets. It's been at school. Studying has always been easy for me, and I was thrilled when the principal said I could skip a grade. But I had a really hard time fitting in with the older kids. They didn't seem impressed with my intelligence, so at first I tried dressing and talking more like they did, even though I knew it didn't honor God. That didn't work either.

I just ended up feeling guilty and more out of place than ever. Turns out they weren't the kind of friends I needed anyway. It's a good thing God has given me an awesome youth group.

My leader and friends there have helped me remember who God says I am.

So who am I, really? You could say I'm God's girl, even though I don't *always* act like it. But I am learning how to honor Him more. And one day I hope to take all the abilities God has given me and use them, maybe to become a veterinarian or zoologist or something. Whatever I do, though, one thing's for sure: I want it all to honor God.

Gracie

Let's just say it's all by God's grace that I'm here. And I'm not just saying that because of my name. If it had been left up to me, I'd still be in my old hometown of Perkasie, Pennsylvania. We're talking beautiful green hills and parks on every street corner. I was born there, and I knew everybody (and everybody knew me).

And then we moved. I thought life was over. I wanted my old friends and old world back, and I was pretty stubborn and loud about it.

In my hometown, my family and I didn't talk about God much. But once we moved here, we started going to this church, and there were some girls in the youth group who were . . . nice. More than nice, really. They were cool. They liked to do fun stuff and all, but they also weren't afraid to talk about things that matter—like what we're supposed to do with our lives. I used to ask myself that question sometimes, like when I was walking through the woods by my house or listening to my music. These girls were able to show me the answer in the Bible. I always knew there had to be a

God who made all those beautiful things. Now I'm beginning to know who He is, thanks to God Himself, those girls, my church, and, yes, even my parents, who moved me here.

Wanna know something else kind of funny? The only time I ever sang back in Pennsylvania was in my shower at home. I loved it, but I was afraid to sing in public. Now I'm in the choir at church, and I'm singing about God to anybody who'll listen!

Faith

Have you ever known anybody who is homeschooled? If you haven't, now you do! My sister and I have been homeschooled all our lives. I miss my friends, but I still love learning at home because I have more time—to finish my work, to hang out, and to think. I've even used that time to start reading the Bible on my own because I really want to make God happy.

But to tell you the truth, I tend to try to please more than just God. I want everyone to like what I do, which has made me quite a perfectionist. Even though my name is Faith, I think a better name right now would be Worry because I'm always worried that I'm going to disappoint someone, including myself. The only time I get away from those thoughts is when I'm painting, my favorite hobby. Fortunately, I find lots of time for that, which is starting to pay off. I've been asked to help the younger kids with their art projects at camp this year, and I've even won some local art contests!

The girls in the youth group are helping me too, and I love spending time with them. They remind me that God already knows all about my mess-ups and sins but loves me anyway. I guess I'm learning that my faith is not a bunch of "dos and don'ts." It's about a relationship with God, who knows the *real* me, and He is working on me to make me more like Him. That's what real faith is all about—believing that God loves me, forgives me, and sees me as His very own work of art, no matter what!

The Youth Group

If God had thought we worked better alone, He wouldn't have invited so many people into His family. We need each other! Just like a body works best when all its parts are connected, God's family is the strongest when all His kids work and worship together.

But a funny thing often happens with a big group of people who spend a lot of time together. The people start to look the same. They dress the same, talk the same, and only welcome other people who are, well, just like them. Think about your body: Can you imagine if your nose decided to be an eye instead? And then, out of peer pressure, your ear became an eye, then your hands, and . . . you get the picture. You'd have a body of eyes without any ability to move, feel, taste, touch, or smell. Plus, you'd creep out a lot of people.

Each one of us has a special way to honor God and help others see Him in ways the rest of us can't on our own. But together, we're even stronger—which is a great part of God's plan.

That's what our youth group is all about: learning how to work together to know God better and to tell other people about Him too. We meet every week to talk, to learn what God is saying to us in the Bible, and to pray about anything and everything—together, the way God's family was meant to be. Want to join us?

When You Grow Up

Live the kind of life that honors and pleases the Lord in every way.

COLOSSIANS 1:10

What do you want to be when you grow up? An astronaut, a lawyer, a doctor, or a teacher? A mom, a ballerina, or a world-famous lion tamer?

That's a question you'll hear a lot over the next few years, and it's important to give it some serious thought. But no matter what sort of job you decide to do, it's even more important to decide *who* you want to be. Do you want to be God's child—or not? It's one or the other; there's really nothing in between.

So choose God. It really does matter, not only for heaven but also for here on earth. Choose God, and choose to be like His Son. Love and serve others. Be gentle with people, and treat them with goodness and kindness. Keep your promises, and keep the peace. Be patient both with others and yourself. That's *who* God wants you to be . . . both now and when you grow up.

Prayer Pointer

Lord, there are so many things I could be when I grow up. But more than anything, I want to be like Jesus.

JANUARY 2

You Are What You Wear

Clothe yourselves with the Lord Jesus Christ.
Forget about satisfying your sinful self.

ROMANS 13:14

"But Mom, I've just got to have those new boots before the party," Jessie pleaded.

"I'm sorry," her mom said. "They're just too expensive. Maybe for your birthday."

"But that's two months from now!"

"Why are these boots so important?" her mom asked.

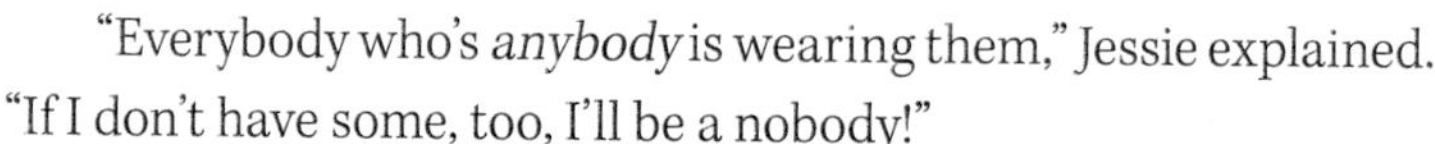

"Everybody who's *anybody* is wearing them," Jessie explained. "If I don't have some, too, I'll be a nobody!"

It's easy to feel like Jessie. You want to fit in, and you just know those boots, those jeans, or that shirt will help you. And the truth is, clothes won't help you make friends—at least not real ones who'll stick by you no matter what. But there *is* something you can wear that will help you make good and true friends—the attitude of Jesus. Wearing His kindness, thoughtfulness, patience, and serving heart will make an unforgettable style statement!

Prayer Pointer

Lord, help me remember to put on a Christlike attitude every day.

On a Role

In Christ we are all one body. Each one is a part of that body. And each part belongs to all the other parts.

ROMANS 12:5

How well would a car move if the tires were flat? What if the steering wheel were missing? Or the lights didn't work? A car only runs well if all the parts are there and doing their jobs.

The same goes for your family. God designed families to work with one another and to roll through the ups and downs of life together. Husbands and wives are to love and respect each other, and children are to respect and obey their parents. And God's Spirit is supposed to fuel us all.

You have an important role in your family. You can be an encourager by serving them. Speak the truth, but do it in love. Seek peace. Follow your parents' direction. And pray that God will help you and your family listen to His Spirit. Through prayer, obedience, and service, you are a powerful and important force of God's goodness, working in your family for God's glory.

Prayer Pointer

Lord, thank You for my family. Help me do my part in supporting and encouraging others.

What Really Matters

To God every person is the same. God accepts anyone who worships Him and does what is right. It is not important what country a person comes from.

ACTS 10:34–35

Hope dropped her backpack on the bus seat and huffed out a big sigh.

"What's wrong?" her friend asked.

"I heard some kids making fun of my little brothers," Hope said, "because they still have a little bit of a Ukrainian accent. Those kids even said some mean stuff about them being adopted. Can you believe that?"

Hope's friend shook her head sadly.

It's easy to look at others and see all the things that make them different from us. They don't look the same, sound the same, or dress the same. And some people use those differences as a reason not to like people, to make fun of them, or to bully them.

But all those differences don't matter one bit to God. It's what a person thinks and does and says that matter to Him. And as long as we try to do what's right, we are perfectly wonderful in God's sight.

Hope

Prayer Pointer

God, help me to see each and every person as someone You love.

Caught by Beauty

It is the evil that a person wants that tempts him. . . . This desire causes sin. Then the sin grows and brings death.

JAMES 1:14–15

JANUARY 5

If you hate spiders, you might want to move to Antarctica—it's the only place without them. Around the world, there are more than forty thousand species of spiders. That may sound creepy, but spiders actually help pollinate plants, keep the insect population down, and are a great source of food for birds, lizards, and other creatures. Some spiders, like the wolf spider and the giant huntsman (with a leg span of one foot!), chase their prey. But most spiders use spinnerets on their abdomens to create silk, which they weave into a sticky web to catch their meals.

Those webs can look beautiful, but watching a spider wrap and eat its prey can be horrifying. How can something so beautiful be so deadly? Sin operates the same way for us. It often looks beautiful and inviting, but sin is a trap just like a spider's web. The good news is that Jesus frees us from sin through His forgiveness and love. Stay away from sticky sin, and stick with Jesus instead!

Honor

PRAYER POINTER

Jesus, help me stay away from the trap of sin, and keep me close to You.

Morning Glory

[God's] mercies never stop. They are new every morning. Lord, your loyalty is great.

LAMENTATIONS 3:22–23

If you look all around this world God has made, you'll see that His creativity is amazing. Flowers are just one way He paints our world, showing us His character. One particularly interesting flower is the morning glory. Morning glories unfurl when the morning sun warms their petals. As long as the sun shines on them, the flowers stay open. But as evening approaches, the petals slowly close up until the next day.

Our spiritual hearts are a little like the morning glory. On our own in a cold, dark world, we stay closed up and afraid to be ourselves or reach out to others. But when we realize that God's love is shining down on us, we open up to Him, showing Him and the world the beautiful person He has made us to be. We bloom as long as we stay in God's light. And every day is a new day to soak up the warmth of His love.

Prayer Pointer

Lord, thank You for Your love that helps me open up to be the person You made me to be.

Stick to What's Good

Test everything. Keep what is good. And stay away from everything that is evil.

1 THESSALONIANS 5:21–22

W*ait . . . what?* Hannah couldn't believe her eyes. She and her new friend Serena were shopping at the mall. But she'd just seen Serena slip a candy bar inside her purse without paying!

"What are you doing?" Hannah hissed at her. "You didn't pay for that!"

"Oh, come on," Serena said, rolling her eyes. "It's no big deal. It's not like the store's going to go bankrupt over one candy bar."

"It's still stealing," Hannah said. "You have to put it back."

"Okay, already," Serena said, slipping the candy back onto the shelf.

Hannah's right. Stealing is wrong—and a sin—whether it's stealing a million dollars or a candy bar. The world often tries to tell us that wrong things are right, that "it's no big deal," or "everyone does it." But God's Word tells us what is right and what is wrong. We should stick to the right and stay far away from the wrong.

Prayer Pointer

Lord, show me what is good and what is evil. And please give me the strength to stay far away from evil.

JANUARY 8

Runway the Right Way

Help each other with your troubles. When you do this, you truly obey the law of Christ.

GALATIANS 6:2

Have you ever watched a fashion show? Typically, models walk down a raised platform wearing designer clothes. Just like any show, a lot of prep work happens beforehand. The stage must be set, lighting fixed, wardrobes chosen, and makeup applied. Lots of different people do lots of different jobs.

In the same way, everyone in your house has a job too—whether it's your parents going to work, your siblings cleaning the dishes, or you taking care of the family pets. God says one of the reasons He puts families together is so we can help carry one another's load. We can make life better for one another, which brings glory to God and joy to our hearts. What can you do to help your family be better prepared for the day ahead? Try these ideas or make up your own!

- Pray together about the day.
- Help make breakfast and clean the kitchen.
- Tell them something encouraging about themselves.
- Give them a hug and tell them you love them.

Glory

Prayer Pointer

Lord, help me lighten the load of others around me.

Tech Tools

Jesus said to the followers, "Go everywhere in the world. Tell the Good News to everyone."

MARK 16:15

There's a lot of talk about the Internet, texting, and social media these days and how bad they can be. And it's true! They can be addictive, and they can take time away from family, friends, and even God. But the Internet and social media are tools, and they can even be used *for* God. Try some of these tips for shining God's light into the digital world. (Remember: always get a parent's permission first, and never share personal information—like your name, address, or school—online.)

- Gather a group of friends and create an e-mail prayer list. Share prayer requests, praises, and answered prayers.
- Text people to say things like, "Have a great day," "Thinking of you," and "Happy Birthday."
- Pick out a Bible verse each day, and post it to your favorite social media site.

How else can you use technology as a tool for God?

Honor

Prayer Pointer

Lord, help me see all the ways I can use technology to tell more people about You.

Smile Power

Happiness makes a person smile.

PROVERBS 15:13

Samantha was feeling pretty down. She'd been looking forward to today's softball game, but now it was rained out. As she walked toward her mom's car, her friend Amanda flashed her a huge smile. As Samantha smiled back, she thought, *Hmm . . . I already feel a little bit better.*

Did you know that if you smile at someone, there's a pretty good chance that person will smile back? It's true! A smile is a powerful thing. Scientists say that a smile can relieve stress, make you look and feel more confident, *and* boost your immune system. Even if you're having a horribly bad day, smiling can help you feel just a little bit better.

Okay, so maybe a smile won't fix everything that's wrong, but it'll help you remember that you've always got things to smile about like family, friends, and a God who loves you. And a shared smile is even more powerful because all those good effects are multiplied. So give yourself a cheerful challenge: How many smiles can you share today?

Prayer Pointer

Lord, help me to smile and remember all the things I have to be happy about.

Knowing Jesus Better

"If someone wants to brag, let him brag about this: . . . that he understands and knows me."

JEREMIAH 9:24

When Jesus was on earth, many people heard about Him, some were able to hear Him speak, but it was Jesus' disciples who knew Him best. Why? Because they lived with Him, ate with Him, and walked with Him all day long. We get to know people better the more we spend time with them.

So how can we get to know Jesus even though He's in heaven now? We spend time with Him. We set aside time each day to read the Bible without other distractions. Then we talk to Jesus in prayer about the verses we've read and about what we're thinking and feeling.

And we can keep the conversation going all day long. When we see a beautiful sunset, we can thank Him. When we're nervous, we can ask Him to make us brave. Whatever is happening in our lives, we can share it with Jesus. When we do, we will soon see a beautiful friendship grow.

Prayer Pointer

Jesus, I want to walk with You today and every day.

Love It or Leave It

We will speak the truth with love. We will grow up in every way to be like Christ, who is the head.

EPHESIANS 4:15

We know it's not right to lie. But telling the truth isn't always easy, especially when the truth might hurt someone. You know what's even harder? Learning to tell the truth with God's love. Check out these scenarios, and see how you rank at truth-telling God's way: with love and humility.

1. Your friend's zipper is down. You:
   a. pretend nothing's wrong.
   b. start laughing uncontrollably and pointing.
   c. whisper the embarrassing fact in her ear.

2. The teacher is writing on the board, and you notice that she misspelled a word. You:
   a. blurt out to the class that she can't spell.
   b. laugh with your friends about her mistake.
   c. raise your hand and go up to her to tell her about the error.

3. Your best friend forgot your birthday. You:
   a. give her the silent treatment for a whole week.
   b. tell all your other friends how awful she is.
   c. wait until she's alone and admit that her forgetting really hurt your feelings.

4. You met a new girl at the park who doesn't think Jesus is real. You:
   a. get really angry and tell her she's stupid for not believing in Jesus.
   b. get scared of her and stop playing with her altogether.
   c. calmly and lovingly explain why you believe that Jesus is God's Son and continue to treat her with kindness and respect.

If you answered *C* for all of the above, then congratulations! You have learned the secret to sharing the truth with God's love. If you chose some other options, think of why those actions aren't very love-filled and can hurt others. Then pray and ask God to help you always tell the truth in love, just like how God speaks to you in His Word.

Prayer Pointer

Jesus, You were never afraid to tell the truth in love. Help me be like You.

A Team Effort

"If anyone wants to be the most important, then he must be last of all and servant of all."

MARK 9:35

"Wow! That was an awesome shot, Hope. You won the whole game!" cheered Ashley.

Hope *was* feeling pretty good about the game, and she *had* made the game-winning basket for her youth group's basketball team. She was just about to head off to celebrate with the other stars of the team when she noticed Sarah cleaning up all the water bottles from the bench. Sarah wasn't the greatest player, but she was a great friend.

"Come on, Hope!" her teammates called.

"Shouldn't we help clean up?" Hope asked.

"We're the stars," they said. "We don't have to clean up."

Hope looked at her teammates and then back at Sarah. "Go ahead," she said. "Sarah and I will be there in a minute." Then she smiled at Sarah and started picking up bottles.

Being the star is a great feeling, and everyone likes to feel important. But we should never feel too important to help and serve. Because when we serve others, that's when we truly shine.

Prayer Pointer

Hope

Thank You, God, for my moments to shine. And help me remember that I shine brightest when I'm helping someone.

We, Not Me

Make me very happy by having the same thoughts, sharing the same love, and having one mind and purpose.

PHILIPPIANS 2:2

JANUARY 14

What do the following scenarios have in common?

- My parents planned a family outing, but I want to spend the day with friends. I argue until my parents give in.
- My mom asked us to clean up the living room. But I'm trying to finish my game, so I keep playing, even though everyone else has started to clean.
- During worship at my church, everyone stands to sing together except me. I'd rather sit and play with the bulletin.

If you guessed "selfish thinking," then you're right! This girl is thinking only about herself, not the needs of her family or what God wants from her. But God didn't create us to care only for ourselves. Instead, He placed us in families, and He placed our families in the bigger family of believers.

God wants all His people to work together as a team, worshipping, serving, and loving each other. Why? Because there's no better way for the world to see God's love than to see His family caring for each other.

Honor

Prayer Pointer

Lord, help me fight my selfish ways and think like a team member instead.

Crown of Creation

God looked at everything He had made, and it was very good.

GENESIS 1:31

Can you imagine those first days of creation? With just a word, God filled the empty space with trees and plants, grass and mountains. Then He made animals—the sweet, fuzzy kind and the great, towering kind. Through the power of His incredible creativity, God made a spectacular world filled with life and color and beauty. And after each day of creation, God said that it was good. But after God made Adam and Eve, He said, "It's very good!"

From the beginning of time, God has been in love with His people. We are the crown of His creation. Even when sin entered the world, God's view of us didn't change. He wanted us to stay close to Him so much that He sent His own Son to die for our sins! Nothing can change God's mind about how great you are. In Jesus, each of God's children is His special treasure, a reflection of His glory, and the receiver of His never-ending love.

Prayer Pointer

Thank You, Jesus, for giving me such a special and honored place in Your heart.

Leah, Who Felt Unloved

You are precious to me. I give you honor, and I love you.

ISAIAH 43:4

Leah probably always knew her younger sister, Rachel, was prettier than she was. And it was Rachel who caught Jacob's attention and won his love. But after Jacob worked for seven years to marry Rachel, Leah and Rachel's father tricked Jacob into marrying Leah instead. This upset Jacob, of course, so he worked another seven years to marry Rachel. All her life, Leah knew she wasn't the prettiest or the most wanted. Yet God loved her. He chose her to be the mother of many of the first leaders of Israel. God had great plans for Leah. (Read more in Genesis 30:16–21.)

Maybe you can relate to Leah. Sometimes people can be mean and make us feel left out or unimportant. And if we believe other people look better than us, we can feel bad about ourselves. But Leah's story reminds us that we're all beautiful treasures in God's eyes, and He has promised us a future full of hope and love.

Prayer Pointer

Father, Your love for me means that I am special. Thank You for making me the way You did.

God's Ways Are Best

The Lord's ways are right. Good people live by following them, but those who turn against God die because of them.

HOSEA 14:9

Read the entire chapter of Hosea 14, which talks about the people of Israel coming back to the Lord. In the past the Israelites had believed in idols and other gods, and they had forgotten who the One True God is. But when they came back to Him, God promised not to be angry with them. He told them they would be protected and would prosper. God also reassured them that He would watch over them.

However, in verse 9 God also reminded them what happens if you turn away from Him. It might sound severe, but this verse is much simpler than it looks. It's saying that if you're wise, walking with God and living for Him isn't that difficult. With God's strength and guidance, right living will come naturally to you. But if you're committed to wrong living—selfishness, greed, rebellion—you'll always stumble on the path of life. In other words, following God's way helps people live good lives, but being rebellious makes a person trip and fall.

Prayer Pointer

Lord, help me keep my eyes on You and live in a way that pleases You.

Gifted

Those parts of the body that seem to be weaker are really very important.

1 CORINTHIANS 12:22

Scenario

Jasmine dazzled the teacher with her answer once again. Lizzy grumbled, "She's such a teacher's pet."

In PE, Jasmine showed her friends some new tricks she learned at gymnastics. While everyone else seemed impressed, Lizzy grew angrier. *I bet I can do more push-ups than she can.*

At home, Lizzy told her mom how annoying Jasmine was. "She's showing off all the time!"

Her mom answered, "It sounds like Jasmine is a pretty special girl. But you know what? God has made you special too. You don't have to compete with Jasmine."

Solution

God has given each of His kids gifts to use for building up His kingdom. He doesn't want us to look at others and wish that we had their looks or personality or skills. God made each of us exactly how He wants us to be. We just have to trust Him and thank Him for making us the way He did.

Prayer Pointer

Faith

Father, forgive me for comparing myself to others. Thank You for making me as You did. Please use my gifts to show Your glory, not mine.

Carried Away

The Lord takes care of His people like a shepherd. He gathers the people like lambs in His arms. He carries them close to Him.

ISAIAH 40:11

Have you ever had your mom or dad carry you? Maybe when you were younger, you were carried up to bed. Or perhaps you were feeling lost and small in a crowd, and your dad lifted you on his shoulders to see. Or maybe you were hurt, and your mom held you until you felt better. It's a wonderful feeling, isn't it?

That's what God does too. When we're tired, He scoops us up and carries us so that we can rest. When we're feeling small and not very important, He lifts us up and reminds us that we're always important to Him. And when we're hurt, He gathers us in His arms and carries us close to His heart until the hurt goes away.

Just like a loving parent takes care of a child, God takes care of His child—and that's you!

Prayer Pointer

Lord, when I'm feeling tired or lonely or hurt, please help me remember You're here with me to carry me through.

Better Than Blue Jeans

Religion that God the Father accepts is this: caring for orphans or widows who need help.

JAMES 1:27

Scenario

Ari and her mom worked hard on the yard sale, selling everything they no longer used. And it really paid off! They made more money than they'd anticipated, even more than Ari needed to buy those new, expensive jeans she wanted.

"What should we do with the leftover stuff and the extra money we made?" her mom asked, curious to see what Ari would say.

Solution

Though tempted to buy shoes and tops to go with her new jeans, Ari had another idea. She knew about a shelter for homeless women and children not too far from their home.

"Do you think they'd want any of these leftover things?" she asked.

"Sure!" her mom answered. "They could use the stuff or sell it at their thrift store."

That gave Ari another idea. "Do you think any of their kids need new clothes? We could use the extra money to help them get some new outfits too."

Prayer Pointer

Lord, help me remember the needs of others and not just myself.

JANUARY 21

Go and Tell

Because we loved you, we were happy to share God's Good News with you. But not only that, we were also happy to share even our own lives with you.

1 THESSALONIANS 2:8

Sharing your faith with a friend can seem scary at first, but try these tips to build your bravery:

- Always pray! Before you ever say a word, ask Jesus to make you brave and wise.
- Ask your friend some general, safe questions about spiritual things, such as "Do you go to a church around here?" or "What kind of things do they do at your church?"
- Get more personal. Ask her what she thinks about her church if she has one, or how she feels about not going.
- Then ask her about Jesus. Who does she say that He is? Is He just a made-up story to her? A good man? A crazy leader? Or the Son of God?
- Explain to her why you believe Jesus is the Son of God who saves you from your sins. Share your favorite verses.
- Ask her if she would like to come to church with you and learn more about Jesus.

Honor

PRAYER POINTER

Lord, use me to tell my friends about Jesus.

Better Together

Two people are better than one. . . . If one person falls, the other can help him up.

ECCLESIASTES 4:9–10

JANUARY 22

Can you imagine what the people in Noah's day must have thought when Noah started building a gigantic boat in the middle of dry land? Everybody probably told him he was crazy.

We know those folks weren't listening to God like Noah was. And their foolishness cost them their lives. Noah's story (Genesis 6–9) reminds us that being friends with God makes a lot more sense than listening to people who don't know Him.

What about you? Are there areas in your life where you are listening to the world instead of to God? How about your choices of music, television, or movies? Do your friends help you love God? Do the way you speak to your parents and the way you spend your free time honor God?

If not, ask God to forgive you, and pray for strength to stand strong like Noah. Join with Christian friends and help each other do the right things. By joining together in the fight against sin, you will stand even stronger.

Prayer Pointer

Hope

Father, help me love good and hate evil. Please give me friends who will help me stand strong.

Tabitha, the One Who Served

I will show you my faith by the things I do.

JAMES 2:18

Tabitha had been busy. She worked with the widows of her town, making robes and clothes and helping the poor around her. But one day, Tabitha died unexpectedly. Her widow friends were so sad! They were mourning and preparing for her burial when they remembered that Peter was in town. They sent for him, and Peter came.

He asked everyone to leave the room where Tabitha lay. Then he knelt beside Tabitha and prayed. Peter said, "Tabitha, get up." And she did! Tabitha was raised back to life to continue her life of love and service to God and His people (Acts 9:36–42).

Now take a moment to think about your life. What do you spend most of your time doing? Are you using your energy to serve God and help others, or do you spend it just on yourself? Ask God to give you a heart like Tabitha's, and start looking for little ways you can make the most of your day today.

Prayer Pointer

Lord, You have asked us to care for the poor, widowed, and orphaned. Show me how I can help.

Beautiful Fragrance

The smell of your perfume is pleasant. Your name is pleasant like expensive perfume!

SONG OF SOLOMON 1:3

What are your favorite smells? Cookies baking, your dad's cologne, freshly cut grass, or new crayons? Do those scents bring back special memories? Our sense of smell often creates our strongest and most lasting memories.

God says our love for Him is like a powerful perfume that He remembers forever. Spending time with Him in prayer, singing songs, and studying His Word all give off the sweet fragrance of your love for God.

And as your relationship with God grows stronger, the people around you begin to notice the fragrance of Christ too! They notice when you help with a service project instead of going to a movie with friends. They see when you stop to encourage a child or help the cafeteria workers clean up a mess you didn't make. People begin to link your love toward others with the God you're telling them about. Before you know it, they'll be giving their lives to God, and He'll use them to spread the fragrance of His love too!

Prayer Pointer

Lord, please make my life a beautifully fragrant perfume in Your world.

The Boy with a Great God

The Lord your God fights for you, as He promised to do. So you must be careful to love the Lord your God.

JOSHUA 23:10–11

All the Israelite soldiers took one look at David and moaned, "He's just a boy! Goliath is a strong and powerful soldier!"

From all appearances, it didn't look like David the shepherd boy was the right choice to go against the great Philistine warrior, and much was at stake. The winner of the fight would win the entire war. The loser would make his nation slaves to the victor. But weeks had passed, and though the giant Goliath came out every day to make fun of Israel and Israel's God, no one had the guts to fight—until David heard what was happening.

David didn't have to think twice. He couldn't stand hearing Goliath say all those horrible things against the God he loved and served. "God will protect me from Goliath and help me win, just as He has helped me many times against the wild animals that have attacked my sheep," David explained to King Saul and the others. They finally agreed, and the rest is history. With a single smooth stone shot from his sling, David struck Goliath in the head and finished him off with Goliath's own sword (1 Samuel 17).

Do you feel too small or young or untalented to do anything great? Then remember David, but not just for the Goliath encounter. David's faith in God was so strong because he had learned how to trust God in the smaller daily tests of life. Today look for God at work in your life, teaching you to lean on Him for strength. Age and size don't matter when you're standing on God's side.

Prayer Pointer

Father, help me learn to love and trust You like David so I'm ready to stand strong for You when the time comes.

JANUARY 26

Being Beautiful

Let us think about each other and help each other to show love and do good deeds.

HEBREWS 10:24

Want to be beautiful? Don't pull out the flat iron just yet. Instead, think about the most beautiful, selfless things your mom or dad, or maybe a sibling or friend, has ever done for you. Aren't those moments worth a million times more than great hair or clothes?

In this exercise, you get to spend some time being beautiful—or at least planning for it. First, you'll need a blank calendar page. (Ask your parents for one.) Fill in each day with something you can do to make someone else's life beautiful. Some ideas are listed below to get you started. You can even repeat your favorite ideas! Then put your "beautiful" plan into practice.

- Give your mom a shoulder massage.
- Write an encouraging note or bring a flower to your teacher.
- Say something encouraging to your sister or brother.
- Clean out the car without being asked.
- Call or text someone who needs a friend.
- Make breakfast or coffee for your dad in the morning.

Glory

Prayer Pointer

God, show me how I can share Your love with the people in my life.

Letting Grudges Go

"Love your enemies. Do good to those who hate you."

LUKE 6:27

JANUARY 27

Honor couldn't believe her eyes as Mandy raised her hand in youth group, saying she wanted to become a Christian. Mandy had been mean to her all year long. She'd even pulled a prank that had left Honor feeling dumb and unloved. Now Mandy was going to accept Jesus and join her youth group. Honor wasn't sure how she felt about it. She had two choices.

Choice 1

I bet it's just another trick to get attention, Honor thought, as she watched Mandy pray with the youth leader. *She'll just go back to her old ways. And if she thinks I'll forget everything she's done to me, she's crazy!*

Choice 2

Wow, Lord, You're really amazing, Honor silently prayed. *Now would You help me forgive Mandy and love her like You do?* Then Honor got up and put her arm around Mandy while she prayed with the youth leader.

Honor

Prayer Pointer

Father, help me forgive and love others—and treat them as You have treated me.

Better Believe It

God is not a man. He will not lie. God is not a human being. He does not change His mind. What He says He will do, He does. What He promises, He keeps.

NUMBERS 23:19

Isn't God amazing? After all, He made the mountains and the oceans. He created stars by the zillions. He tells the sun when to rise and set. He teaches the lions to roar and the puppies to play. He even created each of us. Is there anything He can't do?

Actually, there is! The Bible mentions a couple things that God can't do. He cannot tell a lie, and He cannot break a promise. So when God says He loves us, believe it. When He says He'll never leave us, it's true. And when He says He'll always take care of us, then we can trust Him to do it. Every single word of the Bible is true—so we'd better believe it!

Prayer Pointer

Lord, I'm so glad I can always count on You. You always keep Your promises, and You always know what's best.

The Blame Game

Confess your sins to each other
and pray for each other.

JAMES 5:16

JANUARY 29

If anyone should have been best friends, it was Adam and Eve. After all, Eve was formed from Adam's rib, so they were closely connected to each other and to God. Plus, they lived in paradise where they walked and talked with God every day.

But sin has a way of taking something beautiful and messing it up. When Adam and Eve disobeyed God, they immediately turned on each other. Adam blamed Eve, and Eve blamed the snake (Genesis 2:21–3:13). But it didn't matter whose fault their sin was. Both of them felt the pain of a broken friendship with each other and with God. Sin always makes good relationships go bad.

Even though it's a huge problem, God has fixed this problem through Jesus. When we follow Jesus, we don't need to play the blame game. We know we're all sinners. When we hurt one another, God helps us forgive. And each mended friendship gives us a taste of heaven, where all fighting will end and love will win!

Prayer Pointer

Lord, I know I'm a sinner. Thanks for forgiving me and helping me forgive others too.

JANUARY 30

Sleeping Beauty

The Lord gives sleep to those He loves.

PSALM 127:2

Do you know the secret to being really active? Get some sleep! God created our bodies to need sleep so our cells can prepare for the next day. For example, while our brains shut down our voluntary muscles to rest, our brains also finish firing off thoughts to clear our minds and create new pathways for memory and learning. During deep sleep, the brain releases hormones that help us kids grow taller and stronger. In sleep, all our cells are refueled for the next day. But without sleep, we feel the effects: anger, mood swings, and just not being interested in the day's activities. Sleep is important!

The same is true for us spiritually. God designed us to be really active in sharing the gospel and helping others. We do that best when we rest from trying to do everything on our own. Instead, we trust God to change us, make us new, and use us to show His glory. He'll renew our minds and fuel our bodies to take on the challenges of each new day.

Prayer Pointer

God, thank You that I can rest in the love of Jesus, knowing that His Spirit will fuel me and lead me to do Your will.

Write It Out

WHEN you talk, do NOT say HARMFUL THINGS. But say WHAT people NEED—WORDS THAT will HELP OTHERS become STRONGER.

EPHESIANS 4:29

Words are so very powerful. They can build up, or they can tear down. And it's so easy to use them the wrong way. Think of a time you used words in a way you wish you hadn't. What could you have said instead?

Prayer Pointer

God, help me to talk to others the way I want them to talk to me.

Working with God

We are workers together with God.

2 CORINTHIANS 6:1

Sarah finished zipping up her jacket. She and some people from the youth group were going to serve food at the shelter.

"All right, everyone," their youth leader said, "today is going to be very busy, and there'll be lots of hard work to do. But remember you're not working alone; God is with you. You're not just working with each other; you're working with God."

Working with *God? Hmm*, Sarah thought and smiled to herself. *That's pretty cool. I've never thought about it that way.*

Have *you* ever thought about work that way? After all, we know that God is with us every moment of every day. So whenever we're working—either serving others or just going about our daily lives of chores, school, family, and friends—He's not sitting somewhere else watching over what we do. He's right there with us, cheering us on, leading us in the right direction, and helping us do the things that are right. God's working with us, and we're working with God!

Prayer Pointer

Lord, thank You for letting me be a part of Your wonderful work.

Changing Colors

Do not be shaped by this world. Instead be changed within by a new way of thinking.

ROMANS 12:2

FEBRUARY 2

What color is the cuttlefish? Any answer you have could be right, depending on the day and the cuttlefish's surroundings. God designed this fish to protect itself by changing its colors to match its surroundings, also known as *camouflaging*. Cuttlefish skin is filled with *chromatophores*—special cells that each house a different color. When a cuttlefish wants to camouflage itself, it tightens the muscles surrounding certain chromatophores while relaxing others. As the cells are squeezed, the color rises to the skin's surface, making the cuttlefish's color change. What an amazing way to ward off attackers!

God's people, however, don't need camouflage. God tells us not to blend in with the world because the world isn't following Him. In fact, the more we're following Jesus, the less we'll look like everybody else. And that's okay! People will see a difference in the way we love and care for others. They'll hear what we say about Jesus. And God's colorful kingdom will grow.

Prayer Pointer

Jesus, please help me follow Your lead by loving others well and telling others about Your goodness.

Decide to Try

Whoever loves God must also love his brother.

1 JOHN 4:21

Scenario

"Ewww. I don't want to play with her," Olivia moaned.

"Why not?" asked Elsie.

"Well, Chloe plays with dolls, and I don't. I guess I'm more of a tomboy than Chloe."

"Have you ever asked if she likes anything besides dolls?" Elsie challenged.

"What's the point? I can just tell she's not like me." Olivia huffed and walked off alone.

Solution

We all tend to look at people and make judgments about what they're like. But unless we take time to actually talk to them and get to know them, we could be drawing the wrong conclusions. God wants us to look for ways we can be friends with others. Even if Olivia doesn't agree with Chloe about dolls, they might like the same music or books, or enjoy skating or painting. Who knows? The only way to find out if someone might be a good friend is getting to know her.

Honor

Prayer Pointer

Lord, help me to be brave enough—and caring enough—to reach out to others who seem different from me.

Mending Hope

Trust the Lord with all your heart. Don't depend on your own understanding.

PROVERBS 3:5

Hope was losing hope as she watched the doctor x-ray her arm. "I'm afraid it's broken," he confirmed. "You're going to be in a cast for at least six weeks." Tears filled Hope's eyes as she turned to her mom and said, "But I'm supposed to play in the state championships this weekend!" Hope could react one of two ways.

Choice 1

"I can't believe God let this happen!" she cried. "Doesn't God even care how important that game was to me? How could He possibly work this out for my good?"

Choice 2

Tears fell down Hope's face as she felt deep disappointment. Then she prayed for strength. "God, I don't know why this happened, but I know You're in control. You'll somehow work this out for my good."

Hope

Prayer Pointer

God, help me believe You are good even when things don't go my way.

Otter Delight

Trust the Lord and do good. Live in the land and enjoy its safety. Enjoy serving the Lord.

PSALM 37:3–4

Otters seem to love to play. Twirling and swirling in the water, they chase and swim with beauty and ease.

But otters aren't all play. They also make time to eat, sleep, and groom. Without frequent grooming, otters would lose their oily coat, which helps them glide and float in the water. All their activities are important to help them stay healthy and fun little otters!

We like to play too, don't we? It's a great way to build friendships and knock off some stress. But just like otters, you also have to make time for other important activities in life. Sleep restores your strength. Work at school and home helps you learn needed skills for life. And grooming is important too. Nobody is looking for a grungy friend! So scrub up, work hard, and play with all your might. And when your head hits the pillow at night, thank God for the gift of friends and a fun life.

Prayer Pointer

God, thanks for making life fun! Help me find the balance between play and everything else.

Growing Beautiful

He has made everything beautiful in its time.

ECCLESIASTES 3:11 NKJV

FEBRUARY 6

What do you think it takes to be beautiful? Flawless skin, long eyelashes, lots of makeup, or the latest style of clothes? That's probably what you think if you get your ideas of beauty from movies and magazines. But God has a completely different perspective.

God intends for all of His girls to be gorgeous, but not with makeup or the latest clothes. In fact, He says we don't need to bother with all that stuff, because it only covers the surface. True beauty only comes from God's Spirit living inside us.

True beauty is being nice to someone who's been unkind to you, or helping your brother clean his room. It's sticking up for a kid who's being bullied or making peace between two fussing friends. In other words, true beauty comes from the fruit of God's Spirit living inside you! When we let God's Spirit be our guide, His beautiful fruit grows in our lives so that others can see and taste His goodness through the things we do and say.

Prayer Pointer

I want to be Your kind of gorgeous, Lord.
Please help me grow in Your goodness!

Soak It In

"Martha, Martha, you are getting worried and upset about too many things."

LUKE 10:41

It was a big day! Jesus was coming to Mary and Martha's house to have dinner and teach. Many people were coming to hear what Jesus had to say. So Martha got her game plan together. She knew just what needed to be done.

There was only one problem: Mary, her sister, wasn't helping. Martha couldn't possibly do all she'd planned by herself. Totally mad, she went straight to Jesus and said, "Why don't You tell her to help me?" But Jesus saw something Martha didn't. Mary was happy sitting at Jesus' feet, soaking in all He had to say. Martha was so busy that she was missing the truly important thing: learning from Jesus. "Mary has chosen the right thing, and it will never be taken away from her," He answered gently (Luke 10:38–42).

Did you know that we are a lot like Martha most of the time? Whether it's running to games or recitals or school, we are constantly busy. Even church can be packed with activities. But how much time with your loved ones do you miss because of the busyness? Ask yourself, "Do I just think about God, or even my friends, or do I actually talk to them and listen to them? Do I ever stop running around so that I can spend time with them?" Make an effort today to slow down and spend time with God and those you love.

Prayer Pointer

Lord, I don't want to be distracted from what is most important: You and Your people. Help me spend my days wisely.

Extra Activity!

Record how you typically spend your day in each time block. Are you spending too much time in one area?

6:00 a.m.—8:00 a.m.: ____________
8:00 a.m.—10:00 a.m.: ____________
10:00 a.m.—12:00 p.m.: ____________
12:00 p.m.—2:00 p.m.: ____________
2:00 p.m.—4:00 p.m.: ____________
4:00 p.m.—6:00 p.m.: ____________
8:00 p.m.—10:00 p.m.: ____________

Ditching Distractions

Keep me from looking at worthless things. Let me live by your word.

PSALM 119:37

Scenario

Ashley heard her mom asking for help, but Ashley pretended not to hear her. She was too busy playing a new game on her phone.

Later, when her family loaded into the car to go out to eat, Ashley was still glued to her phone.

"Honestly, Ash," her mom sighed. "Even when you're with us, you're not really here. Can you put that thing away?"

Solution

Ashley has forgotten that real people are a lot more important than the game she is playing, and she's hurting her relationships by ignoring those around her. Here are some ideas that would help Ashley and other brave girls find some needed balance:

- Always make eye contact and speak to people when they first come in the room.
- If you have guests, put the electronics away.
- Never bring a phone or game to the dinner table.
- Set a timer when you play so you know when it's time to move on to something else.

Prayer Pointer

Lord, thank You for technology. Please help me honor You with my use of it.

From a Distance

Do not be fooled: "Bad friends will ruin good habits."

1 CORINTHIANS 15:33

Lexie was struggling. She tried to be friends with everyone, so when a couple of girls from her class invited her to go swimming, she agreed. But while she was with them, the girls started gossiping, and said a lot of things that were both cruel and untrue. *It's like they enjoy hurting people,* Lexie thought. Lexie called her mom to pick her up early. As she left, the girls invited her to come again, but Lexie thought to herself, *I'm not sure that's a good idea.*

Lexie's right. God wants us to try to be friends with everyone, but some people actually seem to enjoy doing wrong. We should still forgive them because that's what God asks. And we should pray for them, but we should also stay away. If we get too close, their bad habits could easily start to ruin our good ones. It happened to Samson with Delilah (Judges 16), and it happened to King Solomon with his foreign wives (1 Kings 11).

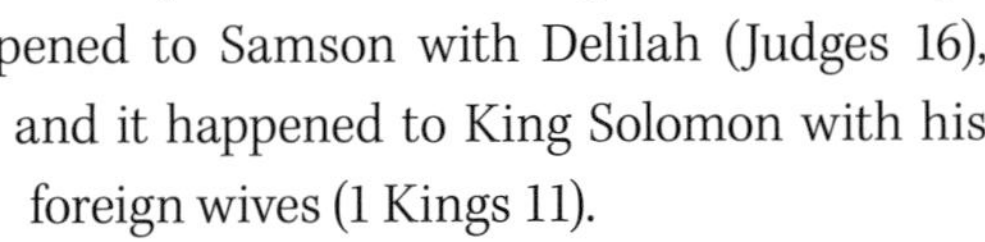

So, yes, be kind to everyone and pray for those who aren't kind—but do it from a

Prayer Pointer

God, help me to choose friends who will encourage me to follow You.

Like Father, like Son

No one has seen God, but Jesus is exactly like Him.

COLOSSIANS 1:15

The disciples had walked, worked, and lived with Jesus for three years. They had seen fish and bread multiplied to feed thousands, the sick healed, the lame walk, and the blind see. They had heard Jesus' teaching, and Peter himself had declared that Jesus was the Son of the living God.

But when Jesus talked about His upcoming death on the cross, the disciples were confused and scared. They must have thought, *What will we do without our leader?* So Philip piped up and said, "Lord, show us the Father. That is all we need." In other words, "Jesus, stop messing around, and let us see God. Then this won't be so scary."

Jesus' answer shocked them: "He who has seen me has seen the Father" (John 14:8–9).

Have you ever wondered what God looks like? Jesus let Philip—and you—know that seeing Jesus' life and love is like seeing God. When we know and love what we see in Jesus, we know and love God the Father too.

Prayer Pointer

Father, thank You for showing Yourself to us through Jesus' life on earth.

Thanks a Lot

Give thanks whatever happens.

1 THESSALONIANS 5:18

Scenario

Brooke was so excited. Her mom had taken her to a painting class where she learned to work with oil paints. She decided to paint a picture for her friend, Brantley. She worked hard on it each week. After a month, Brooke was finished. She wrapped it up, eager to give it to her friend. But when Brantley opened it, she looked confused.

"What is that?" Brantley asked.

"It's a picture I painted for you," Brooke answered.

"Huh," Brantley grunted. "That looks kinda . . . messy."

Ouch.

Solution

Does it even matter what the picture looked like? Brantley missed the whole point of her friend's gift. Maybe that's why God talks so much about thanking Him and the people He's placed in our lives. When we're thankful, we show that we've not only noticed the gift, but also the kindness of the giver. We all need to learn to see the blessings all around, and give thanks to God and others who really need to hear it.

Prayer Pointer

Thank You, Jesus, for who You are and all You do for me. Help me grow a grateful heart.

Sister Success

"Then the King will answer, 'I tell you the truth. Anything you did for any of my people here, you also did for me.'"

MATTHEW 25:40

Do you have a sister? Or a friend who's like a sister? If so, are you two similar, or are you as different as day and night? No matter what your differences may be, sisters can be a total delight if you treat them right. But to build a beautiful friendship with your sister, you first have to learn to lose. Here's what you need to give up:

- The right to always be right. Work to listen and love instead.
- The right to your things. Be willing to share.
- The right to win. Believe it or not, you don't always have to be the best. Look for ways to encourage your sister.
- The right to privacy. Welcome her to your room, and invite her to share what's on her heart.
- The right to be served. Follow Jesus' example, and serve her instead.

Here's what you'll win: a closer walk with God, habits that help with all friendships, and a friend for life!

Glory

Prayer Pointer

Jesus, thank You for my sisters—both in my family and in Christ. Please give us a lifelong friendship with each other and You.

Caught in the Storm

Jesus stood up and commanded the wind and the waves to stop. He said, "Quiet! Be still!" Then the wind stopped, and the lake became calm.

MARK 4:39

Have you ever watched a storm roll in? Ever just sat and watched as it crossed the sky, with its winds blowing, clouds swirling, thunder booming, and lightning flashing? When you're safe inside your warm and cozy home, storms can be amazing things to watch.

Have you ever been stuck *outside* during a storm, maybe at a ballgame or at a park? That's a whole different experience—because *you're* the one getting all blown around!

Storms can be a lot like life. The hard things that happen in our lives—feuding friends, changing schools, a divorce—can make us feel as if we're caught outside in the middle of a terrible storm. That's when it's time to turn to the One who controls the storms: Jesus. When we turn to Him, sometimes He stops the storm and makes everything peaceful. Other times, He doesn't. But during those rough times, He doesn't leave us alone. He stays with us during the storm and makes *us* peaceful.

Hope

Prayer Pointer

Jesus, help me trust that You can calm any storm in my life. Thank You for always watching over me.

Precious Pearls

We have small troubles for a while now, but they are helping us gain an eternal glory. That glory is much greater than the troubles.

2 CORINTHIANS 4:17

Have you ever held a real pearl? It's tough to imagine how something so beautiful was made.

God chose rough, gray oysters to make lustrous pearls. Inside the oyster's shell lies a soft, slippery body that looks like a tongue (gross!). When an irritant, like a grain of sand, gets inside the shell, the oyster coats it with *nacre*, the same chemical it uses to make the "mother of pearl" lining inside its shell. As it keeps coating and recoating the intruder, a pearl is formed!

God uses irritants in your life to grow beauty inside you too. Maybe your brother bothers you or your family struggles with money. Maybe your parents got divorced. Everyone has problems. But each time we trust God to help us, we are like the oyster coating the sand. Before you know it, your life will be a shining example of God's beauty for the whole world to see.

Prayer Pointer

Jesus, thank You for using even my problems to make me beautiful in Your sight.

Winging It

Each part of the body does its own work. And this makes the whole body grow and be strong with love.

EPHESIANS 4:16

Have you ever seen a large group of geese flying overhead? Do you know why they fly in a *V*?

Geese know a little secret about teamwork. If a goose were to try to fly a long distance alone, it would get tired. But when geese travel together with one goose at the point of the *V*, the trip is easier. The lead bird pushes against the wind, resulting in much less resistance for the geese following behind. When the lead goose gets tired, it falls back and another takes the lead. By taking turns, the geese are able to fly smarter and keep going longer.

Geese aren't the only ones who work better in groups. God created people to work together. If you tried to build God's kingdom on earth all by yourself, how far do you think you would get? If everyone worked together, using the gifts God gave each of us, just imagine what we could do!

Prayer Pointer

Father, thank You for adopting me into Your family. Help me work with others to stay strong in You.

Hot Mess

"A person speaks the things that are in his heart."

LUKE 6:45

Did you know that one of the most beautiful places on earth is also home to the world's tallest mountain? Hawaii's Mauna Loa measures more than thirteen thousand feet from its base deep within the Pacific Ocean to its highest peak. And it's no ordinary mountain. It's a volcano that, over time, built itself to grand heights with its many eruptions.

Even though Mauna Loa looks like a regular mountain on the outside, deep inside its core, *magma*—liquid, burning rock—pools and builds. When the earth's crust shifts, magma gets squeezed to the top, overflowing the mountain's sides. Though they may be exciting, eruptions can cause mudslides, avalanches, flash floods, and earthquakes.

Volcanoes are powerful reminders that what lies inside is even more important than how something looks on the outside. Someone could be gorgeous on the outside, but if her heart is full of anger, self-centeredness, or other sin, it can ruin everything. That's why God cares so much about what's inside our hearts and minds. He wants us to be full of His love so we overflow with the beauty of His Spirit.

Prayer Pointer

Glory

Lord, please make me beautiful from the inside out by the power of Your Holy Spirit.

Listening to Beauty

I hope my words and thoughts please you.
Lord, you are my Rock, the one who saves me.

PSALM 19:14

Isabella had started gymnastics at a new gym and loved the music they played. It had a cool beat that made workouts more fun. At home, she found the same station and turned it up loud. After a while, her mom asked, "What are you listening to? Can you hear what that song is saying?" Isabella started really listening. Then she was embarrassed. Now what should she do?

Choice 1

"I don't listen to the words, just the beat," Isabella answered.

"But that trash is filling your mind. You're even singing it!" her mom replied.

"Everybody listens to this. We just have to get used to it," Isabella argued.

Choice 2

"Wow, I wasn't paying attention to the words. They're pretty bad. I'll change the station," Isabella said.

"And I'll talk to your coach about switching the station at practice," her mom added.

Prayer Pointer

gracie

Jesus, help me choose music that doesn't dishonor You.

Peace Talks

"Those who work to bring peace are happy."

MATTHEW 5:9

So you know it's a good thing to be a peacemaker. You've probably been told this a thousand times. But have you ever wondered why God wants His people to be keepers of His peace?

Maybe it's easier to think about the opposite of peace: war. Fighting shows a break in togetherness. People are always divided in fights. But God didn't create people to be against each other or Him. He wants us to be one big, happy family, serving Him and loving each other. What keeps that from happening now? Sin! Ever since sin entered our world, people have been separated from each other and God. It was such a big problem that God sent Jesus to die (and rise again) so that we could have peace. One day, when we're all in heaven, we'll see God's big plan in action. We'll all love Him and each other in perfect unity.

But for now, God wants each of us to play our role in keeping peace here on earth. It helps others see God's plan and want to be with Him too, so it's a really important job for us. But how do we do it? Pray and ask God for wisdom. Then think about some of the following situations, and decide how you would start the peace process.

Your friends have stopped speaking to each other because they're mad. You:

____

Your family is arguing because they can't agree on a restaurant. You:

____

Your sister keeps whispering to you and giggling during the sermon at church. You:

____

You got angry with your brother and said some pretty mean things during the fight. You:

____

You brought home the candy prize you won at school, but now your siblings want some. You:

____

Prayer Pointer

Jesus, please give me Your peace. Help me keep it daily in my life with others.

Talk About Friends

A person who gossips ruins friendships.

PROVERBS 16:28

Scenario

It was late, and the slumber party quieted down. Now the girls were in their sleeping bags, talking in the darkness to one another.

"Hey, did you hear about Emma?" a voice whispered.

"Noooo, what happened?" a girl answered from the corner.

"Well, I heard she likes Ryan and tried to tell him, but he just laughed! How embarrassing is that?"

"Well, what was she thinking?" another girl piped in. "He's really cute and popular, but she's . . . what can I say? Not."

Suddenly, all the girls were giggling—all except Kaitlyn, who was one of Emma's friends.

Solution

If you were Kaitlyn, would you join in the giggling or stay silent? Would you speak up for your friend?

If the girls were talking about you instead of your friend, you'd want somebody to stick up for you, right? Be brave and remind others that it's wrong to talk badly about others. God wants us all to be trustworthy friends.

Prayer Pointer

Lord, keep me from saying things I shouldn't. Help me speak Your truth and love instead.

Tuned In

Look with your eyes and hear with your ears.
And pay attention to all that I will show you.

EZEKIEL 40:4

At dusk, you might see a bat swooping down toward your head. Then, just before impact, it abandons course, only to dive at another seemingly invisible target. What is that bat doing? It's listening! And if it listens well enough, it gets to eat. Bats use *echolocation* to bounce sounds they make off objects around them. This information tells them how close their flying insect meal might be.

Even though people don't hear like bats do, God has given us the ability to hear other people. No, not as potential meals—God wants us to listen for the sound of other people's needs. If we're always talking or busy doing other things, we'll miss it. So as you listen to your friends, ask yourself: "What's my friend really saying?" "Can I help her?" and "How can I pray for her?"

As you pay attention and listen to your friend's heart, you'll be better able to love her like Jesus.

Prayer Pointer

Lord, help me tune in to the needs around me so I can better serve You.

Being Content

Godliness with contentment is great gain.

1 TIMOTHY 6:6 NKJV

Glory was beside herself with excitement. Her grandparents had come to take her and a friend to the local fair. In a day filled with fun, they rode every ride, ate funnel cakes and candied apples, and even got to ride a camel. When it got dark, Grandmom and Granddad were exhausted. "It's time to go home," they said. But Glory and her friend were still buzzing with energy. What should Glory say?

Choice 1

"Oh, come on, it's still early! We're not even tired yet!" Glory rattled off excitedly. "Plus, I really wanted to try to win a stuffed animal!"

Choice 2

"Okay, Grandmom and Grandad. I bet you're tired. Thank you so much for taking us to the fair. It's been awesome!"

- Why is it so important to be content and thankful instead of always looking for more?
- How would your attitude improve if you chose to be thankful and content with what you have instead of always wanting something else?

Prayer Pointer

Glory

Father, thank You for filling my life with so many wonderful people and things. You are so good to me!

Gain Through Pain

I have fought the good fight. I have finished the race. I have kept the faith.

2 TIMOTHY 4:7

February 22

On a scale of 1 to 10, how good are you at finishing a task you've been given?

You might think, *Well, it depends on the task.* We're more than happy to keep playing that video game until we win. But studying for that test until we really understand the material? Not so much! Persevering—sticking to a task until it's done—is easier when the reward is great.

Jesus understands. The task His Father had given Him wasn't easy at all: Leave heaven to suffer on earth while you love and serve people. Then die a horrible death.

Wow! That's a tough task! But Jesus felt the reward was worth it. He would save all the people who loved Him, and He would get to be with them forever in heaven.

Life will not be easy for us either. But God calls us to persevere through every trial, looking to Him for help and trusting in His goodness. When we do, we'll be rewarded with God's peace today and the promise of an eternity in heaven with Him.

gracie

Prayer Pointer

Jesus, help me turn to You for strength whenever I feel like giving up.

Elizabeth, Who Listened

"Those who believe without seeing
me will be truly happy."

JOHN 20:29

Ever since he came out of the tabernacle, Zechariah—Elizabeth's husband and a priest—had been acting strange. He could motion with his hands, but no words came out of his mouth. Turns out, an angel had told Zechariah that he was going to be a father, but Zechariah didn't believe him. God didn't like that, so He took away Zechariah's speech for a while.

Zechariah and Elizabeth's child was no ordinary child. The baby grew up to become John the Baptist, the man God chose to prepare the world for the coming of Jesus. Unlike Zechariah, Elizabeth immediately believed the good news and celebrated God's goodness. When her baby was born, they named him John in obedience to the angel's instructions, and Zechariah got his speech back (Luke 1).

Even though some of the rules or instructions in God's Word might seem too difficult to follow, Elizabeth's story reminds us that if we trust Him fully, God will lead us into the wonderful plans He has for our lives.

Prayer Pointer

Lord, Your understanding is greater than mine.
Please help me trust and obey You.

A Howling Mess

I may speak in different languages of men or even angels. But if I do not have love, then I am only a noisy bell or a ringing cymbal.

1 CORINTHIANS 13:1

FEBRUARY 24

At dawn or dusk, you can hear their screeching cries: howler monkeys. Special vocal chords allow howlers to shriek so loudly that their message can be heard three miles away. And what are howler monkeys trying to say? "Back off! This is our territory!" Their screams tell other monkeys or predators that they're getting too close.

While howler monkeys can be fascinating, no one would want to listen to their screeching 24/7. Yet sometimes that's exactly what we do to one another. God says that when we talk or act without love, we sound like a noisy bell or a ringing cymbal. Always complaining about our lives, our friends, or our situations sounds awful, and it drives other people away. That's why God tells us to soften our words and actions with thankfulness and love. If you find yourself complaining, remember the howler monkey. And ask the Lord to fill you with sweet and gentle words instead.

PRAYER POINTER

Lord, please make all my words pleasing to Your ears.

FEBRUARY 25

Family Functions

God gives the lonely a home.

PSALM 68:6

When you think of the word *family*, what words come to mind?

____

____

How would you describe your family?

____

____

Did you know your family was and you were uniquely created by God and put together to help one another grow closer to Him? It's true!

Sometimes it's hard to see the blessing, though. Parents can seem too strict. Siblings can get on our nerves. Life at home can feel crazy and unsettled. And suddenly God's gift to us might not look so good. But trust God's goodness. Believe that He has given you parents and leaders to guide and help you. Those things that bother you about your parents or siblings will actually help build your character if you handle them with prayer and obedience to God. Take time right now to thank God for your special family. And look for ways to share God's love with those He's placed around you.

Hope

Prayer Pointer

Lord, thank You for my family. Help me learn from them and love them well.

What About Your Words?

Never shout angrily or say things to hurt others.

EPHESIANS 4:31

FEBRUARY 26

Did you know there is one thing that's more powerful than a hurricane, more deadly than any weapon, and also more healing that any medicine? But what one thing could possibly be all those things?

A word.

We must never forget the power of a word, and we must especially be very careful of how we use our words. The Bible says, "Careless words stab like a sword. But wise words bring healing" (Proverbs 12:18). A word shouted in anger can be more destructive to a person's life than any hurricane. And hateful gossip can be more deadly than any weapon. But kind and gentle words? They can be more healing than any medicine. So what about your words? Do they build up or tear down? Do they help or hurt? Always work to make your words be a gift—something that helps and benefits whoever is listening.

Prayer Pointer

gracie

Lord, I know how the words of others can make me feel terrible or wonderful. Help me always use my words as a gift to those around me.

World News

"In this world you will have trouble. But be brave! I have defeated the world!"

JOHN 16:33

Do you ever watch the news? So often it's bad news, and it can make this world seem like a scary place. Terrible things can happen, like fighting, sickness, and storms. All those bad things happen because sin is in our world. But there's also good news—*very* good news.

Jesus has beaten sin!

You see, Jesus came from heaven and was born here on earth as a baby. He was completely God, but He was also completely human, just like us. When He died on the cross, He took all our sins with Him, and sin was defeated! When He rose up from the grave to life again, death was defeated too. Jesus frees us from our sins. Now, instead of death, we have the hope of heaven. Yes, bad things still happen, but we can be brave because Jesus has already beaten this world's two greatest threats. And that's some really good world news!

Prayer Pointer

Lord, when bad things happen, help me remember that You are good, You love me, and You have already won!

Perfect Pairing

Use the gift God gave you.

2 TIMOTHY 1:6

Did you know that vanilla extract comes from a bean that grows from an orchid vine? Originally discovered in Mexico, these delicate vines produce orchid flowers that bloom for only one day. In order for pollination to occur so that vanilla beans can grow, something has to target that bloom at just the right time, lift up a special flap on the anther that houses the pollen, and press it to the stigma that pollinates the flower. But what on earth would know how to do all that at just the right time?

The Melipona bee does! These tiny bees, some no larger than a flea, find the orchids, lift the flaps, and transfer the pollen, all in the nick of time. Without these bees, the vanilla bean would have become extinct long ago.

God created you, like the Melipona bee, for a special purpose. As you follow God, He will lead you to the special work He has planned for you. And God promises that everywhere you go, you'll spread the fragrance of God's great goodness.

Prayer Pointer

Father, everything You have made has a special purpose, including me. Thank You!

The Wrong Kind of Right

The Lord laughs at those who laugh at Him.
But He is kind to those who are not proud.

PROVERBS 3:34

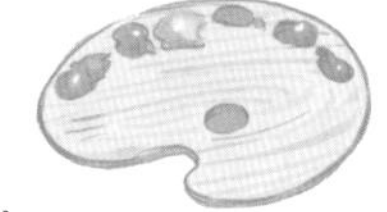

Lie: I always need to be right.

"That's not how you do it," Maggie told Chloe as she was drawing a picture.

"Well, I like it this way," Chloe said.

"Look," Maggie answered, starting to erase Chloe's picture. "If you change it like this, it looks better."

"Leave my paper alone," Chloe mumbled as she took her things back and moved to another table.

The Truth Is . . .

It feels good to be right. But the problem with needing to be right all the time is that we're only thinking about ourselves and not considering other people's needs. And just because something may be true doesn't mean it needs to be said. For instance, comments like "You're wrong" or "You don't have any friends" may be true, but they aren't helpful.

In Maggie's case, a word of encouragement would have been better than a word of correction. Because love and kindness always win out over pride.

Jacie

Prayer Pointer

Lord, You hate pride but love the humble. Help me humbly love the people around me.

Write It Out

You should know that your body is a temple for the Holy Spirit. . . . You were bought by God for a price. So honor God with your bodies.

1 CORINTHIANS 6:19–20

When you choose to follow God, your body becomes the home of His Spirit. So you need to keep that home in good shape. What can you do to take better care of your body—not just your physical body, but also your feelings (heart), your way of thinking (mind), and your time with God (soul)?

Prayer Pointer

Thank You, Lord, for Your Spirit that lives inside me and helps me.

Temple Test

If you eat, or if you drink, or if you do anything, do everything for the glory of God.

1 CORINTHIANS 10:31

Your physical body is a temple for God's Holy Spirit. So it's a no-brainer that you need to take care of it. But knowing what's good and actually doing it aren't always the same thing. Take this quiz to find your level of kingdom fitness.

1. Your friends started a game of soccer outside while you're in the middle of playing a video game you just don't want to quit. You:
   a. don't hear them laughing and kicking the ball because you're so engrossed in the game.
   b. hope they'll still be out there later when you finish this level.
   c. save your progress and join your friends right away.

2. You've just come home from school, and you're hungry. You look in the pantry and choose:
   a. your favorite bag of potato chips and head for the sofa to watch TV.
   b. an apple and a bag of granola, and then you head for the sofa.
   c. an apple and a bag of granola, and then you head outside for a bike ride.

3. On average, you tend to exercise:
    a. only in your dreams.
    b. every now and then.
    c. on a consistent basis.

4. When you exercise or play a sport you:
    a. think watching other people play sports is good enough.
    b. start off with enthusiasm, but often lose steam.
    c. work full-throttle until the time is up.

If you answered mostly *A*s, your fitness is totally flat. It's time to get up, get out, and get moving toward a healthier you. If you answered mostly *B*s, your fitness is fair. Moderation is good, but push yourself a little more to achieve greater fitness. If you answered mostly *C*s, congratulations! Your temple should be fit for whatever adventure God has in store!

Prayer Pointer

God, help me take good care of this body You've given me so I can be ready for whatever you have planned for me.

Taking Courage

"Be strong and brave. . . . The Lord your God will be with you everywhere you go."

JOSHUA 1:9

Joshua was facing some seriously scary stuff. Moses, Israel's trusted leader, had died. Now Joshua was supposed to lead the Israelites into the Promised Land, where many more people lived—people who hated the Israelites.

God reminded Joshua, "It doesn't matter what you face, I will give you the power to overcome when you follow Me." We can be courageous and confident because we know He is our faithful Leader who never fails.

What would it look like for you to be strong and courageous? Maybe you'll trust God to help you tackle the new trick in gymnastics that you have feared. Perhaps it's time you told your friends at school about Jesus. Maybe it's something else.

One way to be courageous like Joshua is to read about other believers who lived boldly for Christ. Some of these believers are Corrie ten Boom, Jim and Elizabeth Elliot, George Mueller, Florence Nightingale, and C. S. Lewis. Learn from their examples, and ask God to strengthen you in the same way.

Prayer Pointer

Jesus, I can be strong and courageous because I know You're always with me.

Treasure God's Word

"I will cause a time of hunger in the land. The people will not be hungry for bread or thirsty for water. But they will be hungry for words from the Lord."

AMOS 8:11

Don't you hate it when your stomach starts rumbling hours before lunchtime? But imagine if lunchtime rolled around and, somehow, the cafeteria had mysteriously disappeared, and all the food with it. Disaster! In the same way, the prophet Amos warns of a time when people will be starving for God's Word and won't be able to find it.

Perhaps you don't open your Bible very often. You have to go to school every day, and then you have sports and parties. You may struggle to find time to read God's Word. But it's so important.

If you are going to know God as He really is and love Him as He wants you to, the Bible must be your best-loved, most treasured book. Make a habit of reading the Bible at the same time every day, and you'll never go hungry for God's Word.

Prayer Pointer

Lord, I'm so grateful for Your Word. Help me want to read it more and more.

Tame the Flame

Anger will not help you live a
good life as God wants.

JAMES 1:20

Scenario

Ashlyn, her mom, and her two brothers were in the car. They were headed for a vacation, but it didn't sound like it.

"Andrew, stop touching me!" Ashlyn yelled, jerking her elbow away from her brother. A minute later she yelled, "Mom, you know I hate that kind of music. Turn it off!" Almost in the same breath, she rudely told Kyle to give her the iPad so she could play her favorite game.

Solution

Sounds pretty terrible, doesn't it? Ashlyn's outbursts are ruining the trip for everybody. So what's her problem? It's a sin we all have: selfishness. When other people block us from getting what we want, we often explode in anger. We've learned that people will give in to our demands if we get angry enough. But that's not what Jesus wants. He wants us to put others first. Ashlyn should have asked to take turns with the music they listened to and shared the iPad with her brother. That way everyone would have fun and keep peace while honoring Jesus.

Prayer Pointer

Lord, forgive my selfishness. Give me
Your patience and love instead.

MARCH 6

Now What?

If we confess our sins, He will forgive our sins. . . . He will make us clean from all the wrongs we have done.

1 JOHN 1:9

Abbie had completely blown it—and she knew it. Her parents had said she couldn't get a certain new app for her phone, but she'd secretly downloaded it anyway, hoping they wouldn't find out. And then they did. Now she was not only grounded, but they didn't trust her anymore. *How do I make this right?* she wondered.

No matter how hard we try, everybody messes up and everybody sins—whether it's on purpose or accidentally. So how do you make it right? First, tell God that you've done wrong and apologize to Him. He already knows, of course, but He wants you to acknowledge that what you've done is wrong. When you do, He promises to forgive you. Next, ask God to help you not repeat that sin. Finally, it's time to try to make things right with the people in your life. Admit your sins and apologize to them too. It might take a little time to regain their trust, but you're off to a great start!

Honor

PRAYER POINTER

God, when I mess up, help me come straight to You to make things right again.

It's Not Fair

Wait and trust the Lord. Don't be upset when others get rich or when someone else's plans succeed.

PSALM 37:7

"It's not fair!"

Have you ever said that? Maybe someone else got the spot on the team, even though you'd worked much harder. Or maybe you studied all night and still flunked the test, but someone else cheated and got an *A*.

The truth is that life isn't always fair. But what we *do* with that unfairness makes all the difference. Do we whine and sulk or throw a temper tantrum? That's not what God wants at all! Instead, God wants us to trust Him. He sees the unfairness—He really does. But God has a plan to use it. He'll take all that unfairness, frustration, and sadness, and He'll use it to make us more like Him. We'll learn patience, kindness, and contentment. And even though life isn't always fair, with God by our side, life is fabulous!

Prayer Pointer

Lord, it's frustrating when life isn't fair. Help me trust You to bring good things even out of unfairness.

Beginning Beauty

God did not send His Son into the world to judge the world guilty, but to save the world through Him.

JOHN 3:17

Have you ever looked closely at a rose? Did you feel its soft, delicate petals? Did you notice how they curl around each other in a swirl of fragrant color? It's a miracle of wonder in every small bloom.

Now picture beautiful, rolling hills covered in flowers of every color. Imagine towering mountains and forests, sandy white beaches and sparkling seas, all in perfect, new condition. Add in rabbits hopping, squirrels scurrying, elephants lumbering, and a host of other animals just filling the earth with God's creative glory. And last, picture Adam and Eve. Can you imagine the beauty they walked in before sin darkened the view?

God's creation is still breathtaking, even though it's now covered with the curse of sin. But here's a beautiful truth: God has made us into new creations through Jesus. And we have the power of His Spirit to help us make everything we say and do a part of making God's world a beautiful place.

Prayer Pointer

Lord, help me to know what can I do today to make this world more beautiful.

MARCH 9

Praying Power

Early the next morning, Jesus woke and left the house while it was still dark. He went to a place to be alone and pray.

MARK 1:35

If God already knows what's going to happen, why pray? Pick your best guess from this list:

a. God tells us to do it.
b. God's peace fills us when we do it.
c. Being still helps us remember who God is.
d. God is with us when we pray together.
e. God listens when we pray.
f. We grow closer to God when we pray.
g. Prayer changes things.

Did you choose them all? You should! Prayer is an extremely powerful weapon God has given us to fight off the enemy, to starve our fears, and to feed on His incredible goodness. So set aside time each day just for talking to God. During that time, use the ACTS tool to help you think of things to tell God: A, *adore* and praise Him; C, *confess* any sins; T, *tell* Him everything you're thankful for; and S, *supplication*, a fancy word for asking for what you need.

Prayer Pointer

God, I'm so glad I can talk to You about anything, whenever I need to!

Everything You Need

Using the Scriptures, the person who serves God will be ready and will have everything he needs to do every good work.

2 TIMOTHY 3:17

God has good plans for us (Jeremiah 29:11), and He promises to give us everything we need to make those plans come true.

Remember Joseph? God had a plan for his hard times. God was always with him, blessing him, so that one day Joseph would save the lives of his brothers (Genesis 45). God also had a plan for Moses—to free the Israelites—and He gave Moses everything he needed, including sending Aaron to help him speak (Exodus 7). And God had a plan for Mary to be the mother of His Son. He put people in her life to help her, like Joseph, Elizabeth, and even the wise men (Luke 1–2).

God has a plan for you too. He'll put people in your life to help you, He'll guide you through His Word, and He'll always be there to help you. His plans may seem difficult at times, but remember: if God asks you to do something, He'll give you everything you need to do it.

Prayer Pointer

gracie

Lord, I want to be part of Your great plan. Please use me to make Your plans come true.

Colorful Impact

You are young, but do not let anyone treat you as if you were not important.

1 TIMOTHY 4:12

Have you ever seen a male peacock fanning his tail feathers to show off his rainbow of colors? Now picture all those brilliant colors poured onto a shrimp. Sound impossible? Not for the peacock mantis shrimp. Not only is it colorful, but it has two eyes that can see ten times more color than ours can. Oh, and another thing—these little guys are fast. They can propel through the water at speeds so fast your eyes can hardly see them, causing deadly damage to the crabs or mollusks they are hunting.

So what would the peacock mantis shrimp tell you (if it could)? Don't worry about your size or shape or age. God designed you to bring beauty, color, and brilliant energy into the world just by being you and doing what you do. When you love and trust God, you're bound to have tremendous impact as He propels you to bring life and love to everyone around you.

Prayer Pointer

Lord, thank You for using someone small like me to do big things with You.

Ripple Effect

"He who believes in me will do the same things that I do."

JOHN 14:12

Have you ever thrown a rock into a still lake? If so, you've seen the "ripple effect." Rings of waves flow out from the spot where your rock landed, making bigger and bigger circles in the water. It's amazing how one little rock can have such a big impact!

In a way, our world is like that lake. It seems too big and we seem too small for our lives to make an impact. But God doesn't see us that way. He uses everything we do, no matter how small, to impact the world. The effects of our actions can reach places we never could've imagined.

What are some stones you can throw into your world for good? Maybe giving your mom an honest compliment and thanking her for her work. Or asking for donations to a charity instead of birthday gifts. Or praying every day for God to use you to spread His Word. Try putting these stones—or some of your own—into action, and see how God uses the ripple effect in your world.

Prayer Pointer

Thank You for using me to show Your love to Your people.

MARCH 13

Brave Face

Be strong and brave. Don't be afraid of them. Don't be frightened. The Lord your God will go with you. He will not leave you or forget you.

DEUTERONOMY 31:6

Scenario

"Mom, I don't want to go in there!" Hayley moaned.

"Honey, your dad and I are going to our Sunday school class, and it's not for kids," her mom said. "You have your own class, and I'm sure it will be fun."

"No, it won't," Hayley argued. "I don't know any of those kids in there, and they already have their friends. I'm just going to be left out."

"Well, you don't really have a choice. I'll come back to get you in an hour."

Hayley then entered the class, staring at the floor, and took a seat off by herself.

Solution

Do you think the Sunday school class is as bad as Hayley predicts? What would you encourage her to do differently?

Have you ever had to be the new person in a group? Maybe you've moved to a new place and started at a new school. Or you've joined a new team or you're trying out a new summer camp. Change can be difficult, and walking into a place with new faces can be really scary. But you are not alone! God, your best Friend, is with you wherever you go. And He always has a way of connecting His kids with the friends they need. You just have to be brave and trust that God isn't going to abandon you. Instead, He has hidden treasures in the people around you that He eagerly wants you to discover. By hoping for the best and trusting that God has put you in this situation on purpose, you can be sure that God is working something really good in your life as you reach out to new people with His love.

Prayer Pointer

Lord, fill me with bravery as I face the challenge of making new friends.

Joint Effort

At the sound of the trumpets and the people's shout, the walls fell.

JOSHUA 6:20

Last night our youth group leader asked us if we'd ever thought about why God's plan to defeat Jericho was so *strange* (Joshua 6). Here's how it went:

Leader: So what did God ask them to do?

Honor: God told them to march around the city one time each day for six days, and on the seventh day, march around it seven times. Then they were supposed to blow trumpets, shout, and rush in to capture the city when the walls fell.

Gracie: I bet those people from Jericho thought they were nuts.

Hope: Yeah, until the walls came crashing down! But why did they have to keep walking around the city?

Glory: And be silent the whole time until the time they could shout? If I'd been there, my big mouth would've ruined the whole thing.

Faith: That's just it! They had to work together to follow God's plan. God wanted them to learn to work together and trust Him.

Prayer Pointer — gracie

God, help me stick with Your people and trust Your plans.

Now Trending

"Everyone who hears these things I say and obeys them is like a wise man. The wise man built his house on rock."

MATTHEW 7:24

MARCH 15

Our culture is filled with trends, but almost all of them are passing. That number-one-hit song that everybody's listening to can be old news in a week or two. Last year's must-have video game is now on the clearance rack, and clothing styles change so quickly it's impossible to keep up. That's why it's important not to build your life on what's popular; instead, build your life on something that never changes.

In Matthew 7, Jesus told a story about two builders. One built his house on the sand. But when the storms came, the sands moved and changed, and the house was destroyed. The other man built his house on rock, which never moved or changed. So when the storms came, his house was safe.

Trends can be fun, and it's not necessarily wrong to follow them. Just don't let fashion, music, or entertainment become the focus of your life. Those things are like sand, always moving and changing. Keep your focus on God. He is our Rock, our Protection, our Savior (Psalm 18:2).

PRAYER POINTER

Glory

Thank You, Lord, for being the Rock of my life.

Top Ten Ways to Build Up Your Faith

So the churches became stronger in the faith and grew larger every day.

ACTS 16:5

Faith is like a muscle: it needs exercise. Try these tips to make your faith grow stronger today.

1. Ask God for more faith.
2. Keep an attitude of prayer all day.
3. Obey what you know from God's Word.
4. Repent when you mess up.
5. Pray for opportunities to share the gospel.
6. Share your testimony with someone you know.
7. Look for ways to serve others.
8. Guard your time. Use it for building something great rather.
9. Use all means possible to share your faith.
10. Remember, reflect on, and thank God for who He is and what He has done in your life.

Can you think of any more faith-builders to add to the top ten?

Prayer Pointer

Lord, every day, please show me a way that I can build up my faith and tell others about You.

Cheating Cheats the Cheater

MARCH 17

When a person gets food dishonestly, it may taste sweet at first. But later he will feel as if he has a mouth full of gravel.

PROVERBS 20:17

It would be so easy, Marcie thought. *No one would ever even know.*

She'd gone into Mrs. Stewart's classroom after school to ask a question about tomorrow's test. Mrs. Stewart wasn't there, but the test was! And all the answers were filled in. Marcie stared at it.

Copying down those answers would sure make my life easier, Marcie thought. *I could get a good grade without having to study so hard, and I could hang out with my friends instead.*

What should she do?

As Marcie thought about it, she realized that copying the answers would mean she'd miss out on knowing the things she needed to learn. Plus, she'd feel horrible about betraying Mrs. Stewart's trust. *Cheating would only really cheat me,* she thought. Marcie turned and left the classroom, deciding to wait in the hallway for her teacher—far away from the temptation of that test.

Prayer Pointer

Lord, sometimes it seems like cheating would be an easy fix for my problems. Help me to remember that cheating only cheats me.

MARCH 18

Mood Management

Be happy with those who are happy.
Be sad with those who are sad.

ROMANS 12:15

Scenario

It was Olivia's birthday, and everybody was ready to have fun. Everyone except Skylar. Skylar didn't get much sleep last night, and now she was in a bad mood.

"Come and join the fun!" her friends urged as Olivia waited to open her presents.

Skylar, though, sat sulking in her chair. "Leave me alone," she answered. "I don't really want to."

Olivia frowned, but tried to keep up the party spirit in spite of Skylar's bad attitude.

Solution

All girls feel the weight of mood swings at times. Sometimes our moods just don't match the situation at hand. What can we do?

Jesus says we should put others' needs before our own. We can decide to obey God and honor others. Even if we don't feel like it, we should participate, or calm down, or wait, or talk, or be quiet—whatever the situation demands. By matching our actions with the moment's needs, we become a blessing rather than a bother.

Prayer Pointer

gracie

Jesus, please help me learn how to be sensitive to the needs of others, even when I'm moody.

Growing by Faith

Only God is important, because He is the One who makes things grow.

1 CORINTHIANS 3:7

As a new Christian, Gracie was getting tips from the youth group and church sermons about how Christians behave. She learned that disrespecting parents was bad and Bible study was good. She also learned about quiet time, prayer, journaling, memorizing Scripture . . . the list went on and on! It was all pretty overwhelming! What should she do?

Choice 1

Maybe I need a checklist to make sure I do everything good Christians are supposed to do, Gracie thought. *Plus, I'll fit in better with the girls who are doing everything right.*

Choice 2

Gracie prayed, *Lord, help! I'm overwhelmed by all these dos and don'ts. Help me remember that I'm completely loved by You because of what Jesus did for me, not what I do for You.*

Prayer Pointer

Glory

Jesus, thank You that I don't have to earn Your love. You give it freely to everyone who trusts in You!

Choosing Teams

In Christ, He chose us before the world was made. In His love He chose us to be His holy people—people without blame before Him.

EPHESIANS 1:4

Angie stared down at her shoes and tried to look bored instead of upset. It was gym class, and the team captains were choosing their teams. As usual, she was one of the last people still waiting to be chosen. *I'm just not that good at volleyball—or any sport really,* she thought. *If they'd just let me sit and* sketch *the game, then I'd be rocking.* But even though Angie understood why she wasn't chosen, it still hurt.

When it comes to choosing teams for a sport or for an academic competition, you are chosen—or not chosen—based on what you can or can't do. But with God, it doesn't matter what you can do. He chooses you every single time because of who you are: His amazing, wonderful child. God chooses you simply because you're you. And all He asks is that you choose Him too.

Prayer Pointer

Thank You, God, for choosing me. Help me choose to honor You in all I do and say today.

Encouragement Exercises

If you have any message that will encourage the people, please speak!

ACTS 13:15

MARCH 21

Becoming an encourager isn't always easy. But the more you do it, the more natural it will feel and the better encourager you will become. Look up the Scripture passages listed below, and write out at least one way you could encourage those around you!

- (Isaiah 1:17) At school, you notice some bullies picking on the new kid. You could pretend you didn't see it and go somewhere else, but instead you:

____

____

- (1 Thessalonians 1:2) Every day your parents go to work so they can make the money your family needs to live. Today you decide to show them how much you appreciate what they do, so you:

____

____

Prayer Pointer

Father, help me see people the way You do, and help me remember to treat them with love.

Food for Thought

You prepare a meal for me in front of my enemies. . . . You give me more than I can hold.

PSALM 23:5

Whether it's just your family dinner or a big dinner party with lots of extra guests, it takes more than just good food for a grand time together. You have to learn the art of conversation. Follow these simple dinner-table tips to make every gathering a success.

- Wait for everyone to be seated, the blessing to be said, and the food to be passed to everyone at the table before you begin eating.
- Thank the person who cooked the meal.
- Talk to the person nearest you, and listen to what others are talking about. Do you have a question or story that goes along with what they're saying?
- While others are talking, you can eat. But don't talk with food in your mouth.
- Pay attention to the people who are being quiet. Ask questions to get them talking, such as, "How are things going for you?" or "How'd you do on that test/project/activity today?"

Honor

Prayer Pointer

Lord, thank You so much for blessing me with good food and good family to share it with. Help me bless others as much as You have blessed me.

Godly Girls

So God created human beings in His image.
In the image of God He created them.
He created them male and female.

GENESIS 1:27

MARCH 23

As a girl, you've probably noticed that all twelve of Jesus' disciples were men. But did you know that Jesus had girls on His team too? Many of His followers were women (Luke 8). One of those women was named Mary Magdalene. She had suffered from seven demons living inside of her, but Jesus healed her. The Bible says she joined Susanna, Joanna, Salome, Mary the mother of Jesus, Mary the mother of James and Joseph, and the mother of James and John, among others. They not only followed Jesus, but they helped pay for the disciples' needs out of their own pockets.

So what did Jesus think about His female followers? He loved them! As He hung on the cross, He made sure John took care of His mother. And when He rose again from the grave, He first appeared to Mary Magdalene, so she could tell everyone the good news. Jesus loves all His people just the same—and we all have an important role to play in His kingdom.

Prayer Pointer

Glory

Thank You, Jesus, for Your love for me—
and for my place in Your kingdom.

Starstruck

"You should be a light for other people. Live so that they will see the good things you do. Live so that they will praise your Father in heaven."

MATTHEW 5:16

Lie: I need to be famous.

Mandy was watching her favorite singing competition show on TV. It was down to the final two contestants.

"I would give anything to be on stage like that," she mused out loud to her brother. "Wouldn't it be awesome to have everybody know your name and think you're really talented?"

"It'd probably be pretty fun for a while," he agreed.

"Yeah, and everywhere you went, people would know you, and you could get whatever you wanted."

"True, but fame does seem to have its drawbacks," he answered thoughtfully.

The Truth Is . . .

It seems like everyone is clamoring to become the next superstar sensation. But why? What is at the heart of wanting to become famous? The truth is that we all have a fear deep inside that we are not special. We think we are just one of billions of people on this planet who doesn't do anything to give our short time on this earth any particular meaning. So we figure if we can get a great career or become a famous performer or politician, we will stand out. People will notice us. We will matter.

But God tells you, child of God, that you *do* matter because He sees you (out of all the billions of people) and loves *you*. And because His Spirit lives in you, you already shine like a star in a dark universe. Even if the people around you can't see it now, all of heaven does.

Don't get stuck in the vain search for fame. Instead, work hard to make God, your Father, known.

Prayer Pointer

Lord, I want my life to reflect how brilliant You are. Thanks for loving me!

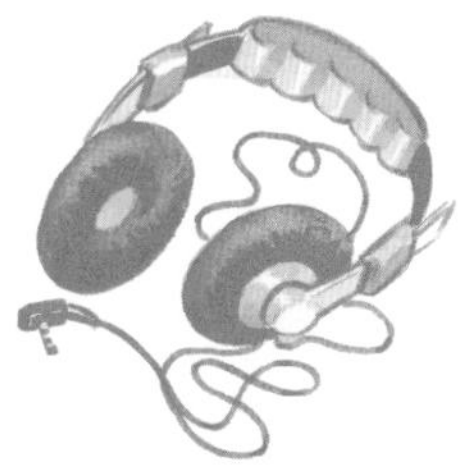

MARCH 25

Creative Genius

The Lord is the God who lives forever.
He created all the world. . . . No one can
understand how great His wisdom is.

ISAIAH 40:28

On a sheet of paper, draw something spectacular.

Was it hard to come up with ideas? Imagine what it must have been like for God before He created the earth. Talk about a blank canvas! Then God spoke, and the most amazing creation appeared. He placed the stars and planets in just the right spots, with the perfect balance of gravity keeping everything in order. Then He zeroed in on Earth, crafting every tiny blade of grass, every great creature, and every breathtaking landscape that exists. God is beyond genius, and His creativity goes beyond our ability to understand.

That same creative God lives in you. When you share your thoughts in a poem or song, you're reflecting His creativity. When you draw or paint, you mirror God's flair for beauty and color. And when you boldly share something God has taught you through His Word, you're helping the world see His glory in a brilliant, new way.

Prayer Pointer

God, please help me share Your love
with the world in creative ways.

Miriam, Who Helped

Respect the Lord your God. Serve only Him.

DEUTERONOMY 6:13

Times were tough. The new pharaoh had ordered that all Israelite baby boys be killed. But Jochebed and Amram didn't obey orders when their baby Moses was born. The mom, Jochebed, nursed Moses until he was too old to hide. Then she crafted a floating basket, put Moses inside, and placed it near the Nile River's edge.

Miriam, Moses' older sister, watched the basket until it was discovered by the pharaoh's own daughter. When the princess saw the baby, she wanted to keep him. But how would she care for him?

"I'll find a Hebrew woman who'll nurse him for you," Miriam volunteered boldly. The princess agreed! So Miriam got their own mom to take care of Moses until he was old enough to go to the pharaoh's courts (Exodus 2:1–10).

Do you like helping your family? Taking in the groceries or vacuuming might not seem as glamorous as Miriam's role, but every part we play in helping God's people *is* important. God uses our kindness to grow His kingdom, one helping deed at a time.

Prayer Pointer

Lord, help me see the needs around me and be quick to help.

MARCH 27

Lean on Me

Good advice from a friend is sweet.

PROVERBS 27:9

Mary was excited, but also concerned. An angel had told her she was going to have God's baby, but she wasn't even married to Joseph yet. She knew the people in her village would probably say bad things about her. Still, she was thrilled to be a part of God's plan to save His people.

But Mary didn't tough it out on her own. She went to live with her older cousin, Elizabeth, for several months. Elizabeth loved God, and she was also pregnant. God had given them each other for comfort and friendship as they trusted Him to work out His mysterious plan for their lives (Luke 1:26–56). What a blessing!

God doesn't want you to go through life all alone either. He made each of us to need one another. Make a list of parents, teachers, or friends who encourage you to follow God.

If the list is shorter than you'd like, ask God to help you find good friends who love God. Then spend time building a good friendship with each person. Like Mary and Elizabeth, you can help each other stand strong in the faith!

PRAYER POINTER Hope

Lord, please help me find friends who can support me in the tough times.

Listen Up!

Always be willing to listen and slow to speak.

JAMES 1:19

"Mom, I really want to go to that art camp," Alison said.

"Well—" her mom tried to say, but Alison kept talking. "Two of my friends are going!"

"I've heard—" her mom tried again.

"And I could help pay for it with my babysitting money, and—"

"Alison!"

"What, Mom?" Alison finally stopped talking.

Her mom laughed. "Alison, I've been trying to tell you that I've already decided you can go."

"Oh! Umm . . . thanks, Mom," Alison said, feeling a little embarrassed.

Alison was so busy talking that she forgot to listen. It's easy to get so focused on what you want to say that you miss what others are trying to tell you. Make sure you take time to listen to what others have to say. And it's the same with your conversations with God. Yes, He always listens to you—and loves to hear what you have to say. But be sure to take time to just sit quietly and listen to Him.

I'm so grateful, God, that you always listen to me. Help me to remember to listen to You.

Mirror Makeover

You will be like a beautiful crown in the Lord's hand.

ISAIAH 62:3

What You Need:

- dry erase markers
- clear tape
- a piece of paper

Directions:

Look in your bathroom mirror. Cover your face on the mirror with a piece of paper, and tape it in place. Now trace the outline of the paper with your dry erase marker. Remove the paper. (You should have a rectangle drawn on the mirror that frames your reflection.) Now decorate the outside of the border, helping your rectangle look like a picture frame. Using dry erase markers, write one of these verses below the frame so you will see it every day:

- I praise you because you made me in an amazing and wonderful way. What you have done is wonderful. I know this very well. (Psalm 139:14)
- God does not see the same way people see. People look at the outside of a person, but the Lord looks at the heart. (1 Samuel 16:7)

Prayer Pointer

Dear God, thank You for making me in Your image as Your beautifully unique child. Help me remember this truth every single day.

Camo Power

We know that in everything God works
for the good of those who love Him.

ROMANS 8:28

You can stare at a fish tank for several minutes without seeing a thing. Suddenly, the sandy bottom looks like it's stirring. Is something swimming? Well, it wasn't really the bottom. It was a flounder, a very flat fish with both eyes on top, camouflaged perfectly in the sandy setting. God designed it to blend in so well that predators can't see it, keeping it safe in a dangerous place.

God is really good at disguising things, including Himself. Sometimes we feel like God is not around, because we can't see Him with our eyes. We get worried when things go wrong and wonder if anybody even cares. Then God lets us see a ripple, like the camouflaged flounder on the move. That ripple might be a friend who calls at just the right time. Or a hug from Mom. Or a kind word from your sibling. God is always with us, even though we can't see Him, and He is always working for our good.

Prayer Pointer

Lord, thank You for being with me,
even though I can't see You.

MARCH 31

Love in Action

"One must love His neighbor as He loves Himself."

MARK 12:33

You've probably heard Jesus' famous command, "Love your neighbor as yourself." What does that really look like? Jesus explained that "neighbor" means anyone God brings into your life. To put the idea into practice, pick one of your actual neighbors this week, and choose from the following:

- Make a meal that you like to help your mom prepare, or bake cookies, then take the food over.
- Write a card that tells your neighbors how much you and God love them.
- With your mom's permission and help, offer to babysit so they can have a night out.
- Plant an herb or vegetable garden in your backyard and give some to your neighbors.

Keep a journal of your visits. Each time, answer the following questions in your journal:

- How did it make you feel to love your neighbors this way?
- How did they respond?
- How can you pray for them?

Prayer Pointer

God, help me to remember to bless my neighbors with Your love.

Write It Out

You will help the blind to see. You will free those who are in prison. You will lead those who live in darkness out of their prison.

ISAIAH 42:7

When Jesus walked on earth, He healed and helped everywhere He went. Now He uses His people to do His work. Where do you see Jesus working in the world? How about in your church or school, and in your own life? In the kindness of your teachers, or in the forgiving attitude of your friends? When your mom makes a sacrifice for you, or when an artist creates something beautiful? Write what comes to mind in the lines below.

Prayer Pointer

Jesus, open my eyes to see all the ways You work in the world—and how you can use me.

APRIL 2

Walking Away

Try hard to live right and to have faith, love, and peace. Work for these things together with those . . . who trust in the Lord.

2 TIMOTHY 2:22

Scenario

Emily was thrilled to be invited to the sleepover. She was new in school and trying to make friends. But during the party, the girls decided to watch a scary movie. Emily knew her mom wouldn't approve, so she asked the girls to pick a different one.

"But we all love scary movies!" the host girl responded. "Plus, you don't have to tell your mom."

Solution

Emily could cave to the peer pressure, but what would she get in return? She'd be building friendships with girls who don't value what she does and hurting her relationships with her mom and God. Though it's hard to walk away, Emily would be wise to say, "Okay. Then I'm going upstairs to read. Please let me know when it's over."

In the search for good friends, sometimes we have to walk away from people who aren't ready to follow God. We can be kind and pray for them, but our deep friendships need to be with those who love God too.

Prayer Pointer

God, give me wisdom to know when I need to choose new friends.

When Things Become King

"Be careful and guard against all kinds of greed. A man's life is not measured by the many things he owns."

LUKE 12:15

Hey, Anna," Becca called. "Did you get the newest one yet?"

Becca and Anna were both collecting tiny, stuffed animal characters. They were really cute. Some were from movies; others wore sunglasses or even earbuds.

"No," Anna sighed. "I've got to save up my money."

"I thought you already had enough," Becca said.

"Well, I did, but it was my brother's birthday, so I decided to get something for him instead."

"Are you crazy?" asked Becca, rolling her eyes. "I wouldn't let my brother's birthday stop me. I've got all of them now. Nobody has more than me. I'm the queen of collectors!" she bragged.

Do you think Becca might be getting a little too wrapped up in her collection? After all, things don't last forever. And there'll probably be something completely new to collect pretty soon. It's fine to have things, but don't ever let things become king in your life. A life filled with God and family and friends is a much greater treasure than any *thing*.

PRAYER POINTER grace

Lord, help me to remember that You and people are much more important than things.

Lights, Camera, Action!

"The eye is a light for the body. If your eyes are good, then your whole body will be full of light."

MATTHEW 6:22

Did you know that you own one of the most complex cameras in the world? And it's sitting right in your face! Incredibly, your eye is designed so that light reflecting off objects shines into your eye, through the cornea (clear), and to the pupil, which regulates the amount of light allowed in. Then the light passes through a lens, which bends the light so the image is flipped and strikes the retina, where rods and cones absorb the light and send the message to your brain. Your brain reads the message, interprets it, and lets your eyes know what you're seeing. Pretty complicated, huh?

God has a lot to say about our eyesight. He wants us to remember that everything comes from Him and to keep our eyes focused on Him. Take time to thank Him for your eyes, and ask Him to help you see and do what pleases Him.

Prayer Pointer

Father, help me keep my focus on You as I enjoy this incredible world You have made.

Sweet Music

Shout with joy to the Lord, all the earth. Burst into songs and praise.

PSALM 98:4

APRIL 5

Hannah sighed as she listened to Gracie finish singing her solo.

"Gracie has such a beautiful voice. I wish I could sing like that," Hannah said. "When I sing, it sounds more like a dying frog."

"Don't be silly," Faith laughed and hugged her friend. "Gracie is great at singing, but you're great at lots of things too. And you don't sound like a frog. Besides, God doesn't care how we sound as long as we're singing to Him."

Faith is right. Some people have a gift for singing, while others . . . well, they have other gifts. But you know what? God still loves to hear them sing. God doesn't care if our voice can carry the show, or if we can't carry a tune. God only cares that we sing our praises to Him with all our heart. Because praises are sweet music to His ears.

Prayer Pointer

Lord, I lift up my praises to You and I thank You for all the gifts You've given me. Help me to use my gifts to bring glory to You.

Tech Talk

"Come to me and listen. Listen to me so you may live."

ISAIAH 55:3

Isn't technology awesome? We can get all sorts of information, play endless games, watch videos, and text people—all with a computer, tablet, or phone. But if we don't watch it, we can lose the beauty of real-life relationships with people and with God if our technology starts to take over.

So has technology taken over your life, or do you have control over this high-tech temptation? Take this quiz to find out.

1. T F I have heard my parents complain about how often I'm on the computer/phone.
2. T F I find it very hard to stop playing and/or texting when it's time to do homework.
3. T F I often forget to look up from my device when someone is talking to me.
4. T F I feel uncomfortable when I don't have my device with me.
5. T F I sometimes look up things or click on links that my parents wouldn't approve.
6. T F I like to use earphones to keep my world to myself and keep other people out.

7. **T F** I often lose track of time when I'm on my device.

8. **T F** I check my device for new information and messages first thing every morning.
9. **T F** I often try to get on my device even after I'm supposed to be in bed.
10. **T F** I get snappy whenever my parents ask me to turn my device off.

If you answered *False* to all of these, then congratulations! You are a tech master and are able to control your time with technology. If you answered *True* to any of the above, ask God to help you take back your time, and turn your focus to Him and the people He's placed in your life.

Prayer Pointer

Jesus, help me to focus on You and doing the things You want instead of focusing on a screen.

The Light Switch

Your word is like a lamp for my feet
and a light for my way.

PSALM 119:105

Can you imagine our world without light? Try this experiment: Let a friend go in another room and set up some objects that you haven't seen, like books, pictures, flowers, or a spice jar. Next, have your friend turn off all the lights and put a blindfold around your eyes. Carefully explore the objects she set up using your other senses, like touch and smell, to help you figure out what they are. When you're satisfied with your investigation, turn on the lights and remove the blindfold. How did you do? Were you able to identify each item, or did some confuse you?

God never meant for us to stumble around in darkness. And God's Word is a light that helps us see what's going on in people's hearts and lives. So don't stumble around in darkness, missing the beauty of who God is and who He has made you to be. Turn on the light of His Word!

Prayer Pointer

Father, thank You for the Bible. It helps me know You and how I fit in Your plan.

Copy Cat

Listen to your father's teaching. And do not forget your mother's advice. Their teaching will beautify your life.

PROVERBS 1:8–9

Did you know that kittens aren't born knowing how to hunt? Even though they look like pros when they're pouncing on some poor, unsuspecting chipmunk, the best hunters learned their skills from their mother. The mama cat trains her kittens to stalk, catch, and kill their prey. Kittens need these skills to take care of themselves.

Fortunately, our mothers don't teach us how to stalk and kill creatures. But there are plenty of skills that we *can* learn from our parents. Their life experiences and time with God give them a better understanding of life situations and how to deal with them. So listen to what your parents say, and follow their example. By imitation and obedience, you will grow up strong in the Lord and be able to lead others on the same path of wisdom. And always show other parents the same respect you show your own. You never know when God will use them to teach you a new skill for life!

Prayer Pointer

Lord, thank You for guiding and training me through my parents.

APRIL 9

Sing, Sing, Sing

They sang a hymn. Then they went out to the Mount of Olives.

MATTHEW 26:30

Today during my devotion time, I read the part in Matthew where Jesus had finished eating dinner with His disciples, right before He was arrested. Jesus must have had so much on His mind—He knew what was about to happen. This time I noticed a tiny part of the story I hadn't seen before.

Before they went to the garden to pray, Jesus led the disciples in singing a hymn to God. What would it be like to sing to God *with* God? And it got me thinking: singing is more than just something fun to do. It's a special way God created for us to worship Him. After all, Jesus' birth was announced to shepherds with a crowd of singing angels. Paul and Silas sang hymns while they were in prison. And throughout Scripture God tells us to sing to Him and on another. Why? Because when hearts are full of thanks, they overflow in songs of joy.

So the next time you turn on the radio or find yourself at church, don't hold back. Sing with all your heart to God who hears you, loves it, and joins with you in song.

gracie

Prayer Pointer

Lord, help me honor You with Your gift of singing!

Lonely Looks

Turn to me and be kind to me. I am lonely and hurting.

PSALM 25:16

APRIL 10

Scenario

It wasn't that she didn't have *any* friends. Bella knew there were plenty of people she could call to invite over. *But how come nobody ever invites me?* she wondered. *I guess they don't really want to be with me.*

Meanwhile, two streets down, Hadley was thinking, *I'm so lonely! Nobody ever wants to hang out with me. What's wrong with me?*

Solution

Both Bella and Hadley feel alone and sad. The truth is, all people feel lonely sometimes. Because of Adam and Eve's sin, our relationships with God and each other became messed up. But God has fixed the brokenness through Jesus. Now we never have to feel alone because Jesus is with us always.

Whenever we're feeling lonely, we first need to talk to Jesus and ask Him to help us know He's there. Then we need to follow Jesus' example. He left heaven to come and invite us into friendship with Him, so we need to reach out to others and invite them to be our friends too.

Prayer Pointer

Glory

Lord, loneliness is difficult, but it reminds me to talk to You and reach out to others. Thank You for being a faithful friend.

Secret Safe

People, trust God all the time. Tell Him all your problems. God is our protection.

PSALM 62:8

Have you ever told your best friend a secret, only to find out later that she blabbed it to someone else? It's enough to make you wonder if there's anyone you can trust.

Jesus understands. A close friend betrayed Him too. Judas was one of Jesus' followers, but he snuck behind Jesus' back and told His enemies where they could find Him to arrest Him. Even though Jesus knew what Judas was going to do, it still had to hurt.

Jesus wants you to know that your secrets are safe with Him. When you tell Him about your worries, those sins you can't seem to conquer, or what you need, He won't make fun of you or tell your secrets to anyone. Instead, He'll listen and comfort you. And He'll answer with real wisdom—either through His Bible or through someone you trust. There's no need to keep all that's bothering you trapped inside. Trust Jesus with your problems, and discover the joy of a truly trustworthy Friend!

Prayer Pointer

Jesus, thank You for being my Friend. I know I can always trust You.

Inner Power

"I will put my spirit inside you. And I will help you live by my rules. You will be careful to obey my laws."

EZEKIEL 36:27

How would you like a bed of saliva? No thanks? Well, you must not be a baby electric eel then. The bed of saliva formed by the male electric eel makes the perfect place for the female to lay more than seventeen thousand eggs. Electric eels have an electricity-producing organ inside them that takes up about eighty percent of their body, making them able to produce up to six hundred volts of electricity when they're attacked or hunting prey. That's enough electricity to light twelve light bulbs!

While electric eels look like ordinary eels, they have a secret source of power inside. Christians, too, look like ordinary people. But the difference lies within us. When we place our faith in Jesus, God puts His Spirit inside of us, filling us with His amazing power. Why not shock the people around you with the remarkable power of God's love for them today?

Prayer Pointer

Father, because of Your power in me, I am empowered to live well for You. Thank You!

Duck Feathers

Love does not remember wrongs done against it.

1 CORINTHIANS 13:5

Have you heard the saying "Don't worry. Just let it roll off your back"? It means to forget the bad things and focus on the good instead. This saying is inspired by our feathered friends—ducks! Unlike mammals, which have hair, ducks are covered with feathers. Feathers are uniquely made to shelter ducks from wind and rain while also providing the lift they need to fly above predators. To become water repellent, ducks use their bills to spread oil from a gland at the base of their tails to coat their feathers. Then they can float on water, dive underneath it, and even stand in a rainstorm—and the water rolls right off.

In many ways, acting like a duck can help friendships. Because your friends are imperfect, just like you, there will be times when they're selfish instead of serving or cruel instead of kind. Instead of dumping them, remember the ducks. Let your friends' actions roll off your back and into the forgiveness Jesus offers both them and you. Offer them kindness and understanding—and your friendships will take flight.

Prayer Pointer

Honor

Lord, help me not take other people's faults so seriously. Help me forgive them as You forgive me.

Share the Spotlight

No one should try to do what will help only himself. He should try to do what is good for others.

1 CORINTHIANS 10:24

APRIL 14

Lexie was the star of the basketball team. If she got the ball, she was almost sure to score. Tonight was the last game, and the team was winning by twenty points. Lexie was playing, but the coach had also put in some girls who didn't get to play often. With just a few seconds left, Lexie got the ball and headed for the basket. Then she saw Angie, who'd never scored before. With a smile, she called, "Hey, Angie!" and passed her the ball. The crowd chanted Angie's name. She went in for a layup and scored!

Lexie could have easily kept the ball and scored again. But she gave Angie a chance to shine. And for Angie, it was a wonderfully special night.

Think of something you're great at, that you can do better than pretty much anyone you know. While it feels good to make every basket, answer every question, or always be first, be sure to share the spotlight—and let others have a chance to shine.

Hope

Prayer Pointer

Lord, thank You for blessing me with my talents. I want to use them to help others shine too.

Mary, Who Worshipped

Praise Him, you servants of the Lord.

PSALM 135:1

Mary, Martha, and Lazarus—a family near and dear to Jesus—had already learned so much from the Teacher. Earlier, Martha had learned that it was better to sit at Jesus' feet and listen than to tire herself out with unnecessary preparations. All of them had witnessed the miracle of Jesus raising Lazarus from the dead. And now they were all together again with Jesus, eating dinner.

But Mary took her love and devotion even further. Taking a jar of very expensive perfume, she broke it open and poured it on Jesus' feet, wiping it with her own hair. Her act showed how much she loved and valued Jesus. Even though Jesus' apostle Judas thought it was a waste, Jesus said it was beautiful (John 12:1–8).

When we humble ourselves and worship God, we touch His heart—whether that's with perfume like Mary or by falling down in prayer and praise like the angels around God's throne. Are you willing to show Him your love through your life and your praise?

Prayer Pointer

Father, You love it when we praise You. Fill my heart and mouth with Your praise.

Who Are We Pleasing?

We must obey God, not men!

ACTS 5:29

APRIL 16

Oh, come on, Annie," Becca pleaded. "We really want you to go to the movies with us Saturday."

"I know," Annie said. "And I want to go, but I've already promised to deliver food with my church group to people who need help."

"Can't you do that any Saturday?" Becca asked. "Besides, I really want you to come and sit by me."

"Yeah, I guess." Annie hesitated. But then she thought about the promise she'd made and said, "But I have to keep my word. I'll try to come with you next time."

It can be hard to say no to friends, but sometimes that's what we have to do. Whether it's saying no to something that's wrong, or even saying no to something good that's just at the wrong time, we have to remember that God should be the One we try to please first. When you're torn between choices, ask yourself whom you're really trying to please.

Prayer Pointer

Lord, help me make good choices, and make my heart want to please You more than people.

Sheltered Sheep

We are His people, the sheep He tends.

PSALM 100:3

What keeps a sheep safe and sound? The shepherd, of course. And Jesus lets us know that we are His sheep, and He is the best Shepherd ever. Look up Psalm 23, and fill in the blanks below, including any worries or thoughts you have on your mind today that Jesus, your Shepherd, can handle.

The Lord is my ____________________.

I have ______________ I need (*including my food, my clothes, my ____________________, ______________, ______________, and ________________________).

He gives me ________________ in green pastures.

He leads me to calm ______________.

He gives me new ________________ (to do the following things: ________, ______________, ______________________, ________________, and even ______________).

For the good of His name,

He ________________ me on paths that are ______________.

Even if I ____________through a very dark ________________ (such as ________________________ or ____________________), I *will not* be _________ because (choose the right answer below)

a. I am a tough kid.

b. My parents will take care of me.

c. God is with me.

Your ____________ and your shepherd's staff ______________________ me. You prepare a _____ for me in front of my enemies.

You pour _______________ on my head (not to make it greasy, but to let me know I am a child of the King).

You give me ______ than I can hold.

Surely your ______________ and ________________ will be with me _________________ my life.

And I will ________ in the house of the _________________ *forever*!

Prayer Pointer

God, thank You for being my Good Shepherd. Help me to be a loyal and faithful follower of You.

A Swimming Idea

Jesus has the power of God. His power has given us everything we need to live and to serve God.

2 PETER 1:3

Want to go for a swim? How about a two-thousand-mile-long swim? If you were an Alaskan salmon, that's exactly what you'd do. Salmon hatch from eggs in a freshwater stream in Alaska. As they grow, they travel downstream until they reach the ocean. They spend between one and eight years swimming more than two thousand miles in the Pacific Ocean. Then, amazingly, they find the stream they traveled down years ago and begin the incredibly difficult journey back upstream, jumping up waterfalls and escaping hungry bears along the way. Once they reach their birthplace, the salmon lay eggs, and a new generation takes over the process.

It takes work and determination for a salmon to swim upstream. Yet God gifted these creatures with the strength for the journey. You, too, might find that swimming upstream—against the culture—is hard. Wearing the same clothes, listening to the same music, and acting the same way as non-Christians might seem easier, but it wouldn't be better. God's way always leads to a greater purpose and new life.

Prayer Pointer

Jesus, please give me strength to swim against the stream and follow Your way instead of the world's.

Looking Up

Seek those things which are above.

COLOSSIANS 3:1 KJV

APRIL 19

Who do you look up to?

If you lived in the savanna regions of Africa, you'd look up to giraffes, the tallest mammals in the world. With six-foot legs, a six-foot neck, and feet the size of dinner plates, these lanky, spotted animals lumber around the savanna searching for food from up high, where the thickest and best acacia leaves grow. To fuel their large bodies, giraffes eat up to one hundred pounds of leaves each day! Not many predators tackle creatures their size, so giraffes can live up to twenty-five years, even in the wild.

Like giraffes, we need to look up for our food too. God is more nourishing to our souls than any food found on earth. If we want our spiritual bodies to grow tall and strong, we need to feed on heavenly things—the truths we find in God's Word. Just like giraffes eat lots of food every day, we also need to look for God in His Word every day. Standing tall and strong, we'll be better able to fight off Satan and any other forces that come against us.

Prayer Pointer

Lord, help me keep my eyes focused on You. Feed me Your truth.

Source of Strength

Some trust in chariots, others in horses.
But we trust the Lord our God.

PSALM 20:7

Can you imagine sleeping while standing up? If you were a horse, you could! It's just one fascinating fact about these beautiful creatures. From the very beginning, people have recognized horses not only for their beauty but also for their power and speed. Able to run shortly after birth, young horses can reach galloping speeds of more than twenty-seven miles per hour. The fastest horse was clocked at nearly forty-five miles per hour!

Armies once used horses to carry troops and supplies into battle. In fact, nations often measured their military strength by how many horses and chariots they had. However, God tells His people not to measure their strength by their possessions. He wants them to trust Him for hope and power. As the Creator of horses (and everything else), God is our most powerful resource, especially in times of trouble.

Whenever you need help, let the horse's beauty and strength remind you of the One who made it. He invites you to come to Him for all you need.

Prayer Pointer

God, my help comes from You alone. Thank You for being everything I need.

Free to Fail

Those who are in Christ Jesus are not judged guilty.

ROMANS 8:1

It's not my fault!" Alyssa yelled defensively as her mother pulled burned cookies out of the oven.

"If you hadn't turned the TV up so loud, you would've heard the buzzer," replied her mother.

"You guys blame me for everything!" Alyssa cried, stomping off to her room.

The truth is, Alyssa was given a task, and she didn't do it correctly. Has that ever happened to you? How did you react?

We sometimes don't like to admit when we've done something wrong. Maybe we're afraid we'll be judged, we'll get in trouble, or people will stop liking us. We might even worry that God will give up on us, especially if we keep repeating the same sin or mistake over and over again.

But God never gives up on you, and His Son, Jesus, has already paid the price for all the sins you've ever made or ever will make. You aren't guilty anymore. You are a forgiven child of God, and the Father always loves and accepts you—in Jesus.

Prayer Pointer

Thank You, Jesus, for covering all my sins and making me right with God forever.

APRIL 22

Pay Attention!

The Lord said to me, "Human being, believe all the words that I will speak to you. And listen carefully."

EZEKIEL 3:10

How well do you know your best friend? Go ahead and ask yourself: *Do I know her favorite color? Her favorite hobby? Things that make her happy or angry? The kind of music she likes?*

Now talk to her, and ask her these same questions. How well did you do?

The truth is we get to know other people by just being around them. We watch them and learn what they do. Most importantly, we listen to what they say. That information helps us understand who they really are and how to be a closer friend.

The same is true about God. We talk to Him through prayer, and He talks to us through the Bible and the Holy Spirit, who lives inside us. The Bible is different from any other book because God inspired all of it, using different people to record His exact words. Because the Bible comes from God, it helps us understand how to be friends with Him. And His Spirit helps us remember and follow what God tells us in His Word.

PRAYER POINTER Hope

Lord, help me grow closer to You by listening and obeying Your Word.

Honor Honesty

"Tell each other the truth. In the courts judge with truth and complete fairness. Do not make plans to hurt your neighbors. And don't make false promises. I hate all these things," says the Lord.

ZECHARIAH 8:16–17

APRIL 23

Doesn't it seem like almost every day you see something on TV or on the Internet that's hard to believe? It's some sort of juicy gossip that people just have to know about, then talk about with their friends. Or maybe you hear something in the halls at school about one of your friends, and you know it is absolutely not true. You know in your heart that you shouldn't join in with the gossip and, better yet, you should even stand up to defend your friend. That's the honest and honorable thing to do, right?

These verses in Zechariah are all about what we should do in that situation and how God's blessings will flow on us when we obey Him. Love what the Lord loves, and hate what the Lord hates. So we are to hate lies and love truth as well. Keep it honest, and you will be blessed.

Prayer Pointer — Honor

God, help me to be brave enough to always tell the truth and to stand up to those who tell lies.

Cooler Than Cool

Do not be shaped by this world.

ROMANS 12:2

Scenario

Emma was usually a calm and respectful daughter. But something happened when her friends came over: Emma became very excited and talked loudly over her family and guests. Her jokes and comments took teasing in a bad direction, often at the expense of her sisters. Worst of all, she argued when her mom asked her to do anything.

Solution

Emma is trying to fit in with her friends. But she's started to think her friends would be more impressed if she made fun of her sisters or proved that her mom is not the boss of her. Do you think her actions will help or hurt her friendships? Why?

Everyone wants to fit in, but God warns us not to act like the people who don't know Him. God made us to be an awesome blessing to our friends and family just the way we are; we don't have to fake it. Emma, like the rest of us, needs to realize that she's a wonderful daughter of God. And what could be cooler than that?

Prayer Pointer

Lord, please help me be real with You and everyone else.

I Can Do All Things?

I can do all things through Christ
because He gives me strength.

PHILIPPIANS 4:13

APRIL 25

A lot of people seem to think that Philippians 4:13 means that God will help you to do anything you want to do. But that's not exactly true. God wants only the very best for you. And He knows (because He knows *all* things) that sometimes what you want isn't what's best. So what does Philippians 4:13 mean?

When God says that you "can do all things through Christ," He means all the things that He's asked you to do. You know, all those really tough things like obeying when you'd rather not, loving your enemies (yes, *her* too!), forgiving others, and speaking up for what's right. It also means Jesus will help you live and love the way He did, like serving others even when you're tired, making friends with people who are different from you, and giving your time and your money. God's got so many good things planned for you to do—and He promises He'll help you do them.

Prayer Pointer

Lord, show me what You want me to do for You today—and thank You for then helping me do it.

Walking Home

What does the LORD require of you but to do justly, to love mercy, and to walk humbly with your God?

MICAH 6:8 NKJV

Have you ever taken a walk by yourself? How would walking that same route with a close friend be different?

When you're alone, you have only your own thoughts to entertain you. But walk with a friend, and a whole new world of conversation opens up. You're no longer taking in the scenes by yourself; you're sharing them. And as you walk and talk, you find that spending time with your friend brings you closer to each other.

Enoch knew all about walking and talking with his best friend. He did it every day of his life. But Enoch's closest friend wasn't from school. His best friend was God! Enoch became so close to God by talking to Him and obeying Him that God decided to take Enoch straight to heaven (Genesis 5:22–24)!

You don't ever have to be alone. God is always with you, ready to walk and talk with you wherever you go. If you answer Him and follow His direction, you'll be like Enoch, walking through life with the Creator of the world at your side.

PRAYER POINTER *Glory*

Lord, please be my closest friend for all my life.

Write It Out

The One who was sitting on the throne said, "Look! I am making everything new!"

REVELATION 21:5

Read Revelation 21. What do you think heaven will be like? What are you most looking forward to about heaven?

Prayer Pointer

Lord, thank You for preparing a place in heaven for me.

Buddy Building

Let each of us please his neighbor for his good, to help him be stronger in faith.

ROMANS 15:2

Jesus says that good friends build each other up and help each other grow stronger. But encouraging others doesn't always come naturally, especially when we don't feel good about ourselves or when we find ourselves competing with friends instead of supporting them. So take this quiz to test your buddy-building strength.

1. Your friend just made a bad grade on a test that you aced. You:
   a. pretend you don't know her score.
   b. laugh and tell her that you didn't even have to study.
   c. give her a hug and tell her you're sorry. Then ask if she'd like to study with you next time.

2. If your friend hadn't missed the last catch, your team would have won the game. You:
   a. throw down your glove and walk off alone.
   b. tell her she should try a different sport.
   c. smile and say, "Don't worry about it! We all make mistakes sometimes."

3. Your friend just got exactly the kind of puppy you've always wanted. You:
   a. act like you don't care.
   b. tell her how much trouble it is to have a dog.
   c. tell her how excited you are for her and ask if you can come over to see it.

4. Your sister has just spent the last hour getting ready for a dance. You look at her and say:
   a. "That outfit makes you look fat."
   b. "Why are you wearing your hair like that?"
   c. "You sure look pretty. I hope you have fun!"

If you picked *C* for your answers, then you're a trained buddy builder! But if you answered *A* or *B* for any of the above, you could use a little strength training. Remember, your words can bring joy or sorrow, so choose them carefully. Ask God to help you find creative ways to build up your buddies.

Prayer Pointer

Jesus, give me words of encouragement so I can build up my friends.

Word to the Wise

There must be no evil talk among you. . . .
These things are not right for you.

EPHESIANS 5:4

Scenario

It wasn't a problem when she was homeschooled, but now that Alli was in a public school, curse words seemed to be everywhere. In fact, taking God's name in vain and adding coarse words to every sentence actually seemed like requirements for fitting in with the cool kids.

It's in all the movies and TV shows my friends watch. I guess it's just unavoidable, she decided.

Solution

If bad language is commonplace in your home or, like Alli, you attend school or play a sport where everyone else says curse words, then you know how easy it is to start talking like that. Does God care about what we say?

Yes! God wants His children to shine like stars in a dark universe. Many people around us don't know God or what is good and true. By choosing our words wisely and honoring God with what we say, we shine with God's purity and love.

Prayer Pointer

Lord, I want all my words to please You. Fill me with Your love so that it overflows in what I say.

Nothing Bigger

Who has measured the oceans in the palm of His hand? Who has used His hand to measure the sky?

ISAIAH 40:12

What's the biggest thing you can think of? A mountain? The Grand Canyon? The moon? No matter what you can think of, there's one thing that's bigger—God! He's bigger than anything because He created everything. He can hold the whole ocean in the palm of His hand. He can measure the sky with His fingers. God is so big that He knows every star and can count every grain of sand.

God is bigger than we could ever imagine—and more powerful too. But the best thing about God isn't how big or how strong or how mighty He is; it's how much He loves each and every one of us. His love for us is bigger than any ocean and stretches even farther than the sky. It's so big that He sacrificed His Son to save us. And there's nothing bigger than that!

Prayer Pointer

Lord, You are so big and so mighty, but You still love someone as small as me. Thank You, God, for making me feel big with Your love.

MAY 1

Rough Days

The Lord hears good people when they cry out to Him. He saves them from all their troubles. The Lord is close to the brokenhearted.

PSALM 34:17–18

It had been a really rough day. Gracie dropped her backpack on the floor and slumped down on her bed. She'd bombed the test and, in her worry, had snapped at a friend. Now she realized that she'd forgotten to put away her laundry, and her mom was sure to be upset. As tears of frustration filled her eyes, she looked up and simply prayed, *God?*

We all have days when nothing seems to go right. But no matter the trouble, if it's our own fault or someone else's, God is there to listen and to help. You don't even have to know the words to say. Just open up and let all those worries, frustrations, and hurt feelings pour out to Him. Then turn to His Word, and let Him pour His answers into you with words like, "I will never leave you" (Hebrews 13:5), "The Lord is close to the brokenhearted" (Psalm 34:18), and "Nothing can separate us from the love God has for us" (Romans 8:38).

Prayer Pointer

God, I'm so grateful that You always listen and understand. I know You'll help me.

More Than a Book

Use the shield of faith. With that you can stop all the burning arrows of the Evil One.

EPHESIANS 6:16

MAY 2

Did you know you're in the middle of a war? It's true. It's a war with Satan, and he's attacking all the time. One of his favorite weapons is telling lies—after all, he's the father of lies. But God protects you. He's given you a shield, the Bible, to protect you from Satan's lies. For example,

- Satan says you're not good enough, but God says you're amazing and wonderful (Psalm 139:14).
- Satan says you're a nobody, but God says you're His very own child when you follow Him (John 1:12).
- Satan says you're not pretty enough, but God says everything about you is beautiful (Song of Solomon 4:7).
- Satan says nobody cares about you, but God says He loves you so much He sent His Son to save you (John 3:16).

When Satan's ugly lies start to haunt you, let God's Word protect you. Make time to read your Bible, study it, and memorize its words—because it's not just a book; it's your shield.

PRAYER POINTER gracie

Thank You, Lord, for shielding me. When Satan tells me his lies, fill me with the truth of Your Word.

MAY 3

Sword Fight

God's word is alive and working. It is sharper than a sword sharpened on both sides. It cuts all the way into us, where the soul and the spirit are joined.

HEBREWS 4:12

Have you ever watched fencing? No, not the stuff that surrounds your yard, but the sport of fencing, where two people with swords battle each other.

Fencing brings to mind the unusual battle between Jesus and Satan that happened in the wilderness after Jesus' baptism (Matthew 4). Jesus had fasted for forty days and was pretty hungry and tired. That's when Satan showed up and the battle began. They didn't fight with metal swords, but with God's Word.

Satan tried to trick Jesus by quoting the Scriptures. He twisted the words just enough to change their meanings. But Jesus answered Satan with the real meaning of the Scriptures. In the end, Satan lost because Jesus knew the truth of God's Word deep in His heart.

What an amazing battle! It shows how important it is to know exactly what God's Word says. God's truth is the sword we need to defeat evil and win.

Prayer Pointer

Lord, teach me Your Word so I can stand up against evil.

Last Respects

Wish good for those who do bad things to you. . . . Do not let evil defeat you. Defeat evil by doing good.

ROMANS 12:14, 21

MAY 4

How would you feel if people you didn't like got in trouble? It would be hard not to feel satisfied watching them leave for the principal's office.

That's one reason why David's funeral song called in 2 Samuel 1:17–27 really caught my attention. He wrote it after Saul, his greatest enemy, and Jonathan, his closest friend, died. Instead of being glad that Saul was gone and wouldn't be chasing him anymore, David wrote kind words about Saul, showing respect for this man God had chosen to be Israel's king. He also honored Jonathan as his loyal best friend. David showed his love and respect for God by how he treated his closest friends and enemies alike.

Honestly, I tend to want revenge when people hurt me. But David's example of respecting his enemy helps me want to love others better! The truth is, no matter what happens, I always have the power to love others because God loved me first.

Prayer Pointer

Lord, help me remember Your love is greater than any hurt I'll ever feel.

MAY 5

Eagle Eye

"People look at the outside of a person, but the Lord looks at the heart."

1 SAMUEL 16:7

How's your vision? If it's really good, your eye doctor would say you have 20/20 vision, meaning you can see objects clearly from twenty feet away. But eagles have 20/4 vision, meaning they can see something that's twenty feet away as clearly as if it were only four feet away. This enables eagles to spot small rodents and other prey scurrying on the ground, even when they're soaring hundreds of feet up in the air. Simply put, eagles see the world a lot more clearly than people can.

Since God made the eagle, can you imagine how strong God's vision is? His sight is so powerful, He can see inside our souls. He can even see a person's thoughts and motives. (Wouldn't that be handy?) When it comes to making and keeping friends, we know God can see our situation better than we can. So instead of blindly going into a friendship, ask God to help you see that person the way He does. And ask for wisdom so you can know if that friendship will honor God.

Honor

Prayer Pointer

Lord, I need You to help me see this world through Your eyes. Please give me Your wisdom.

Studying Beauty and Truth

Be a worker who is not ashamed of his work—a worker who uses the true teaching in the right way.

2 TIMOTHY 2:15

Write down all the reasons you love to do homework:

1. ______________________________
2. ______________________________
3. ______________________________

Are the spaces still empty? Don't worry. While some people love reading difficult passages or discovering how the world operates, others would rather play a game or go out for a run. Yet adults seem to think homework and studying are really important. Why?

True, homework will help you get good grades—but there's much more to it. Guess who made the world you're studying about in school? God! So when you study sea creatures or the way plants produce food, you aren't just learning facts for a test. You're learning more about the amazing God who made this world. You're getting glimpses into His power, perfection, sense of humor, and love when you learn about His quirky and spectacular creation. Add to that knowledge the truth about God in His Word, and you'll start to see how great God really is.

Prayer Pointer — grace

Jesus, help me study hard so I can learn more about You and Your world.

MAY 7

Break the Mold

"So if the Son makes you free, then you will be truly free."

JOHN 8:36

Imagine a creature about the size of a cat. Now picture that animal covered in otter fur with four webbed feet, similar to a duck. Put a duck bill on its face, just below its small ears and eyes. Now add a beaver tail and some sharp, venomous spurs on its hind feet. Sound like something out of a fairy tale? Actually, it's the platypus, a real mammal found in Australia and Tasmania! Unlike most mammals, platypuses are *monotremes*—they lay eggs instead of birthing live babies.

Platypuses remind us that being different—even quirky—can be really cool. Often, people try to fit in by dressing the same, talking the same, and doing the same things as everyone else. But that's boring! Like the platypus, we can enjoy being exactly who God made us to be, even if it isn't what everyone else is like. We're free to be ourselves, keeping our eyes on God and living for His approval alone.

Prayer Pointer

God, thank You for making me. I want to be everything You meant me to be—for Your glory!

Idol Eyes

Some people make idols, but they are worth nothing. People love them, but they are useless.

ISAIAH 44:9

MAY 8

What does the word *idol* make you think of? A golden calf, like the one the Israelites worshipped in Exodus 32? Or maybe those marble statues of Greek and Roman gods? Those *are* all idols, but they probably wouldn't tempt you anyway. After all, doesn't worshipping a hunk of rock seem pretty silly?

But the fact is, we all have idols that tempt us. Idols aren't just hunks of rock. Idols are anything that take our eyes off God. They can even be good things that have taken over too much of our lives: things like the latest fashions, video games, social media, or even friendships. If we choose to play on the Internet and skip our prayer time, our eyes might be focused on an idol. Or if our friends encourage us to go to the movies instead of to church, then those friendships are pulling us away from God. Ask God to help you keep your eyes on Him—and off idols!

Prayer Pointer

God, help me to worship You—and only You—by putting You first in my life.

The Power Box

WHEN A GOOD MAN PRAYS, GREAT THINGS HAPPEN.

JAMES 5:16

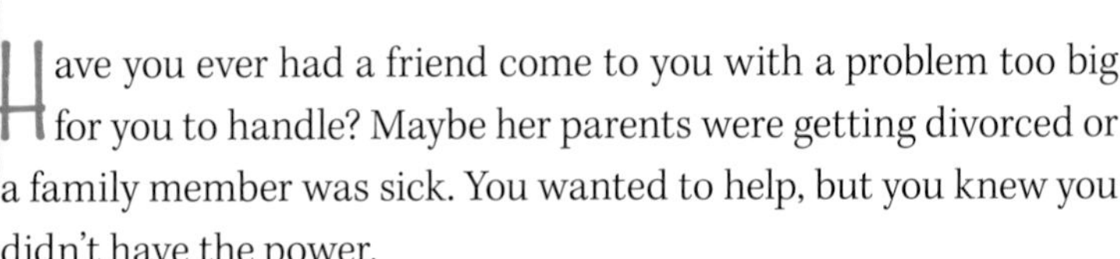

Have you ever had a friend come to you with a problem too big for you to handle? Maybe her parents were getting divorced or a family member was sick. You wanted to help, but you knew you didn't have the power.

Actually, you have far more power than you know. Remember, God loves *you* and lives in you. He wants you to come to Him anytime to talk about anything you need. And He has all the power to fix the problem!

One way to pray boldly and regularly for family and friends is by making a Power Box. No batteries needed—just the mighty power of God. Here's what to do:

- Find a recipe box and some 3 x 5 index cards.
- Write the name of the person you want to pray for on a card, along with specific prayer requests.
- Also write two or three Bible verses that would meet the needs of that person.
- Each day, open your Power Box and choose one or two cards to guide your prayers.
- When God answers your prayers, write down how, and add the date.

PRAYER POINTER

Father, please help me to bring every part of my life to you in prayer.

Joy Full

The Lord is my strength and shield. I trust Him, and He helps me. I am very happy.

PSALM 28:7

MAY 10

Look at the scenarios below. Which of these do you think could bring you joy?

- A new puppy
- Parents telling you what to do
- An *A* on the test
- Winning the game
- Losing the game
- Someone making fun of you
- Chores at home
- Going out to eat

So how many did you choose? If you didn't choose them all, you're missing out! The apostle Paul tells us that Christians look at life very differently from those who don't know God. Those who don't know God can only feel good about life when everything is going right. But God promises that every single thing that happens to one of His children was planned by Him to do us good (Romans 8:28). Of course, tough times never *feel* good. But when we really believe that our loving Father has allowed the situation for our good—even though we don't understand how—then we find joy.

gracie

Prayer Pointer

Jesus, teach me to trust You more so that I can be full of Your joy.

Birthday Blessings

Love each other. . . . Give [each other] more honor than you want for yourselves.

ROMANS 12:10

You watch for it, and you count down the days until it arrives. Finally, it's time! It's your birthday, and you hope everyone else is as excited about it as you are. It's the one day when it seems okay for it to truly be all about you.

But you're not the only one who feels that way. Every kid in your class has the same hopes and wishes when their big day rolls around. So do the kids you know at your church. So do parents and grandparents (whether they admit it or not). Simply put, birthdays are natural occasions to celebrate people we love and let them know we're glad God put them on this earth. After all, God calls us to give honor to others—even more honor than we'd like to receive ourselves! Use birthdays as a prompt to think about other people and their needs, and to send a little love and encouragement their way.

Ask your mom or dad to help you make (or buy) a calendar. Then:

- Call or text your friends and family members, and ask each person when his or her birthday is (if you don't already know it). Write each name on the correct date in your calendar. Go ahead and get their mailing addresses while you're at it.

- Make or purchase a large stack of birthday cards. You could do chores around the house to earn money for the cards and stamps.
- Three to five days before each person's birthday, write a sweet note in a card, letting that person know how special he or she is to you and to God. Address the card, stamp it, and mail it. Your card will be a great reminder of your love and God's love—and that's the best birthday present around!
- Pray for each person on his or her birthday.

Prayer Pointer

Jesus, thank You for always remembering me. Help me share that love with others.

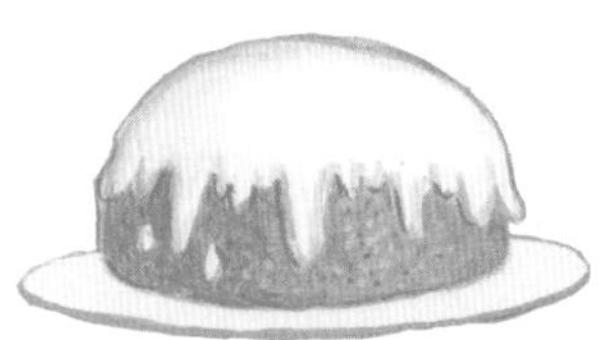

A Giggle a Day

I will be happy because of you. God Most High, I will sing praises to your name.

PSALM 9:2

You've probably heard the saying that "an apple a day keeps the doctor away." Well, a happy heart just might do the same. God says a happy heart is like medicine for our body and our soul. So what's the secret? How do we have a happy heart—especially on days that don't feel so happy?

It's simple: choose to see God and all that is good. Even on the worst days, we have so many things to be thankful for. There are things we can see, like home and family and friends. And then there are the things we can know, like the fact that God loves us, no matter what.

One way God shows His love is by filling this world with wonderful things—even things that make us giggle and laugh. I mean, have you ever watched a puppy play or really looked at a giraffe? God definitely has a sense of humor! Ask Him to help you find a giggle every day.

Prayer Pointer

Lord, thank you for giggles. Help me find things to be happy about every day.

Power Play

Children, obey your parents in all things. This pleases the Lord.

COLOSSIANS 3:20

Lie: I need to get my own way to be happy.

You know the feeling: you want to spend the night with your friend, or you want that candy, or you want to watch that show *all* your friends get to watch. But instead, your parents say no.

Immediately, you want to argue. "Why?" you begin. "Everybody's going," or "You never buy me anything," or "There's nothing wrong with it." With every word, you hope to convince your parents they're wrong.

The Truth Is . . .

You've probably been tricked by the lie of "I need to get my own way to be happy." Actually, you'll feel—and live—better when you obey God's ways, even though you think you want something else.

The next time your parents say no, stop and thank God for giving you leaders who love you and want the best for you. Then ask Him to help you obey with a happy heart. You'll be glad you did!

Prayer Pointer

Father, help me obey my parents so I can live better.

Cool with Kids

"If anyone accepts children like these in my name, then he is also accepting me."

MARK 9:37

Does the idea of playing with little kids make you a bit uncomfortable? Don't worry! Even though some people seem to naturally know how to handle children, the following tricks will help you be the best babysitter in town.

- Get down on their level. Sit down with them so they can get a good look at you and you can talk to them eye to eye.
- Adjust your expectations. Little kids aren't going to talk to you like someone your own age would. Speak in shorter sentences, and use simple phrases.
- Plan a variety of activities. Little kids have very short attention spans. They won't stay on one activity for long.
- As you play, ask them simple questions about what they are doing. For example, if you are building with blocks, ask them, "Are you building a house?"

By the end of your time, you will be their new best friend, and they will have helped you learn that little kids aren't so bad after all!

Hope

Prayer Pointer

God, please help me be a good example to little ones so they can know You better.

Talking Power

You are young, but . . . be an example to show the believers how they should live.

1 TIMOTHY 4:12

MAY 15

All alone in a strange place, without her mom and dad, a servant girl from Israel was faced with a choice. She could have stayed quiet. She could have just done her job and no more. But she had some important information that could save the life of Naaman, her master. So she told Naaman's wife about Elisha, a godly man from Israel who could pray to God and possibly heal Naaman from his leprosy.

Though she was very young, the servant girl convinced Naaman's wife to listen. And in the end, Naaman was healed, God was glorified, and a little girl showed what God could do through her bravery (2 Kings 5:1–14).

This girl's story reminds us that we are never too young to trust God to do great things through us. Often God gives us parents or teachers who will listen to our ideas and pray with us and for us. They become the friends we need in order to be brave and follow God, no matter what.

Prayer Pointer gracie

Thank You, God, for those in charge of me.
Help me work with them to honor You.

Deadly Attraction

Some people think they are doing what's right.
But what they are doing will really kill them.

PROVERBS 14:12

Don't polar bears look so cute and cuddly? Their coat of white fur not only protects them from the freezing cold temperatures of the Arctic but also camouflages them so they can sneak up on unsuspecting seals—their favorite meal. Weighing up to 1,200 pounds each, polar bears have slightly webbed paws that help them paddle through chilly waters for many miles in search of food.

But as soft and cuddly as polar bears may appear, humans who live near them know to keep their distance. Think about it: if polar bears can rip through seals, walruses, and even whales, what would they likely do to people? Exactly!

Just like a polar bear, sin can seem harmless. Telling a lie to get out of trouble or sharing a juicy bit of gossip might seem innocent at first. But cuddling up to a polar bear is dangerous, and so is sin. It can tear your soul to pieces. Just because something looks harmless doesn't mean it is!

Prayer Pointer

Jesus, help me stay away from sinful choices that can hurt me.

Man Overboard!

The Lord spoke His word to Jonah son of Amittai:
"Get up, go to the great city of Nineveh." . . .
But Jonah got up to run away from the Lord.

JONAH 1:1–3

God wanted Jonah to go to Nineveh and preach to the people there. But Jonah didn't want to go. He didn't like Nineveh. So he ran away. You might know the rest of the story: Jonah got on a ship, God sent a storm, and Jonah was tossed overboard and swallowed by a big fish. Inside the fish, Jonah had time to do some thinking. Maybe running away wasn't such a great idea. So when the fish spat out Jonah, guess what he did? He went to Nineveh.

The thing is, Jonah could have saved himself a lot of trouble—and a lot of stink—if he'd just obeyed God the first time. That's true for us too. If we would do the right thing (obeying God and our parents) the first time, it would save us a lot of trouble.

PRAYER POINTER

Lord, I don't always want to obey. Change my heart and my mind so I don't end up in a big mess like Jonah.

MAY 18

Tasty Treat

Oh, taste and see that the LORD is good.

PSALM 34:8 NKJV

What's your favorite ice cream flavor? Now imagine if that were the only flavor in the whole world. Pretty soon you'd be sick of it, right? Isn't it awesome that God created food with so many different textures and tastes?

How does taste even happen? It all starts with your saliva, which breaks down whatever food you're chewing. Then tiny hairs (called *microvilli*) on the ten thousand taste buds on your tongue send your brain messages about what's washing over them. At the same time, special receptors in your nose send messages about what it smells you chewing. Your brain combines messages from the mouth and nose to give you the full flavor—salty, sweet, sour, or bitter—of the food you're eating.

Why does God pack our world with so much flavor? Because it points to how sweet and wonderful He is! God invites us to use all our senses—seeing, smelling, tasting, hearing, touching—to put together the full flavor of His amazing creativity, kindness, power, and goodness. The next time you taste a flavor you love, thank God and think about how His love is even tastier!

Prayer Pointer

God, thank You for yummy foods
and a life filled with Your love!

The Beauty of Forgiveness

"I tell you that her many sins are forgiven. This is clear because she showed great love."

LUKE 7:47

How much is too much to forgive? Which of these situations would be too hard to forgive?

- Your little brother broke your favorite game.
- Your best friend promised to keep your secret, but she didn't.
- Your parents got divorced.
- Your teacher embarrassed you in front of the class.

When someone wrongs us, we often want to punish that person by staying mad. We feel like it's our right to be mad because of our hurt. But God doesn't agree. Peter once asked Jesus how many times we are to forgive others. "Up to seven times?" he guessed. But Jesus said, "Seventy times seven." In other words, every time someone hurts us (Matthew 18:22).

Why? Because Jesus paid the huge debt we owe to God for our sin. And because He died in our place, we are totally forgiven. So every time someone wrongs us, Jesus wants us to remember His goodness and mercy to us. If He forgives our great sin, how can we refuse to forgive others?

Prayer Pointer

grace

Jesus, because You have forgiven me I will also forgive others who wrong me.

Prickly Problems

Stop doing evil and do good. Look for peace and work for it.

PSALM 34:14

Do you know people who lose their temper quickly? You never know what's going to set them off. And once they're angry, it's hard to settle them down. When you find yourself in a prickly situation, remember the porcupine.

Porcupines are large rodents with bushy fur. But their fur is interspersed with sharp, pointy quills—as many as thirty thousand! When a porcupine is relaxed, so are its quills. But when it senses danger, the porcupine's body tenses, and the quills stand on end. Predators who attempt a bite often leave with a face full of quills! Porcupines grow new quills to replace the ones they lost, so they're always ready for battle.

Now think about your hot-tempered friends. Pray and seek God's help for a peaceful way to talk with them. Steer clear of topics you know are upsetting. Over time, they just might learn to trust you and be able to relax in your company, keeping their pointed "quills" flat at their sides.

Prayer Pointer

Lord, help me be patient with others and look for ways to keep conversations honoring to You.

Rush of Proof

"You don't know where the wind comes from or where it is going. It is the same with every person who is born from the Spirit."

JOHN 3:8

You feel it all around you as summer closes, and autumn turns the trees into a swirl of color. Cool wind brushes your skin, and the trees sway.

Really, wind is no mystery. As the sun heats the earth's atmosphere, warm air rises. At the same time, cold air is falling downward. That new air is heated, and the process continues, leaving us with wind.

Everybody believes wind exists, even though they can't see it. If only everyone thought about God in the same way. Like the wind, God can't be seen. But we can see what He does—just look at His incredible creation. And how about love? The existence of love points to a Creator who designed us to love Him and one another. So next time you feel the wind, whisper a word of thanks to the unseen God who made both you and the wind!

Prayer Pointer

Father, even though I can't see You, I feel You working in me, and I see what wonderful works You have done.

Winner Gives All

"It is more blessed to give than to receive."

ACTS 20:35

Jesus shows us that one of the best ways to be a friend is to give up your rights in order to serve others. But living selflessly isn't easy. Take this quiz to test whether you tend to be a taker or a giver.

1. Your mom just brought home a bag of candy from the store. You:
   a. take some candy for yourself and hide the rest so the others won't find it.
   b. go tell your siblings so you can all share the fun.

2. A leader at church asks for volunteers to wipe down tables for a meal. You:
   a. pretend you didn't hear her and start whispering to your friend about something else.
   b. say, "I can do that! Where are the towels?"

3. You feel alone and wish you had someone to hang out with. You:
    a. get angry at your friends for not thinking of you and inviting you over.
    b. pick up the phone and ask your friends to come over.

4. You are listening to music in the car, but your brother wants to hear something else. You:
    a. say, "Too bad. I was listening to this first."
    b. say, "Okay, why don't we take turns listening to music we like?" and turn the station.

Survey Says

Giver: If you answered *B* to these questions, you are growing a servant's heart like Jesus.

Taker: If you answered *A* to any of the above, ask yourself who you are serving in that scenario. Then ask God to give you a servant's heart like His Son's.

Prayer Pointer

Lord, please help me see and serve the world with a servant's heart.

MAY 23

Hide and Seek

The Lord does not ignore the one who is in trouble. He doesn't hide from him. He listens when the one in trouble calls out to him.

PSALM 22:24

Have you ever had a crazy day at school or at home when you just didn't know how to handle a challenging situation? Maybe you saw something happen at school that you knew was wrong, but you hate to be a "tattletale." Or maybe your younger sister was supposed to clean her room, and you saw her just push all the mess under her bed. Now you're torn. You don't want to get somebody in trouble, yet you want to help make things right. You just aren't sure how.

The good thing is that Psalm 22:24 says that you can call out to God and He will listen. You can seek Him, and He won't hide. We can always find answers in the Bible that show us what is right and wrong. And we can pray about what to do, and ask a parent or trusted teacher for advice. Always be honest and caring about the other people involved. Trust that God, along with your parents or teacher, will help you decide the right thing to do.

Prayer Pointer

Glory

Thank You, God, for always answering when I call.

But Honestly

You want me to be completely truthful. So teach me wisdom.

PSALM 51:6

MAY 24

Job wasn't happy. In just a short time, God allowed Satan to send a horrible storm that destroyed Job's home and killed all his children. Then his crops were destroyed, and his health fell to pieces. Even Job's wife encouraged him to curse God and die.

Job didn't curse God, but he did want to know why these things had happened. Without holding back, Job cried out to God, asking for understanding and relief.

And guess what? Even though God didn't answer his question, He talked to Job and comforted him. God wasn't afraid of Job's questions. With power, holiness, and love, God helped Job to grow in his trust and love of Him. (Read the whole story in the book of Job.)

Do you have questions or frustrations about the way God runs His world? Have you had sad things happen that you just don't understand? Don't bother hiding your feelings. Bring them to God. Talk to Him as Job did. You may not get all the answers you're looking for, but God will give you peace and comfort you with His love.

grace

Prayer Pointer

God, thanks for handling my tough questions and loving me in my confusion and hurt.

MAY 25

Puppy Love

My God will use His wonderful riches in Christ Jesus to give you everything you need.

PHILIPPIANS 4:19

Have you ever seen a mother dog give birth? Rarely does she have just one or two puppies. Most larger breeds will have between four and nine little ones, and they all wriggle and squirm around right after birth. Then miraculously, they move toward their mother's belly, where they each find a place to nuzzle and nurse, drinking their mother's life-giving milk.

God wants us to remember the miracle of puppy love in our own lives. Those little fur balls don't need to fight each other for food (though they may have to climb over and under to get a spot!). God provides for all the creatures in His creation, especially you. God brought you into this world with the purpose of protecting you, providing for you, and making you His own. You don't have to fight for the things you need. God is more than able to supply everything you need in life. You just need to stay nuzzled up to Him.

Prayer Pointer

Jesus, You are all I need. Please keep me from being selfish instead of sharing Your love with others.

Wonderful Gifts from God

I thank God every time I remember you.

PHILIPPIANS 1:3

MAY 26

Who are your favorite people? Are they family or friends, or maybe both? We all have special people in our lives. They're the people who love us and take care of us, who make us laugh and hold us when we cry. They're there for us, helping us and cheering us on no matter what. And whenever we think of them, we just can't help but smile.

People like that aren't just wonderful—they're wonderful gifts from God. And we need to thank God for them each and every time we remember them. But we can also do more. We can be God's gift to other people, making them want to thank God for us. We can laugh with those who are laughing and comfort those who are sad. We can love and care for others. And we can always help and cheer others on. Because those things not only make other people smile, they make God smile too!

Prayer Pointer

Lord, I thank You for all the special people You've placed in my life. Help me be the kind of person who makes others thankful for me too.

MAY 27

Deeds Day

Our love should not be only words and talk. . . . We should show that love by what we do.

1 JOHN 3:18

Church gives us so much. It's a place to enjoy youth group meetings, get-togethers with family and friends, and great worship time. So how can you give back to the place God is using to bless you? Take a look at the ideas below, and then talk to your pastor or another church leader. Ask which idea would be the biggest blessing for the church or if there is another need you could fill. Then gather your friends and their families together to help you plan a day of service for the church. Let Deeds Day begin!

- Weed the grounds.
- Clean the pews or worship service area.
- Ask your pastor about prayer requests he has for himself and/or the church. Pray daily for those requests until you see them answered.
- Clean up the playground.
- Wash all the toys in the children's rooms.
- Hold a car wash or a yard sale to raise money for equipment the church needs or to support a mission project.

Hope

Prayer Pointer

Thank You, God, for giving me my church family. Help me serve them.

Write It Out

The Spirit gives love, joy, peace, patience, kindness, goodness, faithfulness, gentleness, self–control.

GALATIANS 5:22–23

MAY 28

The character traits listed in Galatians 5 are known as the Fruit of the Spirit. Which one fruit do you have plenty of? Which ones could you use a little more of? How can you grow the kind of fruit you want more of?

Prayer Pointer

Lord, I pray that the fruit of Your Spirit will grow in me.

Starting Over

"If you forgive others for the things they do wrong, then your Father in heaven will also forgive you for the things you do wrong."

MATTHEW 6:14

As soon as the rooster crowed, Peter knew he'd made a horrible choice. Instead of standing strong and supporting Jesus after the soldiers arrested Him, Peter acted as if he didn't know Jesus. Peter knew he'd been a terrible friend and didn't deserve a second chance (Mark 14:66–72).

But that's not how Jesus saw it. After Jesus rose again, He appeared to Peter and let him know that all was forgiven. Jesus wanted Peter to stay His friend (John 21:15–19).

Have you ever hurt your friends' feelings by doing something mean? Or have they done something wrong to you? Jesus reminds us how important it is to forgive others when they hurt us. If you have a friendship that needs mending, don't wait another minute. Call your friend, and work out the problem. Be sure to admit if you've done anything wrong. Then ask for forgiveness or forgive your friend, and put the past behind you both.

Prayer Pointer

Father, thank You for forgiving all my sins. Help me forgive others too.

Plant Power

My teaching will drop like rain. . . . They will pour down like rain on young plants.

DEUTERONOMY 32:2

Did you know something spectacular is happening right now, right outside your front door? And it's something that should help you breathe a little easier. Plants are making oxygen, and they're using sunlight to do it.

All plants are equipped with cells that act like food factories. As their leaves take in carbon dioxide from the air, they use energy from sunlight, water, and soil nutrients to make a sugar called *glucose*. The plants use the glucose to feed themselves and grow. And when plants create glucose, they also release oxygen, giving us fresh air!

Just looking at a plant, you'd have no idea all that stuff is happening inside. And the same is true for you! God is doing supernatural work inside you through the power of His Spirit. Just like plants soak up sunlight, you can soak up spiritual energy by keeping your heart turned toward Jesus. That energy will help you do what's right—even when you might not want to or think you can!

PRAYER POINTER

Jesus, fill me with Your energy so I can live for You!

Digging Deep

He loves the Lord's teachings. . . . He is strong like a tree planted by a river.

PSALM 1:2–3

Squirrels often bury nuts for winter. But sometimes they forget where they've buried them, and you'll find tiny oak and walnut trees sprouting in your yard, garden, and even flowerpots! Those tiny trees are easy to pull up because their roots haven't dug down deep enough to hold on. But as trees grow, so do their roots, digging deeper into the soil. The deeper the roots, the harder the tree is to pull up.

Psalm 1 teaches a lesson about just that sort of thing. God says that the person who nourishes herself with His Word is like a deeply rooted tree. No matter what storm comes, it stands firm because it has dug down deep. But people who don't read God's Word are like those tiny trees—easily pulled right up.

We want to be like those strong trees rooted deep in God's Word. When we study His truth, we grow stronger and stronger each day, and our lives become filled with the fruit of God's Spirit.

Prayer Pointer

Lord, teach me to love Your Word and to spend more time in it each day.

Think About It

Be very careful about what you think.
Your thoughts run your life.

PROVERBS 4:23

Kelsey dropped her cleats on the locker room floor and plopped down on the bench. Practice had been horrible. She hadn't been playing her best game, but then Amelia had kept laughing and pointing out her mistakes to the rest of the team. At the time, Kelsey hadn't known what to say. But now she couldn't stop thinking about it and what she wished she'd said. She just kept feeling angrier and angrier. Just then, she heard Amelia coming. Furious, she stood up and—stopped. *I was ready to say something terrible,* she thought. *I could have even punched her. That's not me. Lord, help me.*

Kelsey did the right thing. We have to be so careful about the thoughts we let stay in our heads. They can make us do things we'll regret later on. If Kelsey had lashed out at Amelia, Kelsey could've been kicked off the team. God says we should "capture every thought and make it give up and obey Christ" (2 Corinthians 10:5). It's not always easy to do, but it will keep us out of all kinds of trouble!

PRAYER POINTER

Hope

Lord, help me to capture my thoughts
and make them obey You.

Life or Death

"The words I told you are spirit, and so they give life."

JOHN 6:63

Have you ever noticed how a single mean comment from a friend can ruin your whole day? On the other hand, a simple hug or encouraging word can make your spirit sing. Don't worry. We are all that way! God created us to respond to the power of words. It's one of the reasons God gave the Bible to us. Through His words, we learn how to live life and find Jesus. God's words are powerful enough to change lives.

But your words are powerful too. Each time you open your mouth, you can choose to speak words that will help others know how valuable they are or how worthless you think they are. You can speak life to them or words of death. As very loved children of God, we no longer have any need to hurt others with our words. Instead, God has given us the mission to build up others, encouraging them in their faith and lives. Sometimes it can be very difficult, especially when that person or family member says mean things to you. It's natural to want to fight back. But it isn't God's way. God is love, and that's what He wants His kids to communicate to others at all times.

Look at this list of comments. Which ones build up, and which ones tear down?

You're doing great.
You're weird.
That's okay; I mess up too.
You're not going to make it.
I forgive you.
Of course you failed.
I'm happy to help you.
You make me smile.
I can do better than you.
You look great.
I see Jesus in you.
You're an idiot.
You are such a great friend.
I hate you.
You're awesome.
I told you that you couldn't do it.
I appreciate you.
How could you be so dumb?
I'm here for you.
Stay away from me.

Prayer Pointer

Jesus, fill my mouth with loving words that come from Your heart and help others.

"Clicking" Together

Try to live in peace with all people.

HEBREWS 12:14

Have you ever held two magnets together and felt the push or pull? If you put the two ends that repel each other together, they push apart—they just can't come together. But turn one of the magnets around and suddenly they "click" right together!

Relationships are a lot like those magnets. If both you and another person each demand your own ways (for example, "I want to be on the computer first!"), you'll fight and end up hurting each other's feelings. No matter how hard you try to convince the other person you're right, the two of you just won't "click" together.

But Jesus can help you change. He can turn your heart away from wanting your own way to being willing to serve the other person. ("You can go first. I'll play next.") When we allow God to change our hearts, we find that we fit in better with His plan for peace, and we "click" with others around us.

Prayer Pointer

Jesus, help me be willing to put other people's needs before my own so I can be a peacemaker.

Shell-Centered

You are my hiding place. You protect me from my troubles. You fill me with songs of salvation.

PSALM 32:7

Don't take it personally when your pet box turtle hides its head. It's the turtle's way of protecting itself when it thinks it's in danger. Once it feels safe, the turtle will stretch out its head and begin exploring the world again.

Do you ever feel like pulling inside your "shell" because you feel shy or scared around others? Sometimes it feels safer to read a book or play on a phone, because we don't know if others will like us or how they'll respond to us. But you don't have to withdraw like a turtle. You have your own protective shell: God. He loves you and thinks you're wonderful just the way you are. So you can walk with confidence into that room of people or carry on a conversation with anyone. God's love gives you the safety to come out of your shell and make friends with the people He has placed in your path.

Prayer Pointer

Lord, You are my hiding place. Give me confidence to talk and connect with others when I am afraid.

It Depends

By His power we live and move and exist.

ACTS 17:28

You've probably said it a million times to your parents: "I can do this myself!" We all want to show our family and friends that we're growing up and getting better at life. We feel proud when we're able to do things on our own.

And that's natural. But growing up as a Christian should be exactly the opposite. God wants us to learn more and more about how much we *do* need Him. We can't do anything that's

truly important on our own. The Bible even says that apart from God, we can do nothing (John 15:5). We depend on God for everything—and that's a beautiful thing.

What do you depend on God for? Here is a list of some things. Can you think of more?

- the air we breathe
- our lives
- growing faith
- fighting our sin
- the clothes we wear
- knowing what to pray
- loving others well
- getting along with family
- understanding truth
- the food we eat

Prayer Pointer

gracie

Lord, I'm so excited about getting older and getting to do new things. Help me remember these opportunities and blessings come from You.

Dealing with Disappointment

Love is patient and kind. Love is not jealous.

1 CORINTHIANS 13:4

Glory had practiced countless hours to audition for the school play. But when the cast list came out, she'd been given a background part. However, her good friend Gracie—who has an incredible singing voice—had landed the lead role. A flood of emotions washed over Glory as she juggled her own disappointment with trying to be happy for her friend who got the part she wanted. How should she handle this?

Choice 1

Glory let her disappointment melt into anger, then jealousy. *I worked harder than anybody to get that part!*

Choice 2

Glory admitted she was disappointed, but then she remembered the verse about God directing her steps. *Lord*, she prayed, *You must have other plans for me. Thanks for helping me do my best.* When she saw Gracie, she gave her a tight hug and said, "You'll be great."

Prayer Pointer

Glory

God, help me trust You when I am disappointed and give thanks to You no matter what happens.

A Wise Choice

Listen to wisdom. Try with all your heart to gain understanding.

PROVERBS 2:2

Have you ever tried on a pair of your dad's shoes? Did you wonder how feet could grow so big?

Our parents take care of us in lots of ways. They run the house, work, pay bills, and do things we can't do. Their shoes are just too big for us to fill right now!

That's probably how Solomon felt when he took over the kingdom for his famous father, King David. So when God asked Solomon what he wanted more than anything else, Solomon knew just what to ask for. "I want to be wise," he said (2 Chronicles 1). Solomon wanted God to help him rule well more than anything else. God was so pleased that He not only made Solomon the wisest man on earth, but He gave him a lot of material wealth along with it. God always helps us know what to do when we ask Him for wisdom.

Prayer Pointer

Lord, when I don't know what to do, I know I can always turn to You to help me make the right choice.

Ripping Up the Roof

They went to the roof above Jesus and made a hole in the roof. Then they lowered the mat with the paralyzed man on it.

MARK 2:4

JUNE 8

Four men were bringing their friend to see Jesus. Their friend was paralyzed, so they carried him on a mat. But when they came to the place where Jesus was, it was so crowded that they couldn't get in. Then they had an idea.

The four men climbed up on the roof and began tearing into it! They ripped and dug and pulled until they'd made a hole big enough for their friend. Then they lowered him down to Jesus—and he was healed. Nothing could stop these four friends from bringing their friend to Jesus. Not even a roof!

Would we do anything to bring our friends to Jesus? Would we risk being embarrassed, or made fun of, or just told no? Jesus wants us to tell others about Him, and He'll help us do whatever it takes to bring our friends to Him.

Prayer Pointer

Jesus, I have friends who do not know You. Show me how I can bring them to You—and then help me be brave enough to do it.

JUNE 9

A Tempting Idea

When you are tempted, God will also give you a way to escape that temptation.

1 CORINTHIANS 10:13

Look at the list of temptations below. Which ones do you find hardest to fight?

- keeping the whole bag of candy for yourself instead of sharing
- telling that juicy bit of gossip about the new girl in school
- continuing to play your video game because your parents are distracted and won't know
- writing the answers to the test on your hand
- yelling at siblings when they get on your nerves

Making the right choice can feel impossible when everything inside us wants to cave in to temptation. We're only human, right? Who could expect us to do the right thing in that situation?

Jesus could, that's who! But He isn't standing around, waiting for you to mess up. He understands exactly how you feel because when He was on earth, He was tempted too. But Jesus was able to stand strong against every temptation—and He can help you do the same.

Whenever you turn to Jesus for help in a tempting situation, you're trusting in His secret source of strength: the goodness and power of God.

PRAYER POINTER grace

Jesus, thank You for understanding my weakness. Help me be strong in You.

Growing Axolotls

Grow in the grace and knowledge of our Lord and Savior Jesus Christ.

2 PETER 3:18

JUNE 10

Have you ever heard of an axolotl? Also known as a Mexican salamander or a water dragon, these cute little creatures are amphibians that have lungs to breathe air and gills to breathe underwater. They start off small, looking a lot like a tadpole with arms, legs, and five-fingered hands and feet. But don't let their innocent look fool you. You have to keep axolotls separated from one another until they are six inches long. Why? Because they're cannibals. They think the other salamanders are food and not friends. After they grow and learn to eat worms, they learn not to hunt one another.

Kids can be a lot like young axolotls. Some haven't learned how to be friends yet, so they may say or do mean things. Or they might seem selfish. But don't give up on people because of their mistakes. Instead, pray for them. Be kind, and give them time to grow. Then watch to see if God changes their hearts—and yours. You may be surprised to find that you become good friends!

Prayer Pointer

Hope

Jesus, please help me be patient with myself and other Christians as we grow to become more like You.

Lovely Light

"All people will know that you are my followers if you love each other."

JOHN 13:35

If someone asked you to describe a Christian, what would you say? You'd probably mention things like "reads the Bible," "prays," "goes to church," or even "does good things for people." Those are all signs that people might have given their lives to Jesus. But when you think about it, lots of people who don't claim to be Christians live good lives. And many other religions teach that you have to do good works and stay away from bad behaviors.

Jesus says His children will be known by our love—love for Jesus, love for other believers, and love for those who don't know Him. The ability to love like that comes from the Holy Spirit, who lives inside us.

Ask God to help you consider your words and your actions, and make sure they show His love. God will pour out His love through you to reach others who need to know Him! And everyone will know you're His child by your lovely light of love.

Prayer Pointer

Jesus, fill me with Your love for others so they will see You in me.

Noah, Who Stood Alone

"The gate that opens the way to true life is very small. And the road to true life is very hard. Only a few people find that road."

MATTHEW 7:14

If everybody in your class started talking because the teacher left the room, would you stay quiet and work? If your siblings decided to sneak food into their bedrooms (even though it's against Mom's rule), would you disobey too? When lots of people make the same wrong choice, it starts to seem okay, which makes it even harder to do what's right.

Just ask Noah. Everybody was choosing to disobey God. But Noah listened to God and obeyed Him, even though everybody else thought he was crazy for building a boat in the desert.

Only Noah and his family survived the great flood. That's actually pretty scary (read about it in Genesis 6–9), but it's a great reminder of the importance of sticking with God instead of with the world. In big ways (like building a boat in the desert) or small ways (choosing to honor Mom), following God brings blessings to yourself and to those around you.

Prayer Pointer

Father, help me hear Your voice and follow You instead of the world.

JUNE 13

Soul Food

"I was hungry, and you gave me food. I was thirsty, and you gave me something to drink."

MATTHEW 25:35

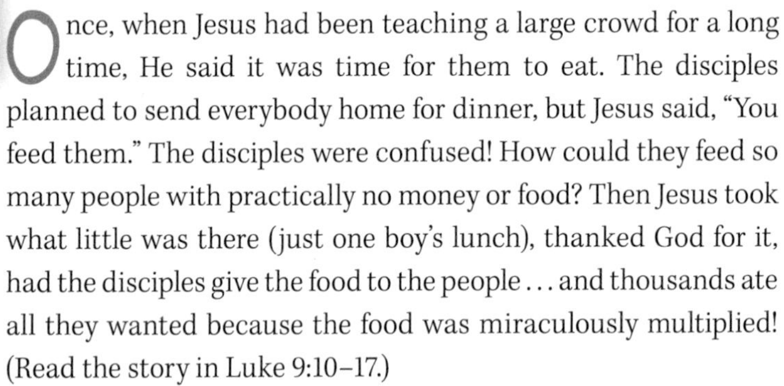

Once, when Jesus had been teaching a large crowd for a long time, He said it was time for them to eat. The disciples planned to send everybody home for dinner, but Jesus said, "You feed them." The disciples were confused! How could they feed so many people with practically no money or food? Then Jesus took what little was there (just one boy's lunch), thanked God for it, had the disciples give the food to the people . . . and thousands ate all they wanted because the food was miraculously multiplied! (Read the story in Luke 9:10–17.)

You can mirror Jesus' love for the poor and hungry by feeding them too. Ask your parents to help you find a food bank or soup kitchen where you can serve. When you go, do the following:

- Learn the customers' names. Smile and tell them your name too.
- Commit to coming back at a regular time so you can build friendships.
- Sit and talk to the people, especially the kids. Find out about their families and their lives. Pray with them.

Prayer Pointer

Father, thank You for caring about the poor and needy. Please use me to show them Your love.

Get Ready

Always be ready to answer everyone who asks you to explain about the hope you have.

1 PETER 3:15

Priscilla and Aquila had listened to Paul preach about the gospel. They even had to flee from their home in Rome because of their Jewish heritage (Acts 18:2). But through all the training and trials, they came to know God and His ways very well.

So when a man named Apollos began teaching about Jesus, Priscilla and Aquila listened closely. Even though Apollos was very educated, he didn't know the full truth about how Jesus had come to save people. So Priscilla and Aquila taught Apollos all about Jesus so he could preach the gospel in the right way (Acts 18:24–28).

Priscilla and Aquila were good friends to Apollos because they listened to him and told him the truth about Jesus. What about you? Do you have friends who need to hear about Jesus? Have you ever asked them what they believe? Learn from Priscilla and Aquila. Be bold and brave. Share what you know about Jesus so your friends can grow closer to God and can help you share the good news with the world!

Prayer Pointer

Honor

God, please help me study Your Word so I know how to share the truth with others.

Mary, Who Pondered

Think about the things that are good and worthy of praise. Think about the things that are true and honorable and right and pure and beautiful and respected.

PHILIPPIANS 4:8

For an ordinary Hebrew teenage girl, Mary had already seen some pretty incredible things in her young life. Out of nowhere, an angel appeared to her, telling her she was going to have a baby by the power of God's Holy Spirit. God also sent an angel to explain things to Joseph, the man she was soon to marry. And the strangeness didn't stop there. God chose for Mary to have the baby Jesus in Bethlehem, a town far from their home, in a cold stable where an animal trough became the baby bed for God's Son. Suddenly, a bunch of smelly shepherds showed up, asking if they could worship Jesus! Mary's head must have been spinning with all the wild things happening to and around her. But she knew that God was in control, and the Bible says she pondered all these things in her heart (Luke 1:26–38; 2:1–19).

Do you know what it means to ponder? It means she was thinking about all that was going on and considering how God planned to use these events to help His people.

Do you have unusual circumstances in your life? Instead of just going through your day without taking special notice, ponder those events in your heart like Mary did.

On the lines below, answer the following questions:

What do you think God is showing you? Where is He leading you? How is God using that situation to bring you closer to Him in faith and trust?

____

____

____

____

____

____

Prayer Pointer

Father, nothing happens to me by accident because You are in control of all things. Give me eyes to see You and a heart that thinks about who You are.

JUNE 16

Choosing Friends

Jesus said, "Come follow me."

MATTHEW 4:19

How easy is it for you to make friends? Is it no big deal to strike up a conversation, or does your heart start pounding in your chest when you try to speak? Even for the most outgoing kid, making new friends can be challenging. But Jesus gives us a great tip. When He was seeking out the twelve men who would become His closest friends and followers, He prayed! During an all-night prayer session, Jesus asked His Father to lead Him to the right people. Then Jesus obeyed and invited each man to be His follower.

Since we aren't Jesus, it would be really weird if we asked someone to be our follower. But we can ask God to help us find the right friends. Then, as we go through our day, we can look for signs of good friend material like kindness, respectfulness, and a love for God. When we see those good qualities in others, we need to be bold like Jesus and strike up a conversation with them. God has a cool way of bringing His people together!

Prayer Pointer

Lord, please help me find good friends who love You too.

Life Is Good!

"A thief comes to steal and kill and destroy. But I came to give life—life in all its fullness."

JOHN 10:10

Did you know that God wants you to enjoy your life? It's true! He created this beautiful, amazing world and filled it with zillions of blessings for you.

Does that mean you'll be happy every second of every day? No, there'll always be troubles, sad times, and hard times. But God promises to help you through those times—and you know God keeps every promise! Sometimes doing what God wants you to do can be difficult. There'll be times when you have to be brave and stand up for what's right. But God will give you courage for that too.

All along life's way, in every minute of every day, God is blessing you. Just ask Him to help you see His gifts, like the love of family, the hugs of friends, and even the tiny wildflower in your path. Yes, life is good—and life with God is even better!

Prayer Pointer

Lord, thank You for filling my life with Your amazing love and blessings. Help me to see them all around me.

JUNE 18

Understanding Honor

Praise the Lord, all you who worship Him. All you descendants of Jacob, honor Him.

PSALM 22:23

The Israelites understood they needed to honor God when they witnessed Him on the mountain. If they hadn't figured it out from all the plagues God sent on the Egyptians, they could see it now: God was bigger, stronger, and holier than anything they could have imagined, and He deserved their full respect (Exodus 20).

When we respect the people in charge of us by following their directions, listening while they speak, and recognizing their position of power over us, we are showing the humble and obedient heart God wants us to have. Read the scenarios below. Which ones show respect, and which one shows disrespect?

- Ashley knew what her mom was going to say, so she interrupted her mom to tell her that she already knew.
- Some people at school were taking God's name in vain. Eva asked politely if they would choose other words that didn't hurt God's name.
- "May I please go get some water?" Adrian asked after the teacher called on her.

Prayer Pointer

Hope

Father, You are awesome and worthy of all my respect. Help me show it to You and others with the way I live.

Order Up

All of you must obey the government rulers. No one rules unless God has given him the power to rule.

ROMANS 13:1

JUNE 19

Imagine a large army led by captains and a general. Every soldier has a job and answers to the man in charge of him. And everything works like clockwork. Now imagine one day the men decide they are tired of doing what they are told. They won't get out of bed, they argue over orders, and they refuse to train. What would happen when that army went off to fight an enemy?

A sense of order, with leaders and those being led, is necessary for armies to work well. The same is true for governments, cities, schools, and even families. You may not like being told what to do by your parents or teachers, but your obedience—even in the little things—is big-time important. When you obey your leaders, you're telling God that you trust the way He's leading you through the people He has put over you. Not only will you reap the benefits of staying safe and growing strong, but the whole group of people around you will function better as well.

Honor

Prayer Pointer

Jesus, help me obey my parents and leaders because I know it pleases You.

JUNE 20

The Gift of Faith

You have been saved by grace because you believe. You did not save yourselves. It was a gift from God.

EPHESIANS 2:8

A dad from Israel came to Jesus and asked Him to heal his son (Mark 9:14–27). The boy had been tormented by an evil spirit since he was a very young child. What's worse, Jesus' disciples seemed unable to cast it out of the boy. So when the man came to Jesus, he wasn't totally sure Jesus could help either. "If you can help him, please do," the man pleaded to Jesus.

"If you can?" Jesus questioned his doubt. "Everything is possible for one who believes."

So there it was: hope. All the dad had to do was believe. The problem was that the man knew in his heart he still had doubts. "Lord, I do believe. Help me to believe more!" he cried out. He knew he needed help in every way, even with having faith. So Jesus answered both requests, and the boy was healed.

We too need help trusting and obeying Jesus. So ask Him for help—He would love to answer you.

Prayer Pointer

Jesus, please help me to believe more, and thank You for always answering my prayers.

With All We've Got

"Love the Lord your God with all your heart, soul and mind."

MATTHEW 22:37

What does love mean to you? Most people would say it's that wonderful, warm feeling we get when we're with someone we care about. But love is much more than that. Love is your mom staying up all night with you when you're sick. Love is your dad patiently helping you build a project for the science fair. Love is the friend who listens to the same joke for the tenth time—and still laughs.

Love isn't just a feeling. It's something we *do* with all we've got. And that's how God asks us to love Him—with all we've got. It's not always easy, especially when we're having a rough day. But loving God with all we've got means praying for peace when we're angry, singing when we're sad, and doing good things for others even if we're tired.

God wants us to love Him with all that we've got and without end. Why? Because that's how He loves us—with all that He's got and without end.

Prayer Pointer

Lord, show me how to love You and others with all I've got.

Sweet-Smelling Prayers

JUNE 22

The smoke from the incense went up from the angel's hand to God. It went up with the prayers of God's people.

REVELATION 8:4

To God, the sweetest smells in all the world are the prayers of His people! The Old Testament talks about people burning incense—a mixture of fragrant herbs—when they worshipped God. And Revelation says our prayers rise up before God's throne, just like incense in the temple. Prayer is a beautiful offering from us to God.

Prayer also connects us to God and helps us realize how much we need Him. Use the ideas below to help you come closer to God and learn to pray about what matters most to Him.

- The book of Psalms is a collection of prayers and songs. Each day, choose a different psalm to read.
- Pray for wisdom to know how and what to pray. Ask the Holy Spirit to lead your thoughts and words.
- Get a notebook with five subject tabs and label them with the words *Me*, *Family*, *Friends*, *Church*, and *World*. In each section, write prayer requests for that subject. Pray for them, and then be sure to note when God answers those prayers!

Hope

Prayer Pointer

Lord, prayer keeps me close to Your heart.
Thank You for listening to me!

Why Bother?

"Love your neighbor as you love yourself."

MARK 12:31

Joseph was one stuck-up brother. At least, that's how his brothers saw it. Whenever he came around, he'd tell about a dream that showed he was better than them, and he was always wearing that colorful coat from their dad. One day the brothers got so mad that they threw Joseph in a well. They planned to kill him, but later decided to sell him as a slave to Egypt.

Of course, that wasn't the end of Joseph's story. He went through many hard trials, but God blessed him. God prepared Joseph to be Egypt's leader and save the people (including his brothers) from starvation (Genesis 37–45).

We all have people in our lives we wish weren't there. Whether it's their personality or habits, there's something we just don't like. We try to avoid them or may even make fun of them. But Joseph's story reminds us that God wants us to love everyone, not just the ones we click with. Instead of trying to ditch the different kids or saying unkind things, ask God to let you see them through His eyes. Everyone has unique qualities that make him or her special.

Honor

PRAYER POINTER

Lord, help me to love others and see them like You do.

JUNE 24

The Great Friendship Challenge

Do not be proud, but make friends with those who seem unimportant. Do not think how smart you are.

ROMANS 12:16

Do you know who Jesus' closest friends were? Well, they were nothing like Him. After all, Jesus was the Son of God. But His closest friends on earth were a bunch of fishermen (including Peter, Andrew, James, and John) who were respectable, but definitely not high society. There was also Matthew, a tax collector—a profession the Jews hated. Jesus also hung out with the poor, the sick, sinners, and outcasts. He wasn't too proud to talk to anyone, and He never made anyone feel unimportant.

Can you say the same about yourself? Or do you only hang out with people who are pretty much like you? Today try taking the Great Friendship Challenge. Talk to at least three kids you don't usually talk to. Invite a new person to join your lunch group. And pick at least one person to try and get to know better. Who knows? You might make a new friend.

Prayer Pointer

Lord, I want to be a friend to everyone, just like Jesus was. Please give me the courage to make new friends.

Swan Song

Thank the Lord because He is good.
His love continues forever.

1 CHRONICLES 16:34

Several birds are known for loyalty, but none are as beautiful as the swan. Elegant white feathers and a long regal neck have earned these birds a place of honor in royal courts, poems, and stories. Equally enchanting is the way most swans choose a partner and stay with their mate for life. Even though they may fly to another place in colder weather, they always return and claim their place together.

Such loyalty is hard to find in the human world. Many friendships break apart because people lose interest or find someone they think will be better. But God's love is forever, and He wants His people to love others the same way. Being a loyal friend means sticking with someone, even when it's hard. Ask God to help you be a good friend and to give you friends who will stick by your side no matter what comes. And most importantly, ask God to help you stay loyal to Him all the days of your life

Prayer Pointer

Father, thank You for always being my friend. Help me be loyal to my family and friends too.

JUNE 26

Heavenly Thoughts

I always pray to the God of our Lord Jesus Christ . . . that He will give you a spirit that will make you wise in the knowledge of God.

EPHESIANS 1:17

Consider this scenario:

Emily was one of the smartest girls in class. She could make straight *A*s without even studying. But at home, Emily wasn't feeling so smart. Her parents fought a lot, and she was worried, but she didn't know what to do. Should she talk to them, or would it be better to stay quiet? Could she trust her friend with this information, or would her friend gossip behind her back? Nothing in her schoolbooks could help Emily solve this real-life problem.

What would you say Emily needs to do in this situation?

Why do you think that?

Emily could sit and think for hours or ask a bunch of different people their opinions on the situation, but how will she ever know which way is right? On her own, she can't. Emily needs wisdom, but she doesn't have it. Wisdom is far different from being smart. Wisdom is understanding life from God's perspective and knowing and following His directions.

Where do we get wisdom? From the wisest One in the universe, of course! God says that if we simply ask Him for wisdom, He'll gladly give it to us. Sometimes He uses the Bible to give us the wisdom we need. Sometimes He guides us through trusted parents or leaders who know His ways. Sometimes He simply works out the situation so we see His power and control. However He chooses to do it, God is faithful to give us the wisdom of heaven to help us through everything that happens on earth.

Look up these verses on wisdom. What do they say? Use them to write your own prayer for wisdom below.

- James 1:5
- 2 Chronicles 1:11–12
- Job 12:13
- Psalm 37:30
- Psalm 104:24
- Psalm 111:10
- 1 Corinthians 3:19
- James 3:17

Prayer Pointer

____

____

____

Choosing Love

We destroy every proud thing that raises itself up against the knowledge of God.

2 CORINTHIANS 10:5

Emma had been waiting all day to go to the pool. Her mom had said they'd go after running errands. But late in the day, her mom said, "I'm sorry, but we'll have to go another time. I'm still not ready for the party we're hosting tonight. I'm going to need your help in the kitchen." How should Emily react to her mom's news?

Choice 1

Emma was furious. "I'm not helping since you didn't take me to the pool like you said you would!"

Choice 2

Emma felt very frustrated, and calmly told her mom she was disappointed. She asked God to help her with her attitude. Then she turned on some music and started putting away dishes. After a while, her anger went away, and she began chatting with her mom about the party.

- Could Emma keep from feeling upset when her plans were changed?
- How does choosing to obey God first have an impact on how we feel?

Hope

Prayer Pointer

Lord, help me choose what is good, even when I don't feel like it.

Write It Out

Let the teaching of Christ live in you richly. Use all wisdom to teach and strengthen each other. Sing psalms, hymns, and spiritual songs with thankfulness in your hearts to God.

COLOSSIANS 3:16

JUNE 28

Singing is another way of talking to God. It can say "Thank You," "I love You," and even "Help me, Lord." It can also encourage you and those around you. What are some of your favorite songs to sing? List them below, and explain why you like them. You could even try writing your own song here too.

____

____

____

____

____

____

____

____

Prayer Pointer

Lord, thank You for the gift of song.

JUNE 29

The Shocking Truth

"I am the vine, and you are the branches. If a person remains in me and I remain in him, then he produces much fruit. But without me he can do nothing."

JOHN 15:5

What do wind, water, and the sun have in common? They're all used to produce electricity! You know, that curious element you use when you watch TV, turn on lights, or curl your hair.

Though we might not totally understand what electricity is or how it gets to our homes, we're certainly glad it does. But what if there's a break in the connection, like when a plug gets pulled out of the wall? It stops working, and we can't get our normal work done.

God wants us to know that He's our biggest power source. When we stay plugged in to Him by reading His Word, obeying Him, and talking to Him through prayer, we'll be filled with His power to do the work He has created us to do. If you feel powerless today, plug in to God through prayer. He'll give you the strength and wisdom you need.

Prayer Pointer

Father, I can't do anything apart from You. Help me stay connected to You.

Stargazing

He counts the stars and names each one.
Our Lord is great and very powerful.
There is no limit to what He knows.

PSALM 147:4–5

Do you know how many stars there are in the universe? On a clear night, you can probably see thousands of them. But with the help of telescopes and satellites, scientists have discovered many different galaxies (oh, about 10 billion), each with its own stars. That leads scientists to guess there are at least 1 billion trillion stars out there!

So when God led Abraham outside to look up and count the stars, God was giving Abraham an impossible task (Genesis 15). Abraham must have known it too because he decided to believe God's promise that his descendants would outnumber the stars, even if he didn't have a son yet. The God who created all those stars was certainly capable of giving Abraham a son, even in his old age.

Like Abraham, we don't have to figure everything out in life. We just need to trust God who knows and controls everything!

Prayer Pointer

God, Your creation is amazing. Help me trust You—especially when I don't have it all figured out.

JULY 1

A New Name

You are all the same in Christ Jesus.

GALATIANS 3:28

How'd you like to be known simply as "the sinful woman"? Not so much, huh? Well, apparently there was a woman in Bible times who had done a lot of bad things around town, and everybody knew it.

But one day she heard that Jesus was going to Simon the Pharisee's house for dinner (Luke 7). Pharisees were religious leaders who were very proud of how good they thought they were. So imagine what they thought when the sinful woman walked in! She went over to Jesus and began crying, wetting Jesus' feet with her tears. Then she wiped them away with her hair. She then broke open a bottle and poured perfume over Jesus' feet. Simon was upset and told Jesus that He must not know who she was.

But Jesus did know. And He didn't see just a sinful woman; He saw a girl who loved God and wanted forgiveness. So Jesus said to her, "Your sins are forgiven" (v. 47). And she wasn't the sinful woman anymore. No matter what we've done, Jesus is always willing to forgive us when we admit we need Him.

Hope

Prayer Pointer

God, I'm so glad You're in my life. I need You every single day.

Sheep Facts

"I am the good shepherd. I know my sheep, and my sheep know me."

JOHN 10:14

Sheep are fascinating creatures. For example, they can see behind themselves without even turning their heads. They have an excellent sense of smell and even have scent glands on their feet. They stress out when they get separated from the rest of their flock. And sheep can recognize human faces—so they know which shepherd to follow.

Doesn't that sound a lot like us? Okay, not the seeing behind our heads or scent glands on our feet part (eww). But the part about being stressed when separated from friends and family? That sounds familiar. And we recognize faces like sheep do, which is important because we need to know our Shepherd too. Jesus is our Shepherd, and He'll lead us where we need to go. Often, He'll use His people to lead us. So it's important that we learn to recognize Him in the people around us. We do that by spending time with Him in His Word. When we know Jesus better, it's easier to recognize His "face" in others and follow His lead.

Honor

Prayer Pointer

Lord, thank You for the way You watch over me. Please help me to always follow You.

JULY 3

Hear No Evil, See No Evil, Speak No Evil

"You will see the difference between those who serve God and those who don't."

MALACHI 3:18

Don't you just love monkeys? They're the cutest little animals. And have you seen those figurines of the three little monkeys sitting together—one with his paws covering his eyes, another his ears, and the third his mouth? This verse from Malachi might remind you of those monkeys. We need to be careful what we let our eyes see, our ears hear, and our mouths say. God wants us to watch out for things that might make us turn away from how He wants us to live. He wants us to listen only to things that are good and to speak with wisdom.

Remember that wisdom is more than having a good vocabulary and knowing the right words to say. Wisdom comes from God, and it's the ability to choose well, to decide between right and wrong, and to know the difference between good and evil people. We should let God lead us in our friendships and in our lives. He shows us what we need to know every step of the way.

Prayer Pointer

Lord, please give me the wisdom to make good choices every day.

Crawling to Glory

God began doing a good work in you.
And He will continue it until it is finished
when Jesus Christ comes again.

PHILIPPIANS 1:6

Migrating monarchs make an extraordinary sight. Tens of thousands of these brilliant black and orange insects take to the sky from Southern California and Mexico and head north. Once they deposit their eggs on milkweed leaves, the butterflies die. But soon, the eggs hatch, and caterpillars emerge. Once the caterpillars mature, they form *chrysalises*, or cocoons. At the right time, they break out of the chrysalises as wonderfully winged butterflies! The monarchs then seek out mates, lay eggs, and the cycle repeats itself.

As amazing as the monarch life cycle is, your life is a million times more miraculous. You are created in God's own image! And God is at work in you, changing you from the inside out. Just like the butterfly crawling from its chrysalis, you become a new creation when you give your life to Jesus. You were made to fly through this life with the warmth of God's love lifting your wings.

Prayer Pointer

Jesus, thank You for butterflies, and thank You for making me a new creation too!

Treasured

"Your heart will be where your treasure is."

MATTHEW 6:21

What's your favorite thing that you own? Is it an expensive doll or a new video game? A trampoline or a closet of clothes? Now imagine your best friend wanting your most prized possession. Would you be willing to give it away?

Jonathan was. He wanted his best friend David, the giant slayer, to know how important David was to him. So Jonathan took off his robe, belt, armor, sword, and bow and gave them to David. Even though Jonathan loved being the prince who would one day be king, he was willing to give it all up to honor David because he loved him as much as he loved himself (1 Samuel 18:1–4).

That's a beautiful picture of true friendship: to put others' needs in front of our own. Are you a good friend like Jonathan, willing to give up your treasures to honor your friends? Or do you tend to hold back and serve yourself more? Ask God to give you a heart like Jonathan's, one that doesn't hold back from doing good for your friends.

Prayer Pointer

gracie

Jesus, thank You for giving up the treasure of heaven to save me. Help me love others as Jonathan did and as You still do.

Defining Beauty

You are beautiful! Oh, you are beautiful!

SONG OF SOLOMON 1:15

JULY 6

What is beauty? It depends on where you live. In the United States, the media prizes slender girls with flawless skin, big eyes, and long hair. But people in Mauritania and Nigeria believe the bigger the woman, the more beautiful she is! If you lived in the Pa Dong tribe near Thailand, you'd want a long neck—a look only achieved by adding metal rings around your neck each year, starting at age six. And if you lived with the Maori in New Zealand, you'd value tattooed blue lips.

The truth is, our ideas about beauty come from what other people around us say—and those ideas change all the time. Trying to meet everybody's expectations is not only exhausting, it's silly! We were made to show our Creator's creativity and love through our different looks, personalities, and styles as we live a life all about loving others. The Bible says to stop comparing yourself to other people, stop trying to be like them or better than them. Instead, God says to be bold, brave, and be-you-tiful!

PRAYER POINTER

Glory

Father, You have told me in so many ways that I am beautiful to You. Please help me to listen only to You!

Love Labors

In all the work you are doing, work the best you can. Work as if you were working for the Lord, not for men.

COLOSSIANS 3:23

Paul's job to spread the gospel around the world wasn't easy. Everywhere he went, Paul met people eager to hear about Jesus, but he also met people who hated him and wanted him to die. Some places weren't easy to reach, requiring long boat trips in bad weather. Sometimes Paul was arrested, beaten, or stoned for teaching about Jesus. But Paul persevered—meaning he kept on working, even when it was difficult.

Paul was a hard worker for Jesus. He knew that if he kept working, God would use his efforts to build the kingdom. What about you? When your parents or teachers ask you to do work that's difficult, what's your attitude? Do you work hard to do your best and finish the task? Or do you find ways to get around the work, stop in the middle, or fail to complete the task? Look at the following scenarios. Which ones show laziness or other wrong attitudes? Which ones show perseverance and hard work?

1. Lindsey's mom asked her to clean up her room. Lindsey had other things to do, so she scooped all the clothes up off her floor and stuffed them in her closet.

2. Allison's chore for the day was cleaning her room. First, she sorted everything she found on the floor and counters. Then she put everything away in the right place.

3. Trysten missed more than half the math problems on her homework. The teacher said she could get more points if she reworked the ones she missed. But Trysten hates math and watched TV instead.

4. Julia had the same problem with her math homework. Determined to do better, she asked her parents to help her. Then she reworked the problems until she understood how to do it.

Prayer Pointer

Father, help me work hard, fight my own laziness, and finish the work You have asked me to do.

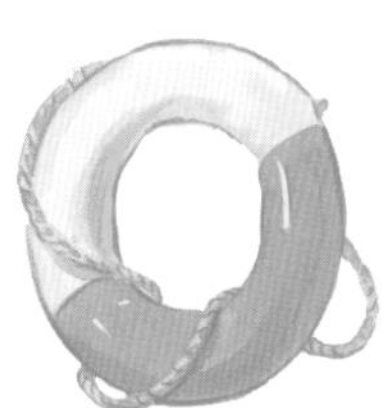

The Woman of Wisdom

But if any of you needs wisdom,
you should ask God for it.

JAMES 1:5

Solomon was the wisest man who ever lived. But the queen of Sheba showed wisdom of her own when she left her kingdom in search of the source of Solomon's great wisdom. She wanted to know God so that she too could rule her kingdom better (2 Chronicles 9:1–8).

Solomon didn't disappoint her. And neither will God disappoint you when you seek to understand and know Him better. The queen of Sheba lets us know that treasures like wisdom and character are far more precious than gold or silver, and they are worth our effort and energy to seek them from their source: God.

So how do you seek wisdom from God? Just ask Him. God says He is glad to give us all we need so that we can walk through this life with confidence in who we are and what we are doing. God Himself is our treasure, the greatest reward for seeking to live a life that honors and pleases Him.

Prayer Pointer

Jesus, all wisdom comes from You. Please give me understanding so that I will follow all Your ways.

To See or Not to See

Faith means being sure of the things we hope for. And faith means knowing that something is real even if we do not see it.

HEBREWS 11:1

Do you believe in things you can't see? Of course you do! In fact, we all do. We believe in things like gravity and air and wind. We can't see them, but we see what they do and how they make things move. We also believe in things like Mars and atoms and deep-water anemone. We probably can't see them for ourselves, but others have. They tell us about them and may even have pictures.

Faith in God is also believing in what we cannot see. We cannot see God's face, but we can see Him in the wonders of this world He's made. We can't hear His voice, but others did. And they wrote down God's words for us to read. We can't touch His hand, but we can feel where His hand touches our lives, with love and joy, with His comfort and His peace.

Prayer Pointer

God, I cannot see You, but I know You are real. Open my eyes to see and recognize the proof all around me.

You Being You

Do not love the world or the things in the world.

1 JOHN 2:15

Sarah stared at herself in the dressing room mirror, tugging at the skirt, and twisting it this way and that. *It's just so short,* she thought.

"Don't you love it?" Becca asked.

"Well . . ." Sarah stalled. "I'm not sure my mom would approve. And I'm not sure it's for me."

"Oh, come on," Becca nagged. "*Everybody* wears them now. Don't you want to be like everybody else?"

Sarah thought for a second, shook her head, and reached for her jeans. "Nope," she said with a smile. "I want to be me."

Did you ever play dress-up when you were younger, pretending to be someone else? A movie star, a teacher, a doctor, or a princess? Pretending to be someone else is a great way to play, but it's a lousy way to live. God created you in an amazing way and blessed you in your uniqueness. Don't be afraid to be who God made you to be, because God made you wonderful!

Prayer Pointer

Glory

Lord, I keep hearing about all the things I should do and say and wear so I'll fit in. Help me not to be afraid to be me.

Loving Light

The glory of God is its light, and
the Lamb is the city's lamp.

REVELATION 21:23

JULY 11

Do you know what I like to do at the beach? After putting on sunscreen, I walk along the shore and soak up the rays. Somehow, the sun's warmth and brightness boost my mood like nothing else can.

So I was pretty shocked when I read in Revelation that the new heavens and earth are not going to have a sun. *What? What about all that warmth and light?* But I read on to discover we won't need the sun because God Himself will be our source of warmth and light! As wonderful as it feels to be outside in the sunshine now, it's going to be billions of times better in heaven because God will be there in all His brilliant glory.

I can hardly wait to see how amazing heaven will be. But until I get there, I want to spend my time here soaking in the rays of God's love and sharing His warmth and beauty. And I don't have to wait for a vacation to do that. I can start right now, right where I am.

Laurie

PRAYER POINTER

God, help me share Your love with others wherever I go.

Just God and You

"When you pray, you should go into your room and close the door. Then pray to your Father."

MATTHEW 6:6

Back in Bible times, people called Pharisees used to make a big show out of their prayers. They'd stand out on the street corners and pray as loudly as they could. They wanted everyone to know they were praying. In fact, they cared more about being seen by people than being heard by God! And God said *that* was not good.

How should you pray? Well, there's a time for praying in public, like when you join with others to praise God, to pray for the sick, or to pray for your meal. But when it's time for just you to pray, find a quiet place—a place where it can be just God and you. Maybe it's in your room, in a special chair, or even up in a tree. No one even has to know you're there. And that's just fine, because God knows. He sees you, and He hears your prayers.

Prayer Pointer

God, I love our times to talk, when it's just You and me. Thank You for letting me pour out my heart to You.

Slug Sleuth

"Stop judging by the way things look! Be fair, and judge by what is really right."

JOHN 7:24

It's time to test your slug knowledge. (Betcha didn't think anybody would say that to you today.) Look at the facts below. Which ones do you think are true?

a. Slugs have more teeth than sharks.
b. Slug blood is green.
c. Slugs can slide over razor blades or cut glass without getting hurt because of their slime.
d. To find their way home, slugs leave a scent trail.
e. Slugs will eat just about anything.

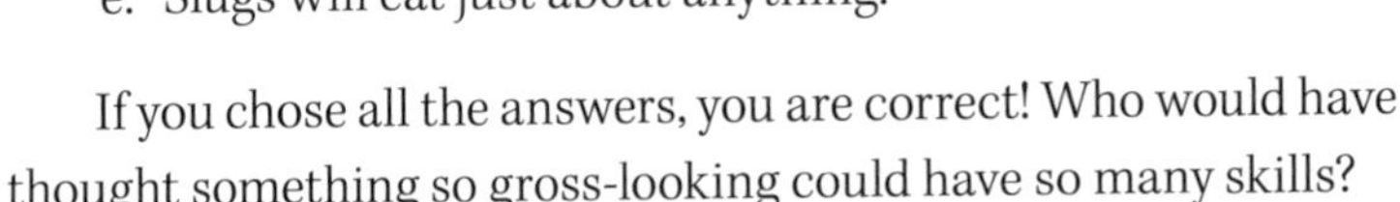

If you chose all the answers, you are correct! Who would have thought something so gross-looking could have so many skills?

The slug actually shows us some important truths. You can't judge animals—or people—based on what they look like on the outside. Every person God makes has a special part to play in this great big world He is running, so ask God to help you appreciate and respect everyone He has made.

Prayer Pointer

God, Your creativity and love are endless. When I respect and love others, I respect and love You too.

Total Connection

At that time Jesus went off to a mountain to pray. He stayed there all night, praying to God.

LUKE 6:12

When should you pray? Which of these times are most worthy of prayer?

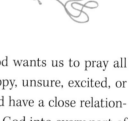

- You are nervous about a test at school.
- You have just woken up in the morning.
- Your parent is sick.
- You won the spelling bee.
- You are scared to share your faith.
- You yelled at your mom.

These are all great times to pray! God wants us to pray all the time—whether we're sad, scared, happy, unsure, excited, or mad. God created prayer so that we could have a close relationship with Him. Through prayer, we invite God into every part of our lives, sharing everything with Him and looking for Him to enjoy it with us or help us through it.

When we live prayer-filled lives, we show that we trust and love God the same way Jesus did when He was on earth. Jesus prayed all the time. And if we want to walk in Jesus' footsteps, we need to depend on God the same way—through prayer.

Prayer Pointer

Hope

Jesus, thank You for inviting me to be close to You through the gift of prayer.

Working for Fun

Do all you can to live a peaceful life. Take care of your own business. Do your own work.

1 THESSALONIANS 4:11

Lie: I need to have fun all the time.

"Mom, I'm bored," Lindsey muttered.

"Well," answered her mother, "I have a mountain of laundry to tackle, and then I was going to take a meal to that lady in our church who had surgery. Want to help?"

"That's not fun," Lindsey moaned.

The Truth Is . . .

Work is not a result of sin in the world, but our bad attitude about it is. Even in the Garden of Eden, Adam had to name the animals and tend the garden (Genesis 2:15, 19–20). Work is part of what God created us to do. But when we let our own selfishness take over, doing work—from homework to yard work to community service—seems like a chore. God wants us to both work and play, all with an attitude of thankfulness and joy.

Bored? Look around and see how you can serve. By working hard, you serve God, bless others, and discover a whole new level of fun and reward.

Prayer Pointer

Lord, help me stop looking for entertainment and start finding ways to bless others.

Pay Attention to Me!

"Your giving should be done in secret. Your Father can see what is done in secret, and He will reward you."

MATTHEW 6:4

Lie: I need to be noticed and appreciated.

Notice anything different?" Taylor asked her sister, Alyssa.

"No, what?" Alyssa answered, clueless.

In a huff, Taylor blurted, "Your toys! I straightened all your mess!"

Then Taylor marched upstairs to her mom. "Mom, no one ever appreciates all the work I do around here."

Her mom answered gently, "I know how you feel, Taylor. But God always sees the good we do. And He's who we work for, right?"

The Truth Is . . .

Taylor's mom was right. Taylor was doing good work by serving her sister, but the kindness was lost when she demanded thanks. Jesus wants us to follow His example instead. He stayed busy serving others, but everything He did was to point people to God. By serving secretly, we get the joy of blessing others in a way that God alone gets the credit. God still sees us and rewards us for the secret good we do.

Prayer Pointer

Lord, I want to point people to how good You are, not to me.

Seek and Find

"You will search for me. And when you search for me with all your heart, you will find me!"

JEREMIAH 29:13

JULY 17

God is *omnipresent*. That's a huge word! It means that God is everywhere all the time. He is in China at the same time He's in Peru. And He's with your dad at work at the same time He's in school with you. Being omnipresent is one of those amazing things that only God can do.

Did you know you can see God, if you know how and where to look? You won't see Him face-to-face as Moses did, but He's still there.

Look for God in the people around you, in their kindness and love. And the proof of God is in His creation. The perfection of every tree, flower, and simple blade of grass is beautiful proof that God is real. Even in times of trouble, God is there for you to see. Just look for all His people, reaching out to help those in need. Seek God and you'll find Him, because He's everywhere!

Prayer Pointer

Lord, You are amazing. You are everywhere. And I'm especially glad You're right here with me.

Think Again

Listen, my child, and be wise. Keep your mind on what is right.

PROVERBS 23:19

God's Word says that what we think has the power to control what we do. The question is: Do you know and believe God's truth? Take this simple quiz to see if your thoughts about God match up with His Word.

1. T F Compared to some other people, I'm actually a pretty good person.
2. T F Sin is a thing of the past. Because of Jesus, God doesn't care about it anymore.
3. T F God will like me more if I work hard to obey Him.
4. T F God will get angry with me if I keep making the same mistake (or sin) over and over again.
5. T F If I sin too much, I can lose my salvation and won't get to go to heaven.

So what do you think? Did you answer True for any of the above? If so, you are missing some vital truths about God's love for you. Every statement above is false!

If you have put your faith in Jesus to save you, here's the truth:

All people are sinners, equally deserving God's anger and punishment. Without Jesus, you have no hope of heaven (Romans 3:23; John 14:6).

God still hates sin because He is still holy. Apart from Jesus, you will have to pay for your own sin, which means punishment forever! Jesus, however, not only takes away your sin, He also gives you credit with His perfect record! Because of what Jesus did for you, even when you sin, God's forgiveness for you doesn't change or end (John 3:16–17; Romans 6:23).

God's anger toward your sin ended when you decided to follow Jesus. God forgives you every time (2 Peter 3:9; 1 John 1:9).

Once you are adopted into God's family through faith in Jesus, nothing can separate you from God's love (John 1:12; Romans 8:38–39).

Prayer Pointer

Jesus, thank You for paying for my sins so I can enjoy friendship with God forever!

Speak Up

Speak up for those who cannot
speak for themselves.

PROVERBS 31:8

Onesimus was in a bit of trouble. He had been a slave, but had run away. Then Onesimus met Paul, who told him about Jesus. Onesimus repented of his sins and turned to Jesus as his Savior.

Now it was time for Onesimus to go back to his master's family. Paul wanted him to return not only to mend the bad relationships, but also to share all the good things God had taught him through Paul. But Paul didn't send Onesimus back empty-handed. He gave him a letter—what is now the book of Philemon—asking the family to receive Onesimus not as a slave, but as a brother in Christ! Since the family members were also believers, Paul trusted they would welcome Onesimus back as a beloved child of God's family.

Paul knew that going back would be difficult for Onesimus. So he helped by speaking up for him. Do you speak up for your friends? Whether it's asking a parent or teacher for help, or remembering to pray for them daily, good friends speak up for one another and are loyal to the end.

Prayer Pointer

gracie

Lord, help me remember to pray for my friends
and get them the help they need.

Ruling Yourself

JULY 20

God did not give us a spirit that makes us afraid. He gave us a spirit of power and love and self-control.

2 TIMOTHY 1:7

Have you ever felt so fidgety you thought you might fall out of your seat? Maybe you were sitting in class for too long, or stuck inside visiting with relatives when you wanted to go outside and play instead. Sometimes it feels like our bodies are telling us what to do. Instead of sitting and listening, we feel like running and talking. Instead of working, we feel like playing. So which side of you wins?

If you're listening to God's Spirit, the self-controlled side will win. Self-control is exactly what it sounds like: controlling your mind and body to make them obedient to God.

Why does it even matter? Because as children and soldiers of God, we're in a lifelong battle against evil and sin. In order to train ourselves to follow God, we need to use God's power of self-control, starting with small things so that we'll know how to stand strong when bigger temptations roll around.

PRAYER POINTER Glory

Lord, sometimes it's so difficult to control my thoughts and actions. Send Your Spirit to give me wisdom and strength to do the right thing.

God's Wonderful Words

The sky was made at the Lord's command. By the breath from His mouth, He made all the stars.

PSALM 33:6

It's hard to imagine anyone making something huge happen just by *speaking*, but that's how God created the world. I guess we can sort of compare it to machines working in response to someone talking. My dad's smartphone finds directions or a phone number when he talks to it (well, as long as my brothers and I aren't making noise nearby). But God created life—something out of nothing—with His words!

God's words are not just noises or sounds; they make things happen. The Bible says, "You were born again through God's living message that continues forever" (1 Peter 1:23). God's everlasting Word, or *message*, is still powerful today. When He speaks through His Word, it creates a new heart in us, and we are born again! Plus His Word, the Bible, tells us who He is—the One so powerful that He made the whole world just by speaking. Once we learn how amazing He is, it's easy to praise Him!

Prayer Pointer

Lord, I want to share Your Word with everyone. Help me tell the world about You.

Seeing Is Deceiving

JULY 22

"People look at you and think you are good. But on the inside you are full of hypocrisy and evil."

MATTHEW 23:28

Nestled in the rainforests of Indonesia is a species of the world's biggest flowers: the *Rafflesia*. Its large red petals stretch three feet across! But step closer, and you'll notice something else: the Rafflesia stinks! This beautiful, enormous flower smells like rotting flesh, which is why it's also called the "corpse flower." This foul odor attracts carrion flies, which help pollinate other Rafflesias.

In the Bible, Jesus warns that people who follow rules just to look good and be praised by others are like empty tombs. Like the Rafflesia, they look good on the outside, but they are full of rottenness inside (Matthew 23:27).

How do you get the rotten stuff out so that you can be a fragrant flower for God? Ask Him to help you be honest about how much you need Him. Then choose to follow God simply because it pleases Him. Then you'll bloom into a fragrant child of God.

Prayer Pointer

Lord, keep me from only pretending to love You. Make my faith real and beautiful in Your eyes.

JULY 23

Hello, Neighbor

"And the second command is like the first: 'Love your neighbor as you love yourself.'"

MATTHEW 22:39

Who is my neighbor?" a man asked, and Jesus told him of a Jewish man who was robbed, beaten, and left for dead along the roadside. A priest and a temple worker passed by, but they did not stop to help. Then a Samaritan (part of a nation the Jews hated) saw the man and helped him. Who was that man's neighbor? The Samaritan who helped him. Then Jesus said, "Go and do the same" (Luke 10:25–37).

You see, to Jesus a neighbor isn't just someone who lives next door. A neighbor is anyone in need. It could be the person who lives next door, across town, across the world, or even inside your own house. How can you be a good neighbor to all these different kinds of neighbors? Think of one idea for each, and try them out this week.

The neighbor next door ______________________
The neighbor across town ______________________
The neighbor across the world ______________________
The neighbor inside my house ______________________

PRAYER POINTER grace

Lord, help me be a good neighbor to everyone I meet.

Building Bridges

God gave us the work of bringing everyone into peace with Him.

2 CORINTHIANS 5:18

When Adam and Eve disobeyed in the garden, the connection between God and His people was broken. And the relationships between His people broke apart as well. But Jesus came to fix that. Through Jesus, we can be close to God and love others the way we were meant to.

As God's kids, we are called to be *bridge-builders.* That means we are to reach out to those who feel separated from God and others. In fact, the Bible says that reaching out to the hurting, such as widows and orphans, is true Christianity (James 1:27). So how can you be a bridge-builder? Try one of these ideas, or come up with one of your own.

- Volunteer in the childcare center in your church one Sunday a month. Choose one child and find out how you could help meet his or her needs.
- Call the widows in your church and ask how you can pray for them. Try to meet them in person.
- Get to know the younger kids in your church. Encourage them and pray with them. Volunteer to teach their class once a month.

Hope

PRAYER POINTER

Jesus, please use me to love those who feel lost, different, or disconnected.

JULY 25

Golden Gifts

The right word spoken at the right time is as beautiful as gold apples in a silver bowl.

PROVERBS 25:11

Have you ever felt completely down in the dumps, but then a friend said just the right thing and turned your whole day around? Or maybe just the opposite happened. You were having the best day ever, but someone's grumpy words ruined it all.

Words are powerful things. One rotten word can be just like a match starting a fire. James 3:5 says, "A big forest fire can be started with only a little flame." And that's exactly what rotten, hurtful, and hateful words do. They burn.

But kind and caring words are beautiful, like golden apples in a shining silver bowl. They are beautiful to the person who hears them, and they're beautiful to God. They lift up, they encourage, they reassure, and they heal. They are a gift—good and golden—to all who hear them. And it's our job to give as many gifts as we can. Challenge yourself to see how many golden words you can give each day.

Prayer Pointer

Lord, let my words be a gift to everyone who hears them.

Perfecting the Past

He has taken our sins away from us
as far as the east is from west.

PSALM 103:12

If you could go back in time and erase a mistake, what would it be? How would your life be different if you hadn't made that mistake or any mistakes at all?

The Samaritan woman who met Jesus at Jacob's Well had a lot of mistakes in her past. But she couldn't do anything about them—until she met Jesus. Jesus told her to ask Him for Living Water.

The Samaritan woman learned that Jesus not only knew everything about her ruined past and her current sins, but He also had the power to wash it all away. Excited that God had come and erased her guilty past, she ran to tell her whole village about Jesus.

If you know Jesus, you don't have to carry around guilt for your mistakes. He's washed your entire life clean and made you right with God. When you think about God's incredibly good news, you'll want to tell everyone—just as the Samaritan woman did.

PRAYER POINTER

Jesus, thank You for freeing me from the guilt of sin and making me beautiful in God's sight.

JULY 27

Impossible Possible

"For people this is impossible. But for God all things are possible."

MARK 10:27

You've got to be kidding me! Alana thought, slamming her books down on the desk. *How am I supposed to work with Tiffany? She's been so mean to me! God,* she silently prayed, *I know I'm supposed to love my enemies, but I just don't think I can do it!*

Tiffany had been making fun of Alana at school all year long—her clothes, her hair, even the way she talked. And now they were assigned to work together on a project. That's a tough assignment! On her own, Alana couldn't begin to figure out a way to be kind to Tiffany, much less work together and help her.

Fortunately, Alana isn't on her own—and neither are we. God is always with us. And those things that seem impossible to us become possible with God's help. Things like being kind to those who've hurt us and forgiving our enemies. When you're faced with an impossible task, reach out to God and ask for His strength and wisdom. He makes the impossible possible!

Prayer Pointer

God, thank You for being strong when I'm not. Help me remember that You're always there to help me do the right thing.

Write It Out

Remember to use the gift that you have.

1 TIMOTHY 4:14

God used His infinite wisdom to design the entire universe—including you! Can you think of any special traits God gave you that you can use to show His love to others?

Prayer Pointer

God, thank You for the gifts You've given me. Help me use them in a way that points people to You.

Character Quest

"I know what you do. I know about your love, your faith, your service, and your patience. I know that you are doing more now than you did at first."

REVELATION 2:19

You know a good friend when you find one, but what exactly are those qualities that make a good friend so great? Look at the list below, and circle the traits you hope to find in your friends.

Kind: answers gently and sees the bright spots in others

Loud: takes control of conversations or simply talks loudly so others will listen

Shy: afraid to say what she really thinks

Encouraging: knows how to make others feel good about themselves

Brave: willing to try new things and venture outside her comfort zone

Curious: asks lots of questions to find out more details about others

Hot-tempered: reacts to small things and gets angry easily

Godly: loves Jesus and isn't afraid to talk about Him with others

Servant-Hearted: seems to look for the needs around her and works to meet them

Sarcastic: uses biting comments to get a laugh or feel important

Wise: looks at people and situations from an understanding perspective

Insecure: seems to need others to tell her she is good at things

Bossy: always tells other people what to do and how to do things

Now take another look at the list and put a check mark beside the traits you see in yourself. Underline the traits you'd like to change, and ask God for help to do it. Can you think of any other character qualities you'd like to see in yourself or others? If so, list them here:

____

____

____

____

____

Prayer Pointer

Lord, please fill me with Your Spirit so I can be the kind of friend I need to be.

Happy Giving

God loves the person who gives happily.

2 CORINTHIANS 9:7

Picture this: You've been saving for weeks to buy those super-cute boots you've been wanting. Then one Sunday, a lady comes to church and tells everybody that the children's home is having trouble. They don't have enough money to support all the orphans. What would God want you to do?

a. Ignore the request.
b. Pray that someone else helps them.
c. Give some of your money while keeping some for yourself.
d. Hand it all over to the lady.

It's not an easy question to answer, is it? Taking care of the poor, orphans, and widows is very important to God. And He loves cheerful givers, because giving shows others His love in a very real way. When we ask God what He'd like us to do and then obey Him, our faith and love grow stronger. And we know He'll always take care of our needs too (even if it means waiting a little longer for those super-cute boots).

Prayer Pointer

Lord, please help me trust You to take care of me so I can cheerfully give to others.

The Tune of Trust

Everything on earth, shout with joy to God! Sing about His glory! Make His praises glorious!

PSALM 66:1–2

Did you know that God writes songs? Check it out in Deuteronomy 31 and 32. Moses was nearing his death, and the time had come for Joshua to take his place as the leader of God's people. So the Lord called both Moses and Joshua to talk with Him. But the news wasn't good. The Lord told them that He already knew the people would forget about Him once they got into the Promised Land. They would think they didn't need God anymore, and they would worship idols instead.

So what was God's plan? He gave Moses a song to write down. It would help the people remember God and all the ways He had saved them. God's great love rings through the verses, even though He already knew they would turn away from Him.

Moses' song reminds us how important it is to remember God and the great things He has done. By singing about God's faithfulness, it will help us stay faithful to Him.

Prayer Pointer

Lord, thank You for the gift of song and how it reminds me of You.

Who Knows You?

Lord . . . You know all about me. You know when I sit down and when I get up. You know my thoughts before I think them.

PSALM 139:1–2

You just don't understand!" Haley wailed as she ran to her room and flopped down on her bed. She'd been trying to explain to her dad why she was so upset about what her friend Sarah had said about her. But her dad just kept saying to be patient and kind, to forgive Sarah. Deep down, Haley knew her dad was probably right, but she was still hurt and angry. And her dad just didn't seem to understand that she wasn't ready to move on.

Sometimes it can be hard for other people to understand what we're thinking or feeling. But there is One who always understands, and that's God. He created you and knows you inside and out. He knows your every thought before you speak it. You can talk to Him about absolutely anything, because He already knows what you're going through. So turn to God. He knows you and He always understands.

Prayer Pointer

Lord, I'm so grateful that I can tell You anything and everything. You understand, and You'll help me sort it all out.

Status Cling

Never become tired of doing good.

2 THESSALONIANS 3:13

Everyone expected Ruth to stay in Moab with her family after her husband died. But when Naomi, her mother-in-law, decided to go back home to Bethlehem, Ruth insisted on going with her. Naomi had taught Ruth about the God of Israel and had become like a mother to her. Wherever Naomi went, Ruth was going too.

God rewarded Ruth's loyalty by leading the two women to Naomi's relative, Boaz. Ruth eventually married Boaz, and they had a son who not only cheered up Naomi in her old years but was also a part of Jesus' family line! (Read the whole story in the book of Ruth.)

Ruth's story shows how rewarding it can be when we stay loyal to our friends, even when it's difficult. When our friends do things that annoy us, it's tempting to just look for another friend. But as long as they're not pulling us away from God, we need to have staying power like Ruth. Be willing to work through the problems with your friend, and trust God to take you and your friend where you need to go.

Glory

PRAYER POINTER

Jesus, I want to be loyal like Ruth and like You. Please help me have staying power when times get tough.

The Perfect Lie

Surely there is not a good man on earth who always does good and never sins.

ECCLESIASTES 7:20

Lie: I can never make mistakes.

"I meant to do that," Sarah lied to her sister, Alli.

"Sure, you meant to fall on your bottom," Alli said and giggled.

"Quit making fun of me," Sarah growled as she stormed out of the kitchen.

"Why can't you loosen up?" Alli called after her. "Just admit when you've messed up! You're not perfect, you know!"

The Truth Is . . .

As much as it might bother Sarah to admit it, Alli is right. Sarah isn't perfect. No one is. And the harder we try to always appear right and without fault, the more miserable we'll be.

God wants us to be humble, understanding that we're all sinners who say and do the wrong things at times and we all need help. Fortunately, Jesus loves to help the humble. So when you mess up, quit the cover-up. Confess it and smile. God's grace is greater than your goof-ups, and His love knows no end.

Prayer Pointer

Thank You, Lord, that Your perfection is good enough to cover all my failures.

Tiny Truth

God, your thoughts are precious to me. They are so many! If I could count them, they would be more than all the grains of sand.

PSALM 139:17–18

Have you ever been to the beach and wriggled your toes in the sand? Have you ever wondered how many grains of sand there are? According to scientists, the answer is more than seven quintillion, five hundred quadrillion.

Now here's another question, and it might seem unrelated to sand, but it isn't. How often does God think about you? The answer is *a lot*. Psalm 139:17–18 says that if we tried to count God's thoughts (which include thoughts about us), they'd outnumber all the grains of sand on earth! That's a number so long it would take up too much space here to write all the zeros!

So if you ever feel forgotten by God, think about all those grains of sand—and remember you're always on God's mind!

Prayer Pointer

Lord, You made the oceans and every grain of sand. I am so amazed—and so glad—that You think about me.

AUGUST 5

No Small Thing

Your love is so great it reaches to the skies.
Your truth reaches to the clouds.

PSALM 57:10

Did you know that Mount Everest is the highest mountain in the world? Its highest peak reaches 29,035 feet above sea level.

The deepest part of the ocean is called the Challenger Deep inside the Marianas Trench of the Pacific Ocean. It's 35,000 feet deep, or approximately 7 miles. If you dropped Mount Everest into the Challenger Deep, there would still be a mile of water on top of it!

The Milky Way Galaxy, where our Earth is located, is so huge that it would take 100,000 years to travel across it—if we could travel at the speed of light. And that's only one galaxy. Scientists believe there are billions and billions of galaxies.

Those are all really, *really* big things. But there's one thing so big it makes Mount Everest look like an ant hill and the Marianas Trench look like a mud puddle. It's even bigger than the entire universe. Want to know what it is? It's God's love for you—and that's no small thing!

Prayer Pointer

gracie

Lord, You created all these huge and wonderful things. But I'm most grateful for how big Your love is for me.

Home Sweet Home

Before the world was made, God decided to make us His own children through Jesus Christ.

EPHESIANS 1:5

Imagine visiting a friend's home. It's filled with comfy furniture and the smell of freshly baked cookies. Then your friend welcomes you into the kitchen and asks if you'd like something to eat. Everything is so wonderful, and you wish that you could stay forever.

Now imagine the same scene, but this time the house is yours. You don't just feel at home; you *are* home. So what's the difference?

Everything! Being someone's guest can be fun, but at some point you know you'll have to leave. But when you're a part of the family who owns the beautiful home, you never have to leave, and you are always welcome.

That's what it's like when you accept Jesus as your Savior. God, your heavenly Father, adopts you and welcomes you as part of the greatest royal family in the universe. Your place in God's kingdom is permanent, because God never leaves His kids. All the benefits and blessings of His kingdom are yours for the taking . . . and for offering to your guests who just might become future family members too.

Prayer Pointer

Glory

Thank You, Jesus, for welcoming me into Your beautiful family forever!

AUGUST 7

Right for Wrong

Do not do wrong to a person to pay him back for doing wrong to you. . . . But ask God to bless that person.

1 PETER 3:9

What would you do if . . .

- your little brother snuck into your room and messed with your stuff?
- someone made fun of you in front of the entire class?
- your best friend forgot to call you when she said she would?
- you were reaching for the last swing on the playground, but another girl snatched it away?

If one of these things happened to you, would you throw a fit or try to get even? Or would you do what Jesus did?

When people wrong us, it's okay to get mad. But what we do with that anger is most important. It's tempting to try to get even, but Jesus wants you to be different. He wants you to pay back wrong with right. Forgive the one who hurt you and ask God to bless that person. Because when you do, God will also bless you.

Lord, when people hurt me, I want to be forgiving like Jesus. But I need Your help to do it!

Defense Downer

My God is my rock. I can run to Him for safety.
He is my shield and my saving strength.

2 SAMUEL 22:2–3

Not-surprising news flash: almost everyone is afraid of skunks. Who can blame us? Skunks can shoot a horribly foul-smelling spray straight from . . . yes, their rear ends. Actually, though, skunks usually give plenty of warning before they spray, like hissing, stamping, or even doing handstands. Spraying is a last resort, and it can cause temporary blindness, vomiting, or illness—not to mention that horrible smell!

People, like skunks, defend themselves when they feel threatened. The result can be as devastating as skunk spray. Have you ever had a close friend suddenly turn on you, calling you names or being mean? Perhaps you've scared or hurt her in some way, and she thinks she needs to defend herself. Or do you tend to lash out when your feelings are hurt? Jesus says we need to let Him do the defending. Our job is to keep loving others—and that works a lot better than skunk spray.

Prayer Pointer

Jesus, help me keep calm when others wrong me, and give me wisdom to work it out.

Shining Stars

You are living with crooked and mean people all around you. Among them you shine like stars in the dark world. You offer to them the teaching that gives life.

PHILIPPIANS 2:15–16

It's time for a trip out into the country where the man-made streetlights end and the beautiful lights of the night sky begin. If you find the right spot, you'll be able to see the heavens stretching overhead like a dark, velvet blanket dotted with brilliant sparkles of light. Individually, each star is only a tiny light in the great big darkness of the night sky. But together, the lights join to brighten up the whole night sky, shining all the way down to earth.

God says that believers are just like those shining stars. Lit up by God's Spirit inside us, our lives look very different from the dark world all around us. The Bible calls people who do not believe in God "lost," because they cannot find a lasting purpose or meaning in life. List below some of the things of this world that people look to for happiness instead of God:

____

____

____

____

____

When people look to the things of the world for happiness, they will always be disappointed—never finding joy, peace, or true life. Their world will be dark. But those people who belong to God have the light of Jesus' hope. We have been forgiven, saved, and honored by God. And we have love to give because we have been loved first. As we show others what it means to know Jesus, His light shines out of us, pierces the darkness of this world, and draws other people to Him.

Prayer Pointer

Father, thank You for filling me with Your light to give lasting joy to others around me.

Mission Fields

"There are many people to harvest, but there are only a few workers to help harvest them."

MATTHEW 9:37

When you think of the mission field, what comes to mind? Dirt roads, palm trees, and people who don't speak your language? For sure, some mission fields look like that. But guess what? Right where you live is a mission field too.

Try one of these activities to help you connect with your neighbors and show them God's love!

- Bake cookies with your mom or dad, put them in a cute container, and include a card that says, "God loves you, and I do too!" Together, take them over to your neighbor's house. Share that you are praying for the people in your neighborhood and see if they'd let you pray with them before you leave.
- Offer to mow your neighbor's grass, rake their leaves, or take their garbage to the curb for free. Tell them you want to serve people just as Jesus did.
- Start a Backyard Bible Club with your friends. Meet once a week to pray and work on projects to help others.

Prayer Pointer

Hope

Jesus, please use me to help my neighbors know Your love better.

Busy, Busy, Busy

"Come with me. We will go to a quiet place to be alone. There we will get some rest."

MARK 6:31

AUGUST 11

Katie stared at the family calendar on the refrigerator. Soccer practice every afternoon, youth group meeting Wednesday, piano practice Thursday, and a family dinner at Grandma's Friday—plus homework and chores. It was going to be a busy week. *These are all great things,* Katie thought, *but I'm already feeling tired, and it's only Tuesday!*

Even as kids, our schedules can get very busy. Jesus understands because His schedule was often *very* busy with teaching, healing, and traveling. Sometimes He and His disciples didn't even have time to eat! But Jesus also knew the importance of rest. He'd often slip away from everyone and everything to simply talk to His Father and rest.

If rest was important for Jesus, how much more important is it for you? Find time every day—even just a minute or two—to slip away, talk to God, and rest. Go to your room, go outside, or simply close your eyes right where you are. God will always be right there, ready to restore your soul.

gracie

PRAYER POINTER

Lord, some days are so busy that I forget to rest. But I'm so glad You never forget me.

Rebekah, the Risk Taker

The Lord God helps me. So I will not be ashamed. I will be determined. I know I will not be disgraced.

ISAIAH 50:7

Rebekah was drawing water for her sheep when she saw an unfamiliar man by the well. Suddenly, she had the strong feeling she should give water to all his camels. So she did. (Little did she know the stranger was praying to God at that moment for the right woman to water his camels.) When she finished, the man rewarded her with beautiful gold jewelry and told her he believed God had chosen her to marry the man's master, Isaac.

"Are you willing to leave your family and follow me back to marry my master?" the servant asked.

"Yes!" Rebekah decided. It was a scary leap of faith, but she knew God had an exciting adventure ahead for her if she obeyed and followed God's plan. Rebekah took the risk because she and her family trusted God and believed He never fails His people. (Read Genesis 24:12–58 for the whole story.)

What has God asked you to do today?

Prayer Pointer

Lord, Your way is always right. Please help me trust and follow You.

No More Tears

He will wipe away every tear from their eyes. There will be no more death, sadness, crying, or pain. All the old ways are gone.

REVELATION 21:4

Have you even seen anyone cry from happiness? It can seem strange, but some people actually cry when they're happy or laughing really hard. Some people even cry when they're yawning! But while there is such a thing as happy tears, most tears come from sadness.

When sin came into world in the Garden of Eden, so did sorrow. And for as long as we live on earth, there'll be hurt and pain and tears. But one day all that will change.

When we get to heaven, Jesus will wipe away our very last tear—and there'll never be another one! No one will ever be sad or hurt again. How amazing will *that* be? In heaven, it will be like our happiest dreams come true, and every fear will be erased. And heaven is our future when we believe in Jesus and follow Him.

Prayer Pointer

God, sometimes my tears keep falling, but I know You're there to help me through. I can't wait for heaven, where I'll never cry again.

AUGUST 14

Getting to Give

"Give, and you will receive. . . . The way you give to others is the way God will give to you."

LUKE 6:38

If you get your life information from TV shows or magazines, it sure seems like getting more things is a lot better than giving up things. After all, who wouldn't want more candy, more toys, more clothes, more . . . whatever, right?

But Jesus warns us that what we think we want can actually make us sick. The more we try to get things for ourselves, the more miserable we become! For example, have you ever noticed how keeping a box of cookies to yourself instead of sharing them ruins your appetite for healthy food, makes you feel gross, and leaves you feeling more alone? Why? Because God designed us to find our greatest happiness in our friendship with Him, not by getting more things for ourselves.

The more we know and love God, the less stuff we feel like we need because we trust God to take care of us. His love makes us want to give what we have to others. And Jesus says we get happiness when we give.

PRAYER POINTER — Honor

Father, give me a generous heart that loves to give like You do.

Sweet Treat

You have good news to tell. . . . Shout it out and don't be afraid.

ISAIAH 40:9

So your mom made her yummiest chocolate chip cookies last night, and you brought some to school. You couldn't wait to pass them around to your friends at lunch! They didn't even have to ask for a cookie because your friends know you always share good things with them.

Now think about Jesus for a minute. He is good, right? Like, *really* good. Better than chocolate chip cookies or a new video game or a vacation, or any of the other things we love to tell our friends about. So if we know that being friends with Jesus means love, joy, and everlasting peace with God, why don't we share the good news with our friends who don't know Him?

We have to admit it: we're afraid our friends might think we are weird. But Jesus wants us to share what we know because it gives others a taste of God's goodness—just like that cookie. When your friends are ready, they'll be glad you were willing to share the sweet treat of knowing Jesus.

Prayer Pointer

grace

Jesus, make me brave to share Your love and truth with my friends.

Seeing Beauty

CHARM CAN FOOL YOU, AND BEAUTY CAN TRICK YOU. BUT A WOMAN WHO RESPECTS THE LORD SHOULD BE PRAISED.

PROVERBS 31:30

Lie: I need to be beautiful.

Jess had been staring at the mirror for half an hour. No matter how she styled her hair, she just didn't think it looked pretty.

"Ugh!" she grunted. "My hair looks awful! My face looks awful! Why am I so ugly?"

The Truth Is . . .

Have you ever heard that beauty is in the eye of the beholder? It means beauty is determined more by the person looking at it and appreciating it than the object itself. Different things seem beautiful to different people.

If you're a child of God, the most important person beholding your beauty is your heavenly Father. He planned your nose, your hair, and even your freckles before He formed the planet! He put a lot of thought into making you in the perfect way that makes Him smile with delight. So forget that magazine cover or what you think the mirror says. The best beauty secret is seeing yourself through God's eyes.

PRAYER POINTER

Lord, help me see myself the way You see me: beautiful.

Count on It!

God does not change.

JAMES 1:17

Does it ever seem like the whole world is changing? Friendships are changing. Some people move away and others move in. We change schools, and our parents change jobs. Even our own bodies are changing. Some days it's hard to know what to expect—or who you can count on!

But one thing is for certain: we can always count on God. He never changes—not ever! The promises He made thousands and thousands of years ago He still keeps today. Like when He told Joshua that He would never leave him (Joshua 1:5), or when He promised in Matthew that He would take care of everything we need (6:25–34), or when He promised to save all of us who choose to follow Jesus. Those promises weren't just for the people of the Bible. They're for us too. And if there's one thing that never changes, it's the fact that God always keeps His promises. We can count on it!

Prayer Pointer

So many things seem to change, God. I'm so glad You are always the same. I know I can count on You, no matter what.

AUGUST 18

Teams Work

The Lord watches over those who follow Him. He frees them from the power of the wicked.

PSALM 97:10

There's something about the story of Esther that you may not have noticed: the rivalry between Haman (the bad guy who wanted to kill the Jews) and Mordecai (the God-fearing Jew who raised Esther). Haman wanted everyone to think he was important. He even made people bow to him. Mordecai wouldn't obey, because he only bowed to God. So Haman plotted to kill not just Mordecai but all the Jews. That's when a new team formed to turn things around. Mordecai and Esther joined together with all the Jews to secretly fast and pray. Then Esther planned a way to alert the king and upset Haman's plans. God was on His people's side, and Haman was defeated when Esther exposed his evil plan.

Esther showed incredible bravery, but her story is also about Mordecai and the other Jews who came together, prayed, and—with God's power—stopped Haman's plan. In other words, it was a total team effort. And that's the same way God wants His people to fight Satan's schemes today.

Prayer Pointer

Hope

God, I want to be part of Your team. Show me how I can work with others to do Your will today.

Like Jesus Did

Do not be lazy but work hard. Serve the Lord with all your heart.

ROMANS 12:11

Jessica stared down at the scrub brush in her hand. When she'd volunteered to help with a service project at the children's home, this wasn't what she had in mind. She thought she'd be rocking the babies or playing games with the little ones outside, maybe even teaching them some songs or stories about Jesus. Scrubbing the bathrooms definitely wasn't her idea of serving.

But then she remembered the lesson she'd heard in youth group last week. They'd been getting ready for the service project, and they'd been talking about serving like Jesus did.

Jesus, on the night before He was crucified, washed His disciples' feet. It was the yuckiest of jobs, and not even servants wanted to do it. But Jesus—the Son of God—washed their feet. Jessica still remembered what Jesus had said: "I did this as an example for you. So you should do as I have done for you" (John 13:15).

Well, she thought, *it's not washing feet, but it's definitely serving like Jesus.* And she went back to scrubbing, but this time with a smile.

Honor

PRAYER POINTER

Lord, teach me to serve with love, just like Jesus did.

A Good Foundation

No one can build any other foundation. The foundation that has already been laid is Jesus Christ.

1 CORINTHIANS 3:11

Look at the list of items below. In what order would you put them on?

- necklace
- scarf
- your favorite shirt and jeans
- bracelet
- boots

Did you put a number one by your favorite shirt and jeans? You should! Because all those other items are the things that go on top. A great outfit starts with a great foundation—like your favorite shirt and jeans. Then you can add all the rest of the pieces like scarves, jewelry, and boots to make a beautiful, stylish outfit.

Believe it or not, the same principle applies to our spiritual lives. Good behaviors like nice manners, working hard, and being kind to others are like a wardrobe of beautiful accessories. But for true spiritual beauty, you need more than accessories; you need a great foundation.

So what's step one in God's beauty process? Jesus. He is our foundation—not just for what we wear, but for our whole lives. His Spirit inside us changes our hearts to help us obey His Word and become beautiful. Once we belong to God and Jesus' Spirit lives in us, then we can apply the truths that God says will make us beautiful in His sight—things like loving and giving, sharing and forgiving.

For instance, instead of staying mad at your friend who didn't invite you over for the slumber party, you can forgive and love her. Instead of demanding your parents give you whatever you want, you can look for ways to spend your time, money, or talents to help people in need. With Jesus' love encouraging us and making us strong, we can follow His example. And that kind of beauty is always in style!

Prayer Pointer

Jesus, I need You to fill me and strengthen me so I can be beautiful like You.

Hagar, Who Was Seen

"God even knows how many hairs you have on your head. Don't be afraid. You are worth much more than many sparrows."

LUKE 12:7

Have you ever felt forgotten, like no one really cared about you? Being lonely can make us feel scared. But sometimes God takes us to those lonely places so that we see He's with us.

Just ask Hagar, Sarah's servant who was forced to bear a child because Sarah couldn't have one. But when God gave Sarah the son she had always wanted, Sarah had Hagar and her boy sent away. Wandering in the desert with her son, Hagar figured she was all alone and would die that way.

But God saw her. In fact, He saved them, showing them where to find fresh water and how to live (Genesis 21:9–20).

Hagar's story is a beautiful reminder that no matter where you go or what you do, God sees, cares, and is with you. He alone is powerful to save you and walk with you all the days of your life.

Prayer Pointer

Lord, because of Your love, I am never alone. Thank You for being my Savior and Friend forever.

Summer Storms

You are my hiding place and my shield. I trust your word.

PSALM 119:114

AUGUST 22

Crash! You are jolted awake by thunder. *Flash!* Lightning illuminates the sky outside your window. And then you hear the sound of rain, slow at first, but then pouring all around. Grateful for the shelter of your house, you snuggle deeper under the covers, waiting for the storm to be over.

Storms can be scary sometimes, can't they? Storms can make us feel powerless and vulnerable, even though we know the rain is good for the earth.

But storms are good for reminding us of God's tremendous power! As big as storms get and as strong as the lightning seems, God is even bigger and stronger. He not only made the world that houses those storms, He created the universe, which holds everything else! Our God is really, really big and powerful. And He's the perfect shelter from the storms—not just rain storms, but storms of life, like sickness, sadness, or separation. God wants us to come to Him whenever we are afraid, and He will keep us safe in His care!

Prayer Pointer

Father, thank You for watching over me and keeping me safe.

Picking Friends, Not Fights

Don't make friends with someone who easily gets angry. . . . If you do, you may learn to be like him.

PROVERBS 22:24–25

Have you ever met someone who seemed nice at first, only to find out she had a really mean, angry side? In the animal world, she'd be a honey badger—a weasel-like creature with a strong love of honey, often considered to be one of the most fearless and ferocious animals around.

The honey badger will steal other animals' burrows and is famous for picking fights with any creature that crosses its path. The honey badger usually wins these fights because of its thick, rubbery skin and exceptionally strong teeth and jaws. And when frightened, it lets out one big stink bomb from the glands near its tail, much like a skunk.

Needless to say, honey badgers deserve some respect, but also some distance. The same is true for people who like to pick fights. You'll recognize them by how much they gossip or by their habit of insulting others. Pray for them and answer with love and wisdom whenever they approach, but otherwise—keep your distance!

Prayer Pointer

Glory

God, please help me choose friends wisely and pray for those who don't know You.

It's a Bug's Life

Lord, you have made many things. With your wisdom you made them all.

PSALM 104:24

AUGUST 24

Did you know that there are more than nine hundred thousand different species of insects in the world? And that's only the ones that have been identified and named. Scientists think there could be anywhere from two million to thirty million more species of bugs that haven't been discovered yet. And for every person on the planet, there are approximately two hundred million bugs. That's a lot of creepy crawlies!

Some people hate bugs and wonder why God even made them. But bugs serve lots of important purposes in our world. Worms churn up the soil so that plants grow better. Some bugs eat up other, more pesky bugs—while still other bugs are food themselves for larger creatures. Bugs help get rid of waste, and they help pollinate plants and trees. So while you may or may not care to meet one personally, our world couldn't exist without bugs.

If God has such an important purpose for something as tiny as bug, can you imagine what He has in store for you?

Prayer Pointer

Honor

Lord, the next time I see a bug, help me remember that You have a purpose for it—and for me.

Truth Telling

"You must not tell lies."

EXODUS 23:1

We know we should tell the truth and lying is bad. But have you ever wondered why? Jesus says that when we tell a lie, we are acting like we belong to Satan instead of God. But when we speak the truth, we're talking God's language—and His words are powerful!

Look at the situations below. Write out how you would respond with the truth.

- You accidentally broke your mom's necklace. You could hide it back in her jewelry drawer, but instead you: ________________________.
- The kids at church were complaining that church was dumb. You want them to like you, but you don't agree with them. So you say:________________________.
- Your friend hurt your feelings when she ignored you at lunch. You could pretend everything was okay, but instead you bravely and lovingly tell her: ________________________.

It isn't always easy to tell the truth, but God will always help you do what's right when you ask Him.

Prayer Pointer

Lord, please keep me from telling lies, even in what seems to be small ways. Make me truthful always.

Write It Out

Create in me a pure heart, God.
Make my spirit right again.

PSALM 51:10

God wants us to live lives that show His goodness and love to the world around us. Are there things you need to work on in your life so you can better show God's love? Things like being unselfish, thankful, and forgiving? When we acknowledge the things we need to work on and lift them up to God, He helps us. List below the traits you really want to be part of your character, and then pray for one each day:

____

____

____

____

____

____

____

____

Prayer Pointer

Lord, show me if there is anything in me that doesn't please You—and then help me to get rid of it.

AUGUST 27

Hang in There!

I will still be glad in the Lord. I will rejoice in God my Savior. The Lord God gives me my strength.

HABAKKUK 3:18–19

Nothing going right?

There are going to be days when it seems there is a black cloud hanging over your head. Your mom's car wouldn't start, and you were late to school. When you got there, you found out you'd left your homework on the kitchen table. When you got home, your sister had eaten the last of the cookies.

Habakkuk 3:18–19 is part of a song of praise during the storms of life. The author was struggling just to make it through, but he still praised God and had hope. It's easy to have hope when things are going smoothly, but to have hope when things are bad is an exercise in faith. So give your faith muscles a stretch! Take a deep breath, say a prayer, keep doing right, and trust God to make something good out of the wrong. And remember, soon the sun will set on this day, and God will give you another chance to start fresh in the morning.

Prayer Pointer

Lord, some days it seems like nothing is going right. But I know that with You by my side, everything will be okay.

Undivided Heart

Teach me Your way, O LORD; I will walk in Your truth; unite my heart to fear Your name.

PSALM 86:11 NKJV

Judas traveled with Jesus. He listened to the same sermons and saw the same miracles as the other eleven disciples. He was even in charge of handling their money (John 13:29). So what went so tragically wrong?

Judas had a double heart. No, not two physical hearts! His spiritual heart had two very different interests. Judas liked hanging out with an important person who might end up as Israel's king, but he didn't really believe Jesus was God. He was in the friendship for what he could get out of it, not because he loved Jesus. So when the religious leaders offered Judas money to betray Jesus, Judas chose money (Matthew 26:14–15).

Judas gives us a pretty clear picture of what a fake friend looks like. And if we're not careful, we can be the same way. If we only follow Jesus when it's easy, or only make friends with people who give us what we want, then we have a double heart like Judas. And divided hearts can never love like Jesus.

Honor

PRAYER POINTER

Jesus, help me be true to You and my friends. Give me an undivided heart.

Wardrobe Choices

The God we serve is able to save us.

DANIEL 3:17

After her Sunday school lesson, Hope thought to herself, *Okay, I'm supposed to always obey my parents, love others, and answer with a kind word. Got it!* Confident that she was good enough and strong enough to do those things, Hope left class and got in the car to ride home with her family. Immediately, one of her brothers grabbed her video game that she'd left on the seat.

How do you think Hope will respond?

Like all God's kids, Hope has a choice to make. She can choose to serve herself or to serve God in the next few moments. It's a lot like choosing which outfit you are going to put on and show the world. Is she going to put on anger and selfishness, or instead is she going to throw those attitudes in the trash and put on patience, obedience, and love?

Read the options below and circle the wardrobe that shows God's glory best.

Wardrobe Option 1

"Give it back!" She scowled at her brother.

"But I got it first," he replied.

Then Hope's mother said, "Hope, honey, please let your brother play for a little while."

"No!" she argued. "It's my game, and he shouldn't have it!"

Wardrobe Option 2

Hope remembered her Sunday school teacher's lesson and knew she'd need help to obey. *God*, she prayed, *I want to do what's right, but I am weak on my own. Will You please give me strength to follow You?*

Hope was tempted to argue with her brother, but God's Spirit nudged her to be kind. "You can have it for now," she said to her brother, "but I'd like it back when we get home."

Which wardrobe above would you choose in this situation?

Prayer Pointer

God, I can never be good on my own. Please fill me with Your Spirit so I can do what is right.

Fatherly Wisdom

"You will know that I say only what the Father has taught me."

JOHN 8:28

Imagine walking into church with your parents, and it looks like you are the only kid around. Some adults are walking up, about to start a conversation. You have to decide quickly what you'll do. Will you hide behind your parents and stare at the floor? Or will you smile and introduce yourself?

Chances are you know that smiling and introducing yourself is the thing to do, because your parents or a teacher has taught you how to interact with others.

Jesus tells us that His Father, God, taught Him too. He prayed and talked to God all the time, and He listened to everything God told Him. He always knew what to do because He had learned everything from His Father.

If we want to lead others to God just as Jesus did, then we'll need to spend time with Him. As we pray and study His Word, God's Spirit will give us the wisdom we need to talk and walk like Jesus.

Prayer Pointer

Lord, thank You for teaching me! Show me how to follow Your lead and be like You.

Light Up the World

"I am the light of the world. The person who follows me will never live in darkness. He will have the light that gives life."

JOHN 8:12

AUGUST 31

Darkness is the absence of any light. It makes it hard to see and to know where we're going. And it makes it easy to stumble and fall.

Spiritual darkness works pretty much the same way. Since Jesus is light, spiritual darkness is the absence of Jesus. Spiritual darkness makes it hard to see what's right and what's wrong, or to know which path to take. It can also make it very easy to make bad choices. Think about it: If you're walking in the wilderness in the pitch black, what's to keep you from falling off a cliff?

But when we choose to follow Jesus, love Him, and obey His Word, darkness isn't something we have to worry about. In fact, He promises that we'll *never* have to live in darkness. That's because the light of Jesus is big enough and strong enough to light up our whole world.

Prayer Pointer

Jesus, please fill my life with Your light so I can shine it into the lives of everyone around me.

Looking Deeper

Every good action and every perfect gift is from God.

JAMES 1:17

Have you ever seen the optical illusion where there's a page full of rectangles, but if you look hard enough, your eyes adjust to actually see an image? There's one where, after your eyes adjust, you suddenly see the name Jesus! Pretty cool, right? But some people never see more than black rectangles.

The same is true in life. Many people think God can't be seen. They go through each day as if they have to solve all their problems on their own. Good and bad things happen, and they assume it's just chance or luck. They can't see God's hand in it.

But God has given His children special eyes to see life more clearly. Though we can't see Him, Jesus is always there! His Spirit is inside us, and our heavenly Father watches over us and guides our every step. God promises to work out everything that happens for our good.

So don't miss the bigger picture. Celebrate every bird that sings, every tasty bite you eat, and every hug from family and friends as proof that God loves to love you!

PRAYER POINTER

Father, give me eyes to see all the ways You love and care for me.

When It's You

"Do for other people the same things you want them to do for you."

MATTHEW 7:12

Can you believe Emily?" Sadie huffed. "Not only did she not want me to sit with her, she acted like I didn't even exist!"

Anna listened to Sadie complain about Emily. And it was true—Emily could be mean, leaving people out, gossiping, and making fun of other girls. But the problem was, sometimes Sadie did the same thing to Katelyn, one of Anna's friends.

Anna said a little prayer to herself, and softly replied, "You're right about Emily. But you know, you kinda do the same thing to Katelyn."

Sadie's eyes widened, and she started to act mad, but then she remembered laughing at Katelyn's outfit just yesterday. *Oh . . .*

There's a lot of talk about how to handle mean girls. But what if *you're* the mean girl? Maybe you're trying to fit in or make yourself look better than someone else, but that doesn't make it okay. What should you do? It's a simple fix—treat everyone the way you want them to treat you. Oh, and be sure to apologize to God and to those you've been mean to.

Prayer Pointer

Glory

Lord, help me treat everyone the way You would want me to.

Beauty Rest

"Come to me, all of you who are tired and have heavy loads. I will give you rest."

MATTHEW 11:28

Have you ever stayed up really late, or maybe even pulled an all-nighter at a lock-in? If so, did you have any of these symptoms?

- dark circles under your eyes
- extreme tiredness
- grouchy attitude
- feeling gross in general
- dry eyes
- unable to think or speak clearly

Sometimes an event seems like it's going to be so much fun that it's worth missing sleep for it, but our bodies eventually tell us a different story: you need sleep more than you realize! Sleep helps our bodies reset and restores all our cells to proper working order.

The same is true for our spiritual lives. Sometimes we get so caught up in our daily routine of school, homework, and activities that we completely miss spending time with God. Taking time to be with Jesus gives your spirit the good rest it needs to recharge. God's Word renews our minds and fuels us with the energy we need to follow Him throughout our busy day.

Prayer Pointer

Lord, thank You for offering me much-needed rest through spending time with You each day.

On the Hunt

Be careful! The devil is your enemy. And he goes around like a roaring lion looking for someone to eat.

1 PETER 5:8

Who's the king of the savanna? The lion, of course. Why? Because lions are the top of the food chain, if you don't count people. Ranging from 250 to 500 pounds, these massive cats aren't the fastest creatures, but they are rather sneaky. Lionesses (female lions) do most of the hunting. They work in groups to surround a herd quietly, trying hard to remain hidden. Then, when a weak or slow member of the herd breaks away from the group, the lionesses pounce and almost instantly kill their victim.

God says Satan is like a roaring lion who wants to destroy you. Just as the lioness hunts her prey, Satan wants to separate you from the group—God's family—so he can trick you with his lies. If you start listening to him, he can crush your faith. That's why it's so important to stay connected to God and His people at all times. We help one another stay safe!

Prayer Pointer

Lord, help me stay connected to You, and protect me from Satan's schemes.

SEPTEMBER 5

Light of the World

"You are the light that gives light to the world."

MATTHEW 5:14

Have you ever wondered why sunrises and sunsets are so beautiful? Blue skies erupt into flaming colors of red, orange, yellow, and even pink. So what makes the change happen? Light. Yep, the same sunlight that made the sky look blue can make it appear as all those other colors too. Sunlight contains all the color wavelengths, but different conditions in the atmosphere absorb certain colors, leaving the remaining color wavelengths to reach our eyes. For instance, when the sun is low on the horizon, light waves must travel farther to reach our eyes. Shorter blue waves get scattered and lost, while longer wavelengths of red and yellow reach our eyes.

Jesus says God's kids are the light of the world. We don't create the light, but we channel it into its beautiful colors when we share a lunch with the kid who forgot his, take cookies to the firemen and thank them for protecting us, pray for a hurting friend, or tell someone how much Jesus loves her. Every day is a chance to paint the world with the colors of God's love.

Laura

PRAYER POINTER

Lord, let Your light shine through me in the most colorful and beautiful ways.

Endless Devotion

In your lives you must think and
act like Christ Jesus.

PHILIPPIANS 2:5

Jesus knew what was about to happen. Soldiers would arrest Him. His closest friends would desert Him. And He would be crucified on a cross. You would think He would have spent His last night on earth as a free man doing whatever He wanted.

And He did! Jesus took off His robe, put on a servant's outfit, and washed His disciples' feet. Even in His last hour, Jesus wanted His friends to know how much He loved them and loved serving them. And He wanted them to do the same for others (John 13:1–17).

One way to grow a servant's heart is to ask yourself: What do you like other people to do for you? How have your parents or others shown their love to you? Ask God to help you be creative in thinking of ways to love and serve those around you. Each day ask Jesus to help you find new ways to share God's love for the world with creativity and selflessness.

Prayer Pointer

Glory

God, please show me how to spread Your love to the world in new and loving ways.

SEPTEMBER 7

Social Slowpokes

People love and trust those who plan to do good.

PROVERBS 14:22

With long, gangly arms and full-body fur, sloths seem made for hugs. And in a way they are—because they love hugging trees. Sloths are uniquely designed to hang from tree limbs, where they can slowly eat a meal of leaves. That's not all sloths do slowly. It can take a month for a sloth to digest one meal! They also sleep fifteen to twenty hours a day, which doesn't help with their friend-making. Most sloths don't really socialize with other sloths, except for sometimes sharing the same branch.

If we want to become friends with someone and stay friends, we can't just sit back like a sloth and hope things work out. We have to work at it. What is "friendship work"? It's talking together, listening, and finding time to hang out. If you wait for the other person to do all the work, she might just leave you hanging—and that's only fun for a sloth! Ask God to help you reach out to all the people He puts in your path.

Prayer Pointer

Father, keep me from being lazy in my relationship with You and my friends.

A Bigger Plan

"I have good plans for you. I don't plan to hurt you. I plan to give you hope and a good future."

JEREMIAH 29:11

Wow! Amy thought. *Today did not turn out the way I wanted. I worked so hard on that science project. I just knew I'd win and get to go to the state competition. But everything went wrong. I am so frustrated and disappointed! This whole thing is completely hopeless!*

Amy's had a really bad day. It happens to everyone. We work hard and try to do what's right, then it blows up in our face. But it's okay—or, at least, it will be. That's because God's got a bigger plan.

When things don't work out the way you think they should, be grateful. Yes, *grateful*! Because that means God has something even better planned for you. You might see it right away, or it may take a little while. Until then, trust God. He'll only do what's best for you.

Prayer Pointer

God, I know You've got good things planned for my life. Help me trust that Your plans are the best plans of all.

Icebreakers

The Lord sees the good people. He listens to their prayers. . . . The Lord hears good people when they cry out to Him. He saves them from all their troubles.

PSALM 34:15, 17

Do you remember the first time you met your best friend? Chances are the first conversation was a bit awkward. But the more you talked, the more you found you had in common with each other. And now finding things to talk about is no trouble at all!

The same is true when you are hanging out with God. At first, it might seem really weird to talk to someone you can't see. Many kids *and* adults wonder, *What should I say?* or *How does this work?* or *What if I mess up?*

But relax! God is super interested in whatever you have to say. You will be surprised how quickly you become comfortable telling Him whatever's on your mind. Soon, you'll be talking out loud or in your heart all day long and including your new best Friend in everything you do.

So what are you waiting for? Here are a few icebreakers just to get the conversation going:

- **Praise**: "God, You are so ____________ (fill in with words that describe who He is, such as *powerful, forgiving, faithful,* or *kind*)."
- **Confess**: "Lord, I admit that I have ____________ (name your thoughts, attitudes, or actions that go against God's directions in the Bible). Please forgive me. Thank You for always forgiving."
- **Thank**: "Jesus, thank You for ____________ (name the good things you have in your life). Everything I have comes from You!"
- **Ask**: "Lord, You are all powerful and good. Would You please help me ____________? Also, would you please help ____________ (my family, friends, the poor, the missionaries, our leaders, etc.) who need ____________?"

Prayer Pointer

God, thank You for always listening to what I say. I know I can trust You with whatever I'm thinking or feeling.

A Sore Subject

Give thanks to the God of heaven.
His love continues forever.

PSALM 136:26

If you're squeamish, don't ever look up pictures of leprosy, the terrible skin disease that we read about in the Bible. Moses' sister Miriam had it for a time, Naaman had it, and so did the ten lepers who came to Jesus to be healed.

Leprosy is a disease that affects the nerves, lining of the lungs, skin, limbs, and eyes. It's caused by bacteria that can actually go unnoticed for many years until symptoms start to surface. Leprosy can cause skin to change colors and develop lumps, and can stop the nerves from working (which can cause other injuries). Today leprosy can be cured with medicine, but back in Bible times there was no cure.

When Jesus healed the ten lepers (Luke 17), you would think they all would've been really grateful to be freed of the disease. But only one told Jesus, "Thank You." Our health is so important, and so easy to take for granted when everything is going well. Let's be sure to thank God for our health—and for all that He blesses us with.

Prayer Pointer

Thank You, Lord, for my health. Help me take good care of my body.

Getting to Give

Do not be interested only in your own life, but be interested in the lives of others.

PHILIPPIANS 2:3–4

It was Saturday, and Amanda was looking forward to going shopping, but her dad had other plans. "Honey, a family is coming over who could use some encouragement," he explained. "The father is out of work, so I invited them over so you could play with the kids while the grown-ups talk." How should Amanda handle this change of plans?

Choice 1

Amanda crossed her arms. "I don't even know those people," she whined. "It's not my fault they have problems. I had plans today. We can help them some other time."

Choice 2

Amanda thought about how that family must feel. She realized that even though she really wanted to go shopping, she didn't need anything. So she said, "Okay. How old are the kids? I'll plan something fun to do while they're here."

Prayer Pointer

Glory

Jesus, You have said it's better to give than to receive. Help me believe it and live it!

First in Beauty and Grace

We were spiritually dead because of the things we did wrong against God. But God gave us new life with Christ. You have been saved by God's grace.

EPHESIANS 2:5

At first sight, Adam was amazed by Eve—God's answer to Adam's need for a companion equal to himself. When God had realized what Adam was lacking, He'd made Eve from Adam's own rib.

Eve was the first woman, and the beginning of a beautiful work. Sadly, Eve's reign as queen of Eden ended when she disobeyed God's instructions, listening to the crafty snake (Satan) instead. Adam joined her, and their sin separated them both from God.

But God loved His people too much to end the story there. God promised to send a Savior who could erase their sins and reunite them with God. (Read the story in Genesis 2–3.) Many years later, Jesus came and fulfilled God's promise (1 John 3:8). Because of God, Eve would no longer be known only as the first woman who sinned. Now she was also known as the first woman to know God's saving grace.

Prayer Pointer

Lord, thank You for Your beautiful grace and forgiveness.

God's Got This

All the days planned for me were written in your book before I was one day old.

PSALM 139:16

Are you a planner? Lots of people are. They plan what to wear, what to do, what to say. Plans can make us feel more comfortable and in control of what's happening around us.

But no matter how carefully we plan, there'll be times when life doesn't go according to our plans. Maybe it's something small like a rip in your favorite jeans, or something bigger like a pop quiz. Or maybe it's something really big like a move, an accident, or someone in your family getting sick. Whatever it is, it's thrown your plans all out of whack, and now you're not quite sure what to do.

Well, first, stop worrying. Seriously, God's got this. That thing that surprised you didn't surprise Him at all. In fact, He's had a plan to take care of this since before you were even born. So just relax and trust God—because He's got this.

Prayer Pointer

Lord, my plans have gotten all messed up, but I know you've got this. I'll trust You because You know just what to do.

Perfect Party Planner

May He give you what you want.
May all your plans succeed.

PSALM 20:4

So you wanna throw a party? Awesome! But parties take lots of prep—and prayer! So take a look at these party to-dos and ask your parents to help you get started:

1. Decide how many people you want to invite.
2. If you can't invite everyone, mail invitations to each person. Ask your friends not to say anything to others about it. Feelings can get hurt if you aren't careful!
3. Plan the food. How many people do you need to feed? What will you serve? When should you start cooking?
4. Plan the activities. Will you have a themed party or just casual fun? Plan lots of options, like board games, movies, nail-painting, and outdoor adventures.
5. At the party, be a great host. Listen to what your guests want to do. Make sure everyone is included, and try to talk to everyone. Thank each person for coming, and have lots of fun. And don't forget to clean up!

Prayer Pointer

Glory

God, thank You for celebrations that allow me to get together with my friends. Please show me ways to serve them and You better each day.

The Art of Encouragement

Comfort each other and give each other strength, just as you are doing now.

1 THESSALONIANS 5:11

Have you ever noticed how many different greeting cards there are? That's because people want to find one that has just the right words for the moment.

And that's often why we buy cards—because it can be hard to think of the right words on our own. But encouraging others is actually a kind of art. And the more we practice writing and saying words to help others feel better, the better we become at it.

Try one of these activities, and put your art into practice today:

- On a few sheets of heavy paper, paint a simple picture and write your favorite Bible verse below the picture. Then hand these out at a local nursing home, or give them to older people at your church. Be sure to include a hug!
- Write fun, encouraging messages on sticky notes. Stick them in surprising places for your parents or siblings to discover.
- Write a letter to your pastor, teacher, or youth group leader to say thank you for all he or she does for others.

Prayer Pointer Hope

Jesus, give me words of encouragement so I can always build up others.

SEPTEMBER 16

Creation Care

"Tell the people of Israel this: 'I will give you land. When you enter it let it have a special time of rest. This will be to honor the Lord.'"

LEVITICUS 25:2

Our Sunday school teacher shared a great lesson with us from Leviticus 25:1–7. God wanted the Hebrews to give the earth a twelve-month break (Sabbath) from farming every seventh year. So what if... as Christians we simply made our weekly Sabbath (day of rest) an environmentally friendly day? We could have a huge impact on the world, just by doing simple things like the following:

- walking instead of being driven
- turning off the light when you leave the room
- not running the faucet while your brush your teeth
- using as little paper (and paper products) as possible
- recycling
- drinking tap water instead of bottled

What other things can you think of that you could do to help your home, community, and world?

Prayer Pointer

Lord, please show me creative ideas to care for Your creation and give me bravery to start making them happen.

The Potter's Hands

Lord, you are our father. We are like clay, and you are the potter. Your hands made us all.

ISAIAH 64:8

Have you ever worked with clay on a potter's wheel? First, you place your lump of clay onto the center of the wheel. Then you gently press into the center of it as the wheel turns, using your fingers to gradually shape a bowl, a cup, or a vase.

God says that people are like clay, and He is the Potter. Just as He formed Adam from the dust of the ground, He shapes who we are. He presses in—using the people in our lives and our experiences, both good and bad—to mold us and make us fit for the purpose He has planned for us. We might not always like the molding and shaping part, but God knows exactly what He's doing.

Your life is safe in God's hands. Instead of fighting the way He is shaping you, open your eyes and heart to His plans for you—they'll always be perfectly designed.

Prayer Pointer

Father, I trust You to use every moment in my life to shape me into the person You want me to be.

I Don't Want To!

Do everything without complaining or arguing.

PHILIPPIANS 2:14

"No, I don't want to!"

"I won't."

"This is boring."

"I hate doing the dishes."

"Why do I always have to clean my room?"

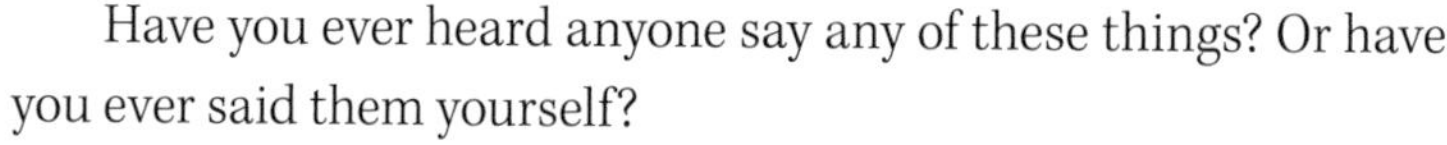

Have you ever heard anyone say any of these things? Or have you ever said them yourself?

We all have things we don't want to do, but some things just have to be done. Imagine if no one ever emptied the trash, washed the dishes, or took out the dog. Things would get very yucky, very quickly!

God wants you to obey your parents and do what's right. In fact, the Bible says He's "working in you to help you want to do what pleases him" (Philippians 2:13). That's right—God's helping you. And there are things you can do too. Try to make those unpleasant chores more fun. Turn on your favorite music, or sing your own song. Or promise yourself a treat when the job is done, like playing with the dog after you take him outside. Some things just have to be done, but we can figure out ways to make them more enjoyable.

Prayer Pointer

Lord, help me think of ways to make the chores I don't want to do more fun. I want my attitude to please You!

Trading Places

Christ had no sin. But God made Him become sin. God did this for us so that in Christ we could become right with God.

2 CORINTHIANS 5:21

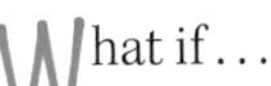

What if . . .

- you made a 100 on the test and then traded grades with someone who flunked it?
- you left behind all your friends and traded places with that shy, new girl who doesn't know anyone?
- you got up from your dinner table and traded places with a homeless person begging for food?
- you left your nice, comfortable home and traded places with a girl who lived in a patched-together shack at the edge of a trash dump in South America?

Would you want to trade places? Probably not. But you know what? Jesus did. He did everything right, and He traded places with those who did everything wrong. Why would Jesus do those things? So we could trade all our sins and mistakes for the mercy, grace, and forgiveness of God, and so we could get to know Him. That's how much Jesus loves us.

grace

Prayer Pointer

Jesus, thank You for loving me so much that You traded places with me.

Mental Muscles

I have taken your words to heart so
I would not sin against you.

PSALM 119:11

If a snake crawled up to you and tried to convince you to disobey God, would you listen? After freaking out, saying no would be the super easy part. Although Satan doesn't sneak up on people in serpent form anymore, he does try to trip up God's people and keep others away from God's life-saving truth. To make matters worse, our own sinful hearts often enjoy the lure of Satan's lies over the beauty of God's ways. So how can we stay on track with what's true?

God's Word! The Bible is God's letter to us, and it still packs amazing power for today's world. That's because the words in it all point to Jesus, building us up in our relationship with Him and His Spirit, who lives inside His people. But what good is a bunch of armor if you never put it on and don't learn how to use it? Don't be a sitting duck. Gear up for the war games that evil wages with our minds by learning God's truth first. Here's the plan of attack:

- Choose to memorize an entire passage of Scripture or book of the Bible one verse at a time.
- Locate a memory verse system. If you have a smartphone or tablet, you can download apps that give you new verses to memorize each week, plus quizzes and songs to help you remember the Scripture verses.

- Use Biblegateway.com or other online Bible search engines to look up verses that help you face the things you're dealing with. Write out the verses and work to memorize them. Find a parent or friend who will test you on your verses.

Over time, your mind will be strengthened by knowing God and His truth. When the enemy tries to trick you into following him, God's Spirit will help you remember what you've learned and help you answer evil just like Jesus did—with God's own words of truth.

Prayer Pointer

God, help me to commit Your Word to memory, and help me to always turn to it for guidance.

The Best Loser

Everything you say and everything you do should all be done for Jesus your Lord.

COLOSSIANS 3:17

Lie: I need to win to feel good about myself.

"Let's play one more round," Livvy insisted.

"Nooooo," Marlie moaned. "We've played this game, like, three times now!"

"I know, but it isn't fair," Livvy said, growing irritated. "You always get the good cards, so we have to play until I can win."

The Truth Is . . .

While some people are more competitive than others, nobody likes losing. Yet someone has to lose in order for someone to win, right? Since it isn't likely—or even fair—that you'll always win, then it's important to learn to lose well.

Losing well means not having a temper tantrum, accusing others of cheating, or having a bad attitude. It also means being grateful for the chance to play and being happy for the winners. Remember, winning doesn't make you a better person. But winning or losing with a good attitude makes you the kind of person other people like to play with.

Prayer Pointer

Lord, help me win, lose, and play in a way that shows Your grace.

The Perfect Hiding Spot

I will come to you as a bird comes for protection under its mother's wings until the trouble has passed.

PSALM 57:1

SEPTEMBER 22

Do you ever feel like playing hide-and-seek (minus the seek part) with the whole world? Maybe it's been a really bad day, or you know someone is upset with you. Or maybe it's been a great day, but now you're just plain tired and you want to hide away for a little while. It happens to us all, and God understands. He's even got the perfect hiding spot for you.

Where is that hiding spot? It's under His wings. Imagine a baby bird, all snuggled up under its mother's wings. She's safe and warm and loved. Nothing can trouble or harm her there. Now imagine that baby bird is you. When you turn to God for help and for rest, He pulls you in close and snuggles you under His wing. You're safe and warm and loved. And you can rest when you're under God's wing.

Prayer Pointer

Thank You, Lord, for giving me a place to hide away from the world for a while. I know I am safe and loved when I'm under Your wing.

The Very Best Gift

THEN A POOR WIDOW CAME AND GAVE TWO VERY SMALL COPPER COINS. THESE COINS WERE NOT WORTH EVEN A PENNY.

MARK 12:42

Casey couldn't help but feel disappointed as she placed her money in the basket. Her church was collecting money to help some people whose homes had been flooded by storms. Casey knew a couple of her classmates had lost everything, and she really wanted to help. She'd done extra chores and babysitting to earn some money, but she'd only come up with twelve dollars. *That won't help very much*, she thought.

Perhaps that's what the poor widow in the Bible thought when she gave her two small coins. Compared to what others gave, it was nothing. But Jesus saw her gift, and this is what He said: "She really gave more than all those rich people. The rich have plenty; they gave only what they did not need. . . . But she gave all she had" (Mark 12:43–44).

Your gifts don't have to be big to be important to Jesus. He can turn a small gift into something that makes a big difference, as long as it's given in love. And that's the very best gift of all.

PRAYER POINTER

Jesus, please bless me with a giving heart and teach me to give all my heart to You.

Scents of Greatness

The teaching about the cross seems foolish to those who are lost. But to us who are being saved it is the power of God.

1 CORINTHIANS 1:18

Lemurs are ring-tailed primates from Madagascar known for their good looks, lively antics, and leaping abilities. But what lemur lovers may not know is how they smell. Male lemurs use scent glands to coat their tails with a pungent and powerful secretion to make them more attractive to females. Though to us the scent is terrible, the female lemur thinks it's terrific! The male with the strongest scent usually wins the girl.

God says our lives can have a similar effect when it comes to telling people about Jesus. For those people still fighting God, who don't want to follow Him, they think the message of the gospel stinks! But for those people who are ready to hear about Jesus, it's a sweet scent. And Jesus says that sharing His message with others is like a beautiful perfume to Him too. Don't worry about how people may react to God's message—just fill the world with the fragrance of Christ!

Prayer Pointer

Honor

God, Your plan of salvation is a beautiful message of hope that I want to share with others.

SEPTEMBER 25

Sweet Contentment

Your teachings are worth more to me than thousands of pieces of gold and silver.

PSALM 119:72

Lie: I need to have money to be happy.

"Mom, Casey's family is flying to Colorado to go skiing this spring break," said Hadley.

"That's nice," Mom answered.

"Mom?" asked Hadley. "Why don't we ever go skiing for spring break?"

"Well, hon, we have a pretty big family, and we don't have that kind of money."

"Sometimes I wish I lived in Casey's family," Hadley muttered.

The Truth Is . . .

God not only meets our needs—He's what we need most! While some people have more money than others, real joy doesn't come with a price tag. We receive the ticket to peace and joy when we choose to thank God for His presence in our lives and trust His promise to meet our needs. Being content with what God has given us allows us to think more about helping others. And when we live by God's economy, we never run out of what we need most: Him.

Prayer Pointer

Father, I need You more than anything in the world. Thank You for providing for me!

Write It Out

In Christ Jesus you are brought near to God.

EPHESIANS 2:13

Do you ever tell yourself lies like "I have to be perfect" or "I have to make everyone around me happy so they'll like me"? Write down some of your favorite verses that replace those lies with God's truths. You can start by looking in your Bible's concordance, or searching an online Bible study guide for key words like *perfectionism* or *people pleasing*.

Prayer Pointer

God, help me to recognize Satan's lies and to remember Your truths.

SEPTEMBER 27

We're Talking Grown-Up

The Lord said to him, "Who made man's mouth? . . . Now go! I will help you speak. I will tell you what to say."

EXODUS 4:11–12

Sometimes you have to talk to grown-ups. Maybe you find yourself seated next to a grown-up at the dinner table. Or maybe your friend's parent is driving you home. What on earth are you supposed to say?

First, remember that adults were once kids just like you. So instead of shrinking into your seat, sit up tall and start up a good conversation using these tips:

1. Start with something polite, such as, "How are you doing?"

2. Ask them something about themselves, such as, "What do you do when you're not driving kids around?" or "What's your favorite kind of food?"

3. They'll probably ask you a question in return. Don't give a yes or no answer. Instead, explain with more details. Then ask them a related question.

Before you know it, dinner will be over or you'll have reached your destination, and you'll have made a new friend in the process!

Prayer Pointer

grace

Lord, please give me courage when I'm nervous and the wisdom to connect well with others, no matter what their age.

Planned with Purpose

I praise you because you made me in
an amazing and wonderful way.

PSALM 139:14

Have you ever just sat and watched people at the mall or at a football game? What are some things you've noticed that make people different from each other?

Isn't God's creativity amazing? While everybody might look kind of the same in magazines, in real life people come in all different shapes, sizes, and personalities. Noticing those differences can be fun. But sometimes watching other people can have a bad effect. That's because it's tempting to look at others and think they're smarter, funnier, or prettier than we are. We can even start to think they're better than us and that we'll never be as special as they are.

But that's not true! God says in Psalm 139 that He carefully crafted each of us. That means you are specially designed by God to display His genius and brilliant creativity in a way only you can!

And since God's creative and powerful Spirit lives in you, who knows what wild and wonderful purpose God has planned for your life! With God as your guide and power, not even the sky is the limit!

Prayer Pointer — Glory

Jesus, thank You for making me perfectly unique to show Your glory.

Study Strength

Our only goal is to please God.

2 CORINTHIANS 5:9

Everybody has to deal with school. But not everybody has a good attitude about it. Whether we're straight-*A* students or not, we should do our best. *Why*? Because God says we should love Him with all our minds, as well as our hearts, souls, and strength. Even when we're studying math, science, English, or history, we're learning about how God made this world. Everything points to Him, so we should learn as much as we can. How are your study habits? Take this quiz and see.

1. You're supposed to read a lengthy book for English, but it's very difficult. You:
   a. read it anyway and go online, to your parents, and to your teacher for help.
   b. read the first chapter and give up.
   c. never open the book. You ask your friends to tell you about it.

2. You're ready for school and have a few minutes to spare before leaving (or starting the school day at home). You:
   a. spend some time in the Bible and prayer.
   b. tell everybody else to hurry up.
   c. play your video game.

3. Your teacher assigned a project that's due in two weeks. You:
   a. plan what needs to be done and start right away.
   b. relax because nobody else is working on it.
   c. wait until the night before it's due to start on it.

4. You work hard on your school work because:
   a. it honors God.
   b. good grades make you look smart.
   c. you're competitive and want to beat the other kids.

If you answered *A* in the above questions, you get an *A* for your study habits! Answers *B* or *C* show that you tend to wait until the last minute, which keeps you from doing your best. Ask God to help you care about His Word and the world He's made by doing your very best in your studies—all for His glory.

Prayer Pointer

God, I want to honor You by working hard to be the best person I can be.

Abraham, the Believer

Abraham believed God, and God accepted Abraham's faith, and that faith made him right with God.

JAMES 2:23

When God told Abram to go to a new land, Abram went. When God said he would have more descendants than stars in the sky, Abram believed it—and God changed his name to Abraham, which means "the father of many." When God said he'd have a son, Abraham watched and waited. And when God asked him to sacrifice Isaac, that beloved son, Abraham obeyed until God stopped him at the last second (Genesis 12; 17; 21–22).

What makes Abraham so remarkable? Abraham believed that God would keep every promise He made. His story reminds us that pleasing God isn't about what we can do for God. Rather, it's about believing in who God is and trusting what He says.

So what about you? Do you trust that God has a plan for you and that it's every bit as good as what He promised Abraham? Then tell God! And you'll be walking in Abraham's footsteps of faith.

Prayer Pointer

Father, I believe that You are faithful to keep all Your promises. Thank You for loving me so much!

Moses, Who Spoke for God

"Say the things God gives you to say at that time. It will not really be you speaking. It will be the Holy Spirit."

MARK 13:11

Do you like to talk in front of crowds? Moses didn't. But when he met God at the burning bush, God gave Moses a clear command: "Go to Egypt and tell Pharaoh to let My people go."

Gulp! Moses didn't want to go back to Egypt. (He had killed an Egyptian years ago, and Pharaoh wanted him dead.) He especially didn't want to tell Pharaoh to let God's people go.

Yet that's what God wanted Moses to do. And God promised to help Moses in his weakness. He even allowed Aaron, Moses' brother, to come alongside and speak for him. And God used them both to defeat Pharaoh and free His people. (Read about Moses in Exodus 3–14.)

So what do you think your greatest weaknesses are? Remember Moses' story, and know that the God who helped Moses helps you too. God will give you everything you need to succeed in whatever He calls you to do.

Prayer Pointer

Father, when I am weak, You are strong. Give me the strength to obey You.

OCTOBER 2

Smarter Thinking

"I am the Lord your God. I am holding your right hand. . . . I will help you."

ISAIAH 41:13

Lie: I have to be smart to have value.

Sarah looked at the giant *D* on her paper and panicked. "Oh no!" she gasped. "My parents are going to kill me." Then her mind began to race: *I'll probably flunk fourth grade. I don't know how I'll make it to middle school or high school. Forget college. I'm just a dummy, and that's all I'll ever be.*

The Truth Is . . .

It's tough when it feels like everyone is smarter than you. Teachers and even parents can add to the pressure by trying to help you succeed. But don't worry. God—you know, the One who created your brain—has a plan for your life.

More important than landing an *A* is learning to trust God with our weaknesses and believing He can take us wherever we need to go. So stop beating yourself up, and thank God for making you as He did. Ask Him to help you do your best while depending on Him to take care of the rest.

Prayer Pointer

Honor

Lord, the smartest thing I can do is trust You. Thank You for taking care of me.

Forever Love

Yes, I am sure that nothing can separate us from the love God has for us.

ROMANS 8:38

How do you know when you're loved? When do you feel loved? Is it when you get hurt, and your mom or dad puts a bandage on you and holds you close? Is it when your best friend stops what she's doing to listen to you? Is it being forgiven when you've messed up?

Though love can show itself in a million different ways, it always makes us feel warm, safe, important, and secure. But, because people are sinners, they can't always love perfectly. It can even feel as if some people will stop loving you if you aren't good enough.

God isn't like that. God *is* love. When you trust Jesus as your Savior, you join His family as God's child, and all your sins (past, present, and future) are forgiven. Because you're God's child, He loves you like He loves Jesus—and that's forever.

Best of all, nothing—not even death—can separate us from God's love. His children are always safe, important, and secure. God's love never ends. And there's nothing more beautiful than that.

PRAYER POINTER Glory

God, help me believe that Your love for me never changes, and it lasts forever.

Everywhere We Go

Jesus went everywhere doing good.

ACTS 10:38

Jesus made a point of doing a particular kind of thing everywhere He went. Whether He was teaching in the temple or leaning against a Samaritan well, Jesus never skipped it. Do you know what it was? Jesus always did something good—He improved the situation. Always. Everywhere He went.

Sometimes He prayed, sometimes He healed, and sometimes He taught about God. But there was never a place Jesus went where He didn't do something good and leave people better off.

We can do the same thing! Wherever we go, we can do something good to make things better. It can be something big, like working in a soup kitchen or giving clothes to people who need them. Or it can be something small, like sharing a hug and smile, carrying a bag of groceries, or offering an encouraging word. There are endless opportunities! Everywhere we go, we can leave a bit of goodness behind. Why should we? Because that's what Jesus did—and it creates a whole lot of joy.

Prayer Pointer

Jesus, I want to be more like You. Show me all the opportunities I have to do good each day, and then help me do them!

Give or Take

A friend loves you all the time.

PROVERBS 17:17

Delilah was beautiful, and Samson was incredibly strong. The perfect match, right? But their hearts were very different. Samson served God, but Delilah served the Philistines, Samson's (and God's) enemies.

Eventually, Delilah tricked Samson into telling her the secret of his strength, which was his hair. She told that secret to his enemies, who cut Samson's hair, put out his eyes, and locked him in prison. Samson's decision to choose Delilah as a friend was a bad one. But God was Samson's true Friend, and He gave Samson his strength one last time to put an end to two thousand Philistines (Judges 16).

Building good friendships begins with finding others who love God. To keep friendships growing strong, look for ways to encourage, support, and build up your friends. If you discover that you only like them when they're doing what *you* want, then you've stopped loving them God's way. Like Delilah, you're just using them. Ask God how you can better serve your friends. You'll all be happier in the end!

Prayer Pointer

Lord, I don't want to use people to get my way. Please help me love them well.

OCTOBER 6

A Cut Above

"They shall be Mine," says the LORD of hosts, "on the day that I make them My jewels."

MALACHI 3:17 NKJV

Have you ever visited a jewelry store? Glass cases are filled with gems, each one specially cut and set in rings, earrings, bracelets, and necklaces to add beauty and color to the person who gets to wear them. Since almost the beginning of time, people have recognized certain gems—like diamonds, rubies, emeralds, and sapphires—as rare and precious. Though they come out of the ground looking rough and cloudy, these special gems are cut just the right way to reveal the incredible beauty within.

Did you know that God views you as a precious jewel? Though you may not always see the beauty of your soul, God does. He has formed you and filled you with His own Spirit so that your life will sparkle with His light and love. Just as gems must be cut to reveal their deepest beauty, so God works through the difficult times in your life to shape your character. Trust Him. God is using every moment in your life—even the toughest ones—to transform you into a beautiful gem!

PRAYER POINTER — Glory

Thank You, Jesus, for making me valuable and beautiful to You and Your world.

Growing Gratitude

Pray and ask God for everything you need.
And when you pray, always give thanks.

PHILIPPIANS 4:6

We know we should give thanks at meals and before we go to sleep. But did you know that God wants us to give thanks in *all things*? That's right! Giving thanks for whatever happens in our lives shows that we trust God. God even uses the tough times in our lives for our good so we can thank Him for those too.

Growing a thankful heart is a lot like growing a tree. Ask God to plant seeds of thankfulness in your heart. Water and nourish them by noticing the little acts of kindness all around you. Look at the incredible creation God has made and all the creativity it shows, and thank Him.

Write down specific things for which you are really thankful, such as "my dog," "my heartbeat," or "God's Word." How many can you find today? Tomorrow? The next day?

Be on the alert, ready to write something down as soon as you spot evidence of God's smile in your day. Then read your list back to God, and thank Him for His everlasting goodness.

Prayer Pointer

Hope

Jesus, please keep me from complaining.
Help me give thanks in all things.

Servant's Heart

"The Son of Man did not come for other people to serve Him. He came to serve others. The Son of Man came to give His life to save many people."

MATTHEW 20:28

Do you have a servant's heart? Which answer best describes you?

1. When you come home from school and see dishes piled up in the sink, you:
   a. get a snack and then add your plate to the pile.
   b. run past the kitchen and hope your mom gets to them soon.
   c. take a few minutes to rinse the plates and load the dishwasher.

2. When a crowd of kids is loading into the van, you:
   a. call shotgun and try to ride up front.
   b. make sure you get a seat with your friends.
   c. offer to sit in the back so it's easier for everyone else to find a seat.

3. Saturdays are the perfect days for:
   a. sleeping late and watching TV.
   b. going to the mall and shopping.
   c. volunteering at the children's home.

Did you answer *C* for all of the above? If you did, your life is a beautiful example of how Jesus loved and served others. He set that example for us when He, as God of the universe, humbled Himself to come to earth to help us.

*A*s and *B*s, listen to a way Jesus once showed His disciples how important humble service is to God: He took off His outer robes, picked up a servant's towel, and then washed His disciples' dirty, smelly feet. Peter was actually horrified that Jesus would stoop so low for him. But Jesus told Peter that all His people must humble themselves just as He had, and they must work hard to make life better and brighter for others.

When we look for ways to serve others instead of ourselves, we shine God's light and love into a dark world, and we help people see the love of Jesus.

Prayer Pointer

Jesus, help me humbly serve everyone You put in my life.

Rahab, Who Started Over

As for me and my family, we will serve the Lord.

JOSHUA 24:15

Rahab was supposed to be one of Israel's enemies. Living in Jericho, she had probably done many of the evil deeds that had made God angry at the nation. But when she heard about God, she wanted to change sides.

So when Israel sent spies into Jericho, she hid them in her home. Then she helped them escape in exchange for her family's safety when Israel attacked the city. Because Rahab chose to side with God, only she and her family survived when God gave the city to the Israelites. Best of all, Rahab was accepted into the Hebrew family of God (Joshua 2; 6:22–25).

Sometimes we can find ourselves in a situation like Rahab's. We realize we've been living a life that displeases God. But Rahab's story gives us great hope! God always welcomes us when we turn to Him for help. So confess your bad choices to God, and ask Him to help you become the person He wants you to be.

Prayer Pointer

Father, please forgive my sin of ____________.
Save me, and make me Your own.

True Colors

"When the rainbow appears in the clouds, I will see it. Then I will remember the agreement that continues forever."

GENESIS 9:16

Try this experiment on a sunny day: get a glass of water (or a crystal vase or pendant) and a plain white piece of paper, and go to the window. Hold the glass at different places just above the paper in front of the window. What do you see? If you find the right spot, a rainbow will appear! Your glass is clear, and the sun is white, so where are all those colors coming from? Though your eyes can't detect it, white light is actually made up of all different colors. When light passes through the glass, the water droplets bend it, separating the white light into a beautiful display of colors.

Rainbows show the difference between how we see ourselves and how God sees us. We may think we're ordinary, but when God is in us, it's like the light shining through the glass. And our lives are colored with His beautiful love, joy, and peace.

Prayer Pointer

Lord, please shine the light of Your love through me, and make me beautiful in Your sight!

OCTOBER 11

Helping Hugs

There is a time to hug . . . . There is a time to be silent and a time to speak.

ECCLESIASTES 3:5, 7

Emily watched her mom put down the telephone and sit down on the couch. Her eyes were filled with tears.

"Mom, are you okay?" Emily asked.

"Oh honey, I just found out a friend of mine is very sick," her mom said, wiping her eyes.

Emily didn't know what to say, so she just sat down next to her mom and wrapped her in a big hug. In her heart, she prayed for her mom and her friend.

Have you ever found yourself in a situation when you didn't know what to say? Maybe your mom had an upsetting phone call, like Emily's mom did. Or your dad had trouble at work, or a friend just had a really rotten day. You know you can't fix the problem, and saying "I'm sorry" doesn't seem like enough. Then it might be time for a hug. When the people we love are hurting, a hug helps them know they're not alone, and that we care about them. So the next time words fail you, try a hug instead.

Prayer Pointer — gracie

Lord, when I'm hurting You give me comfort. Help me comfort others too.

Foolish Rebellion

Get rid of all evil and all lying.
Do not be a hypocrite.

1 PETER 2:1

Ava's family had a rule about not chatting with friends online, which was what Ava was doing. When her dad came in the room, Ava closed the chat window and pulled up her homework page. "What exactly have you been doing, Ava?" her father asked over her shoulder. What should Ava say?

OCTOBER 12

Choice 1

"It's just my homework, see?" Ava said.

"Then what are those other tabs?" her dad asked.

"Just some research I had to do," Ava lied.

Choice 2

"Well, I was doing my homework earlier. But I was also talking with some friends online," she admitted.

Her dad said, "I appreciate your honesty. But you disobeyed our rules, and it's going to cost you privileges for the rest of today."

"Yeah . . . okay, Dad," she answered.

Prayer Pointer

Glory

Lord, whenever I feel myself sneaking,
I know I'm sinning. Help me stay
truthful with You and others.

An Egg-cellent Idea

No one has ever imagined what God has prepared for those who love Him.

1 CORINTHIANS 2:9

Can you imagine a world without chicken eggs? Cakes would go flat, and cookies would be thin and hard. Before long, chickens would disappear from the earth! Not only are eggs a staple for all kinds of baking, but they're also a good source of protein and nutrients like choline, which helps our brains develop, and lutein, which improves our eyesight. It's amazing how much those oval shells filled with goopy stuff have to offer!

The egg does something else too. It reminds us that God can create something powerfully important inside a fragile shell, just as He does with us. Though our lives might seem small and even a little messy at times, God has created us perfectly to house His Spirit and to enrich the world around us with divine flavor.

So don't be so hard on yourself, trying to figure out what God could possibly do with you. Just look at the egg and remember that God is cooking up an incredible recipe for your life!

Prayer Pointer

Father, just as You do with an egg, You turn my messy life into an amazing masterpiece!

Busy Bodies

God says, "Be still and know that I am God."

PSALM 46:10

OCTOBER 14

Lie: I need to be busy.

"So, are you going out for the soccer team?" Kate asked.

"N—not sure," Lizzy stammered. "I mean, I haven't decided."

"How about the drama group, then? Or choir?"

"Probably not."

"Wow. I guess you just like being boring," Kate concluded.

The Truth Is . . .

People today *are* very busy. Just ask anyone. They're busy with activities, sports, and projects. But are people *too* busy? God says that He wants us to be still and know that He is God. When we can barely catch our breath from our activities, we're missing what's most important: time for our friendship with God.

Why do we stay so busy? Maybe because everyone else seems to be doing it. Maybe quiet time makes us nervous. Maybe we feel more important if we're busy. But remember what Jesus told His busy friend, Martha, in Luke 10: more important than filling our time with activities is filling it with Him.

Prayer Pointer

Lord, help me make time for You by saying no to activities I don't need in my life.

OCTOBER 15

Better Than Best

The Lord Himself will go before you. He will be with you. He will not leave you or forget you.

DEUTERONOMY 31:8

Imagine for a moment the best kind of friend in the whole wide world. What would she be like?

Certainly, she would love you all the time. She would know what makes you happy and, when you're sad, she'd know just how to cheer you up. And if someone or something tried to hurt you, she would try her best to defend you. Best of all, she'd always be ready to talk, listen, and spend time with you.

Do you have a friend like that?

If you trust in Jesus, you do! Jesus is the very best Friend you could ever have. He loves you more than anybody on earth. He knows everything about you, and He thinks you're wonderful! He proved how much He cares when He gave up His life and rose again so you could be in God's family. He is eager to be your best Friend. Simply put, Jesus is crazy about you. Best of all, Jesus never changes, and His friendship is forever.

Prayer Pointer

Hope

Jesus, I am amazed that You care so much about me. Help me grow closer to You each day.

Slumber Party Solutions

I go to bed and sleep in peace.
Lord, only you keep me safe.

PSALM 4:8

It's always fun to be with friends. But it's even better when the fun doesn't have to stop. Sleepovers are the perfect solution. Not only do they extend the party, but they also allow time for friendships to grow deeper and stronger. Here are a few tips to make your slumber party a hit:

1. Ask your parents in advance for permission. Work with them to plan a good evening.
2. Invite girls whom you know like one another.
3. Schedule different activities for the evening, such as doing manicures and pedicures, cooking dinner, making s'mores, or swimming.
4. As it gets late, change to quieter activities, such as board games or watching a movie.
5. Make a place for everyone to sleep near one another.
6. Turn off the lights so people can sleep.
7. In the morning, help your mom make a good pancake breakfast before your guests go home.
8. Thank everyone for coming!

Prayer Pointer

gracie

God, thank You for giving me such great friends to hang out with. Help everything we do together honor You.

Secret Service

"Be careful! When you do good things, don't do them in front of people to be seen by them."

MATTHEW 6:1

Jesus didn't have to come. He could have stayed in the comfort of heaven where He ruled as King, served by obedient and honoring angels for the rest of all time. But He didn't. His love for us drove Him to come to earth to live, serve, and even die so we could be with Him forever. Can you imagine that kind of cost? Yet giving our lives for others—serving their needs instead of our own—is exactly what God's kind of love makes us want to do.

Do you have Jesus' Spirit living in you? Then you get the joy of experiencing the secret service life that Jesus did. Everywhere you look, there are opportunities to encourage others, pray, comfort, give, and help meet needs. But the mission starts with prayer, asking God to open your eyes to see it and help you act just like Jesus. So why not ask Him for that right now? If you do, then you're ready for your first mission. Remember, though, this is secret service. Don't tell them what you're planning to do or why (just yet). Only God and you will know the plan.

Pick a family member you want to target this week. Spend the first day just watching what he or she does, looking for ways to serve and love that person better. Ask God for creativity, and consider trying these ideas:

- Each day, say something encouraging about that person.
- Help with the laundry, or put away laundry for someone.
- Clean out the car, or take out the trash each day.
- Volunteer to read a book or play a game with a younger sibling.
- Choose your own idea!

Each week, pick a new family member or friend, and repeat the process. And keep serving the person from last week too!

Prayer Pointer

Father, I'm so glad You give me opportunities to serve those around me. Help me to serve with a cheerful, thankful heart.

Joseph, Who Forgave

Forgive each other because the Lord forgave you.

COLOSSIANS 3:13

Have your siblings ever been mean to you? Maybe they broke your favorite toy or called you a bad name. When the people closest to us hurt us, the pain can be deep and difficult to heal.

Imagine how Joseph must have felt. One day he went out to the field where his brothers were tending sheep, and then they threw him in a dry well. Some even wanted to kill him. His brothers finally decided to sell Joseph to Egyptian traders. In Egypt, Joseph was put in prison, though he did nothing wrong.

But Joseph knew God was in control and loved him. Years later, when Joseph was put in charge of Egypt's food, his brothers came to him because they were starving. Instead of being angry, Joseph said, "You meant to hurt me, but God turned your evil into good." (Read the story in Genesis 37–45.)

No matter what happens, God promises to work out everything for our good (Romans 8:28). God gives us the power to forgive others and to love everyone He puts in our lives.

Prayer Pointer

Jesus, help me forgive others the way You have forgiven me.

Shepherding Sheep

The Lord is my shepherd. I have everything I need.

PSALM 23:1

Throughout the Bible, God often compares His people to sheep. And He tells us He is our Good Shepherd. But have you ever wondered why sheep need a shepherd?

Sheep have a, well, sheepish nature. They scare easily. Left alone, sheep will follow one another, even though none of them knows where they need to go. They end up wandering aimlessly and become easy targets for predators such as wolves.

Now can you see why God calls us His sheep? As long as we keep our eyes on our Shepherd, we know where to go and what to do. But when we quit watching Him and start looking at all the people around us—copying their behavior and going where they go—we are in danger of getting lost. Friends can be a great help to us if they love God and are following Him too. Ask the Great Shepherd to surround you with His flock—friends who listen to His voice—so that you can all follow Him together.

Prayer Pointer

Jesus, thank You for leading and watching over me. Help me keep my eyes on You!

Uniquely You

We are His workmanship, created in Christ Jesus for good works.

EPHESIANS 2:10 NKJV

Imagine having a super-wide head; a long, pointed nose; large lumps all over your body; and huge fins. Top it off with almost fluorescent red lips. What would you be—other than horrifying? A red-lipped batfish!

At first sight, the batfish seems to have gotten a bad deal at creation. Not only does it look strange, but it can't even swim. It walks on the ocean floor using its fins.

But God made batfish that way for a reason. Its strange dorsal fin sticks out like a fishing rod to lure in prey. Those awkward walking fins keep it low to the ocean floor, making it harder for its enemies to see it. And its bright red lips attract other batfish. Its oddities actually protect and help the red-lipped batfish.

Do you have some features you wish you didn't? God didn't make a mistake in your design. Your unique features fit in perfectly with His plan for your life—which God promises is a good plan. So trust Him! And bravely be the unique person God made you to be.

Honor

PRAYER POINTER

God, help me appreciate Your creativity in my design and use me for Your kingdom.

3-for-1 Special

The grace of the Lord Jesus Christ, the love of God, and the fellowship of the Holy Spirit be with you all.

2 CORINTHIANS 13:14

Did you know that water comes in three different forms? If you think you know what they are, circle the right answers below:

rivers	oceans	vapor	jelly	liquid
candy	fire	solid	soda	rain

If you picked vapor (like steam), liquid (like rain), and solid (like ice), you're right! Isn't it weird that water can look and act so differently, depending on the situation? But no matter its form, it's still water!

If you think about it, water helps us know how God can live and work as three different persons—Father, Son, and Holy Spirit—but still be just one God. All three persons of God, also called the Trinity, work, love, and serve each other perfectly. When you join God's family by trusting Jesus to be your Savior, you get a heavenly Dad (God the Father), a Savior and Friend (God the Son), and a Helper who lives inside you to lead you closer to God (God the Holy Spirit). You are completely surrounded by God's love, inside and out!

Hope

Prayer Pointer

God, thank You for being everything I need. I love being in Your family!

OCTOBER 22

Kind of Thought

"I love you people with a love that will last forever. I became your friend because of my love and kindness."

JEREMIAH 31:3

Take a minute and think about your mom. Think about what her mornings before school are probably like. Can you guess? What must it be like to take care of kids, do laundry, work, and cook and clean? What makes her happy or sad?

Congratulations! You've just exercised your unique ability to think about life from someone else's perspective. Instead of just thinking about what *you* do and think, you've started to think about the thoughts and needs of someone other than yourself. This important skill is called *empathy*. Empathy helps us learn how to love others better. Understanding others and thinking about their needs helps us be kind. Being kind is caring for others according to their needs. The Bible says that when God's Spirit is ruling our hearts, we will be kind to others. As you go through your day today, practice your empathy—it'll make God smile and others too!

Prayer Pointer

Jesus, help me notice the needs of others so I can show them kindness like You do.

Write It Out

Children, obey your parents the way the Lord wants. This is the right thing to do.

EPHESIANS 6:1

Sometimes home can be the most challenging place to love and serve others, but God put you in your family for a reason. How can you be a more helpful daughter? How about a better sister, niece, or granddaughter?

Prayer Pointer

Thank You, Lord, for my family. Please show me how I can better serve them.

Mining for Treasure

"I will give you hidden riches. I will do this so you will know I am the Lord."

ISAIAH 45:3

For years, there was something secret hidden underneath a mountain in Chihuahua, Mexico. Can you guess what excavators found one thousand feet below the mountain? An incredibly huge crystal cave. Imagine how surprised they were when they dug into the cave, pumped out the water, and discovered giant crystals—some as large as thirty-six feet long—sticking out in all directions from the cave walls . . . which were also covered in crystals! It was like a crystal palace! Who knew such beauty could grow so far below the surface?

God did, that's who. And the crystal cave is a beautiful reminder that what we see on the outside doesn't always give us the full picture. God wants us to dig deeper into people's lives—beyond outward appearances—and look for the hidden treasures of character and God's Spirit that may be growing there. God is doing a beautiful work in each believer's heart, and we don't want to miss the miracle because we're too distracted by what we see on the surface.

Prayer Pointer — Glory

God, help me see the beauty of Your life and love in the believers You've placed around me.

The Invisible Girl

The slave girl gave a name to the Lord who spoke to her. She said to him, "You are 'God who sees me.'"

GENESIS 16:13

Megan stood by her locker watching all the other girls laughing and talking around her. They were talking about some big slumber party one of the girls was throwing this weekend. And Megan wasn't invited. She tried not to let the girls see that she was upset, but it probably didn't matter anyway. They didn't even notice her—it's like she was invisible.

Have you ever felt invisible like Megan? Some people can leave us feeling unwanted, unimportant, and completely invisible. But that's not true. God sees you. And this is what He says about you:

- "Everything about you is beautiful. There is nothing at all wrong with you" (Song of Solomon 4:7).
- God "even knows how many hairs you have on your head" (Luke 12:7).
- God has "written your name on [His] hand" (Isaiah 49:16).
- "He will not leave you or forget you" (Deuteronomy 31:8).

You're never invisible to God, never unwanted or unimportant. You are His beloved child, and He sees you.

gracie

Prayer Pointer

Lord, when I feel invisible, help me to remember You always see me and love me.

Online in Time

God has planned a time for every thing and every action.

ECCLESIASTES 3:17

Lie: I need to be on top of the latest technology trends.

"Mom, I need you to help me set up a social media account," Camryn said.

"An account on which site?" her mom queried.

"It's not a big deal. I just want to post some pictures."

"Aren't you a little young for that?" her mom responded, growing concerned.

"No, all my friends are doing it."

Her mom frowned. "That may be what everybody else is doing, but I don't think it's wise for you—not at this age, anyway."

The Truth Is . . .

Timing is important. Unfortunately, learning to wait for the things we want right now can be really difficult, especially when our friends or older siblings *aren't* having to wait for them. So many social media sites look like fun, with pictures of all the great things it seems like everybody (but you) is doing. But age restrictions on those sites exist for a reason. And your mom, despite her possible lack of tech know-how, *does* know a thing or two about staying safe on the Internet.

Instead of rushing to be like everyone else, learn self-control, and try building relationships face-to-face. As you grow in God and learn how to relate well to others in real life, you will be better equipped when the right time comes to handle the perks and problems of online life.

Prayer Pointer

Lord, help me be patient and trust that You've given my parents the wisdom to guide me.

Small Wonder

"When you are weak, then my power is made perfect in you."

2 CORINTHIANS 12:9

At first glance, the hummingbird looks like a fragile bird because it is impossibly small with a very long beak. But did you know that hummingbirds have an amazing memory? They can remember each flower they've visited and how long it will take for that flower's nectar to refill. And when a hummingbird takes flight, its wings flap so fast you can't even see them move. While they're zipping, diving, hovering, and even flying backward, it's easy to see that God packed a lot into this tiny package.

God does the same thing with you. It doesn't matter if you feel too young or small to make a difference in your world. God has packed you with amazing power and skill—coming from His own Spirit in you! Just as a hummingbird looks for flowers, you are to look for people who need God's love. God will give you everything you need to spread the joy of His love, making the world a more beautiful place.

Prayer Pointer

Thank You, Lord, that Your grace and power in me make me strong and able to do Your work.

Safe and Secure

God has said, "I will never leave you;
I will never abandon you."

HEBREWS 13:5

Have you ever gotten lost in a store? One minute you were exploring all the new clothes, feeling safe and fine. But the next minute, you were all alone—and all those good feelings vanished. Panic set in as you wandered up and down aisles, hoping to find your mom or dad so you could feel safe again.

Sometimes we feel that way even when we aren't lost. Facing hard times—like sickness, death, or divorce—can cause that same lost and lonely feeling. Jesus' followers felt that way when He was crucified, and again when He rose up into heaven.

But Jesus didn't want them to feel alone, and He doesn't want you to either. He promised to never leave us—and He doesn't! When we follow Him, He puts His Spirit inside us. So no matter where we go, Jesus is right there with us. Feelings of loneliness and sadness are signals for us to stop and remember that He is with us—even if we can't see Him.

OCTOBER 28

Prayer Pointer

Jesus, thank You for always being
with me—now and forever.

A Second Look

Try to understand each other. Love each other as brothers. Be kind and humble.

1 PETER 3:8

Scenario

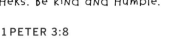

"Ugh! I'm so mad at her!" Libby complained to Abbey about their friend, Amanda, who was supposed to join them at the park today. "I mean, we've been planning to get together for weeks. And now, she says she has to stay home to babysit her little brother? Come on! That's just so rude."

"Well, she has a good explanation," offered Abbey.

"I don't care. She shouldn't do that," Libby snapped back.

Solution

Clearly, Amanda's decision to stay home changed Libby's plans, so her frustration is understandable. But perhaps Libby isn't seeing the whole picture here.

Maybe Amanda's family had a crisis come up, and Amanda was being unselfish and kind by giving up her fun day to watch her brother. Libby could only see Amanda's actions as selfish because they hurt her plans. If Libby had taken time to ask more questions or trust her friend's heart, maybe she could've seen the situation from Amanda's perspective. Looking at life from the other person's perspective helps us understand, love, and know better how to pray.

Prayer Pointer

Hope

Lord, help me see and love other people the way You do.

Personality Plus

We all have different gifts. Each gift came because of the grace that God gave us.

ROMANS 12:6

Lie: I need to have a better personality.

"I wish I were like her," Sophie admitted to her friend Avery.

Both girls watched Lexi, the new girl, who seemed to have the entire class wrapped around her finger. She was the center of attention, laughing and smiling and talking with the popular kids, like it was the most natural thing in the world.

"Yeah, she's just so outgoing and funny," Avery agreed.

The Truth Is . . .

Now imagine if everyone in the world were like Lexi. Sure, everybody would love to talk and entertain, but who would be listening? How would any work ever get done? Actually, God designed each of us for His purposes—and most of His work isn't center stage.

No matter what kind of personality God has mixed into your character, He'll use it for His glory if you give your life to Him. Just ask Him to use little ol' you—in the spotlight or behind the scenes—to shine out His glory like only you can do.

Prayer Pointer

Lord, I'm here to glorify You, not me. Please use me to help others see You.

Beauty Reborn

If anyone belongs to Christ, then he is made new.

2 CORINTHIANS 5:17

What would you like for your birthday? New clothes or old tennis shoes? A new art set or some used pencils? A new phone or your brother's flattened basketball?

You probably don't want any old or broken stuff. After all, birthdays are supposed to celebrate life and new beginnings. People give new and special gifts for birthdays.

God feels the same way about birthdays. When you were born, you were new and beautiful. However, you were also born under the curse of sin that started when Adam and Eve disobeyed God. But when you open your heart to believe that Jesus is the Savior and your only hope for heaven, something amazing happens: your spirit is born again! It's like a new birthday, and God has gifts for you.

You might not look new on the outside, but inside, God makes you an entirely new creation by sending His Spirit to live inside you. The Spirit helps you pray, read the Bible, and understand God better. Best of all, He guarantees your place in heaven forever!

Prayer Pointer

Father, thank You for making me a beautiful, new creation in Jesus!

"Do You Love Me?"

Counsel in the heart of man is like deep water, but a man of understanding will draw it out.

PROVERBS 20:5 NKJV

Peter had blown it in the worst way imaginable. After spending years with Jesus, he abandoned his Lord when the soldiers arrested Jesus. He ran away in fear and told everyone who asked that he didn't even know Jesus!

After Jesus was crucified and rose again, He appeared to Peter. But Jesus didn't say, "I told you so" or "You're a terrible friend." Instead, He asked Peter, "Do you love me?"

His question reached deep into Peter's heart. Peter thought about it and said, "Yes, I love you."

"Then feed my sheep," answered Jesus. Jesus was telling Peter that he was forgiven, and if he loved Him, then he needed to take care of the people who loved Jesus.

Jesus asks you the same question. "Do you love Me, Brave Girl?" Think about it and be completely honest. If the answer is yes, then you're completely forgiven too. Now Jesus wants you to join Him in bringing lost sheep to the Great Shepherd.

Prayer Pointer

I want to show that I truly love You, Lord, by obeying and following You.

First Things First

Then the king said to me, "What do you want?"
First I prayed to the God of heaven.

NEHEMIAH 2:4

When you're faced with a difficult choice or a tough situation, what do you do first?

Nehemiah, a Jew, was in a tough situation. He'd been taken from his home in Jerusalem and was now a servant to the king of Persia. But he had heard that Jerusalem was in terrible trouble. Its walls were falling down, and enemies were threatening to attack. He wanted to go home to help. But first he had to get the king's permission. He was so nervous.

Later, when Nehemiah was serving at the king's table, the king could tell something was wrong. "Why does your face look sad?" the king asked. "What do you want?" But before Nehemiah answered, he prayed to God. And as it turned out, Nehemiah convinced the king to help!

When you're not sure what to say or what to do, follow Nehemiah's example and pray first. God promises that if you ask Him for wisdom, He will give it to you. In fact, the Bible says He enjoys giving to His people (James 1:5). So talk to God—first!

Prayer Pointer

Lord, help me remember to turn to You first when I have troubles.

Mending Matters

Happy is the person whose sins are forgiven, whose wrongs are pardoned.

PSALM 32:1

Scenario

Kylee's eyes narrowed as her younger sister Kasey came into her room for the billionth time. "What do I have to do to get through to you?" Kylee asked angrily. "All you ever do is bother me!"

Tears filled Kasey's eyes as she turned around and closed the door.

Solution

Kylee's hurtful words may have gotten her sister to leave, but at a terrible price. If you ever find yourself in Kylee's situation, try these actions instead of exploding:

- Go ask your mom to help keep your sister out if you *really* need private time.
- Ask your sister what she needs. If she just wants to play or talk, give her ten minutes and then explain that you need your privacy.
- Find a game or toy that can entertain your sister for a while.

Whenever we lose our tempers like Kylee did, we need to ask, "Will you forgive me?" and try to make things right.

Prayer Pointer

Father, help me be humble and ask for forgiveness when I hurt others.

Time to Talk

Never stop praying.

1 THESSALONIANS 5:17

When do you like to pray? Do you find prayer easy or difficult? Like most things, prayer becomes easier and more natural the more we do it. But when you're first learning how to talk to God, it can seem strange. Just think, though, you're talking to the God of the universe—*and* He's listening to you! More amazing still, His Spirit, who lives inside you, will use God's Word to answer you back, keeping the conversation going from the time you wake up until you go to sleep. And that's exactly what God wants: to share every part of your day, guiding, encouraging, talking, and listening as you learn to walk with your unseen best Friend. Here are some practical ways to get that conversation with God going:

1. Before you get out of bed in the morning, say good morning to God. Thank Him for being with you all the time.
2. Choose a certain time of day specifically for prayer. Start off with just five minutes. Then, as you grow stronger in your prayer life, lengthen the time. Don't let anything crowd out that time with God.
3. Pray out loud. Find a place where others won't hear you, and talk to God as if He's standing right beside you—because He is!

4. Write down prayer reminders, and stick them places like the bathroom mirror or refrigerator to help you remember to talk to God.
5. People often pray at mealtimes, but don't get stuck in the routine of only praying at these times. Let your mind think about how much God gives you, and anytime you feel thankful about something, give your thanks to God.
6. Are you excited about something? Sad? Confused? Bored? Talk to God about it. In fact, talk to Him about everything. He cares, and He always knows just what you should do.

Prayer Pointer

Lord Jesus, help me pray without stopping. I want to be as close to You as possible.

Parent Praise

"Honor your father and your mother."

EXODUS 20:12

Your parents have fed and clothed you since you were born. They clapped when you crawled and videoed your first steps. In fact, they've celebrated you not only on your birthday but also when you were in the school play or game, made a good grade, and in all those wonderfully ordinary moments in between. Or maybe instead of your parents there have been others who have made you feel loved in special ways.

In any case, without you even realizing it, the people caring for you have made your life more beautiful than it ever would have been without them. And by their example, they've been showing you how to make other people's lives lovelier too.

Today let the people who care for you know you notice and appreciate their love. Look for ways to add beauty to their day. Clean the kitchen, paint a picture of a favorite memory, or make a banner telling everyone why they're so great. How could you honor those special people today?

Prayer Pointer

Thank You, Lord, for my parents and people who care for me like parents. Help me honor them as I honor You in what I say and do.

Humble Hearts

Humble yourself before the Lord,
and He will honor you.

JAMES 4:10

You've seen it before. Maybe it was a rich kid in class who made another child feel bad for wearing unfashionable clothes. Or at church, perhaps there were people who acted like they were better than everybody else. Even at home, pride rears its ugly head when siblings or parents fight and then refuse to apologize or compromise. Pride is feeling that you're somehow better than others and deserve special treatment. In case you were wondering, God says He hates pride (Amos 6:8).

What God loves, though, are people who are humble. Being humble is the exact opposite of being prideful. Humble people recognize how good God is and how much of a sinner they are. Strangely, understanding that we aren't perfect helps us not only appreciate God's amazing grace more, but it also helps us see others with more compassion. Instead of looking at someone and thinking we're better than her (for whatever reason), we simply see that everyone needs Jesus' love and forgiveness as much as we do.

Prayer Pointer

Father, please forgive my pride. I desperately need You. And You alone deserve glory.

The Up Side

A happy heart is like good medicine. But a broken spirit drains your strength.

PROVERBS 17:22

Scenario

"Want to go fishing with me?" Erika asked her friend Taylor.

"No, I don't like to hook worms," Taylor responded.

"Okay, you want to go swimming then?" Erika asked.

"I don't really like to get wet," Taylor answered.

Starting to feel frustrated, Erika said, "How about a game of checkers?"

"No, I hate that game because I always lose."

At a loss for what to do, Erika got up to leave. "Just let me know if you want to do something," she said, feeling disappointed.

Solution

The problem is that Taylor isn't willing to try anything Erika suggests, and Erika isn't going to want to hang out with her anymore. If Taylor wants the friendship to work, she should make an effort to be with her friend. For example, she could say, "I don't like worms, but I'll go to the lake with you," or "Sure, I can read by the pool while you swim." By staying positive, Taylor can keep the connection with her friend strong while they both find something to do together.

Prayer Pointer

Jesus, help me make my friendships strong by keeping a good attitude.

Moonlight Madness

He gave us light by letting us know the glory of God that is in the face of Christ.

2 CORINTHIANS 4:6

NOVEMBER 8

If you're watching at just the right time of night, in just the right place along the beach, you can witness a marching miracle. Hundreds of newly hatched baby sea turtles poke through the sand and start their quest for the ocean.

Baby sea turtles have a problem, though. Instinct tells them to head toward the light, which is a wonderful GPS feature when the moon is full and bright. But sometimes they hatch near streetlights that give off a bright glow that looks a lot like the moon to a baby turtle. Confused, the turtles tragically flip and flop onto busy streets instead of into the sea!

In some ways, we're like those turtles. We're drawn to the fake beauty of sinful things—just as those baby turtles are drawn to the fake "moon" of streetlights. We can get confused and dazzled by the very things that can hurt us the most. God tells us to fix our eyes on Him and His perfect light. He'll always lead us to where we need to be.

PRAYER POINTER Honor

God, Your Word is a light for my path.
Thank You for leading me to life!

Ask the Animals

Ask the animals, and they will teach you. . . . Every one of these knows that the hand of the Lord has done this.

JOB 12:7, 9

Want to know more about God? Ask the animals. Okay, so you can't exactly sit down with your dog or cat and say, "Tell me about God." But we can learn so much about God by looking at the animals and all the other living things on earth.

Just take a walk around your neighborhood. How many different plants do you see? And how amazing is that sky—whether it's sunny or cloudy or raining? Only God could make that! Then there's the animals. How many different ones do you think there are? Hundreds, thousands, millions, or more? And they all have the features they use to survive, like your cat's claws or your dog's sense of smell. They didn't just happen by random chance, or pop up for no reason. Only God could create all that.

Some people say there's no God. But we know that can't be true. Just ask the animals; they'll teach you.

Prayer Pointer

Lord, help me to see the wonder of Your creation all around me!

Beauty from the Inside Out

Our physical body is becoming older and weaker, but our spirit inside us is made new every day.

2 CORINTHIANS 4:16

Have you ever been in the makeup aisle at the store? There's every kind of powder, cream, and lotion imaginable, and they all promise to make you beautiful. But real beauty doesn't come in a jar or a tube. Real beauty is becoming who God wants you to be—and it happens from the inside out.

God is slowly changing us from the ugliness of our sin to the beautiful goodness of His Son. The more we trust and obey God, the more we realize how much we need Jesus and the more beautiful we become. We actually begin to think, talk, and act more like Jesus and less like our old, selfish selves. And we become beautiful mirrors of God's neverending affection for His people.

True beauty can't be bought in the makeup aisle. It only comes from loving Jesus. And this kind of beauty not only makes us shine, but it also lasts for all eternity in heaven with Jesus.

Prayer Pointer

Lord, change me from the inside out, and make me Your kind of beautiful forever.

NOVEMBER 11

Kindness Doesn't Cost a Thing

Be kind and loving to each other.

EPHESIANS 4:32

Allie listened to the speaker from the homeless shelter and felt sad. Not only did she feel terrible about the children at the shelter, but she didn't think she could help them—or anyone. *Lord,* she prayed, *I want to help, but I'm just a kid. I have an allowance, but it's not enough to really help.* Allie looked back at the speaker, only half listening, until something the lady said caught her attention: "Kindness doesn't cost a thing."

That's it! Allie thought. *I may not have lots of money, but I can always be kind!* She tugged a piece of paper out of her notebook and began writing down ideas.

- Invite that new girl to come to the youth group dinner.
- Smile at the cafeteria workers at school.
- Help my little brother tie his shoes.
- Thank my mom for fixing us dinner, and help her clean up.
- Give my dad a hug when he gets home from work.

Maybe you'd like to try some of Allie's ideas. What can you add to her list?

PRAYER POINTER

Lord, I know there's lots of things I can't do yet. But help me remember that I can always be kind.

Going for Glory

God, you are supreme over the skies. Let your glory be over all the earth.

PSALM 108:5

Glory was thrilled. She had created bathing suit designs that were not only super stylish but also modest. So she invited all her friends over to see her designs. To her delight, her friends were amazed.

"These are incredible!" Gracie said.

"How did you ever come up with such creative designs?" Honor asked.

What should Glory say?

Choice 1

"Well, I'm good at fashion, you know," Glory answered proudly. "I've been working really hard so I can be famous someday. I want my name to be the brand everybody buys."

Choice 2

"Thanks, guys! I'm super excited about them too," Glory answered. "You know, I pray all the time for God to give me creative ideas that can be used to help others, and I think He's done just that!"

Prayer Pointer

Glory

Jesus, let my life be a beautiful reflection of Your glory in all I say and do.

Look at Love

Whoever does not love does not know God, because God is love.

1 JOHN 4:8

You've heard that God loves you, but what does *love* really mean? Look at the words of 1 Corinthians 13:4–8. It has been printed out three times to give you a new look at love. The first passage shows what love is, as recorded in 1 Corinthians.

> Love is patient and kind. Love is not jealous, it does not brag, and it is not proud. Love is not rude, is not selfish, and does not become angry easily. Love does not remember wrongs done against it. Love takes no pleasure in evil, but rejoices over the truth. Love patiently accepts all things. It always trusts, always hopes, and always continues strong. Love never ends.

Think about the fact that God *is* love. That means everything written about love in this passage reflects how God is. In each blank, fill in the name Jesus or God. Then read the passage again.

> ____________ is patient and kind. ____________ is not jealous, ____________ does not brag, and ____________ is not proud. ____________ is not rude, is not selfish, and does not become angry easily. ____________ does not remember

wrongs done against [Him]. ____________ takes no pleasure in evil, but rejoices over the truth. ____________ patiently accepts all things. ____________ always trusts, always hopes, and always continues strong. ____________ never ends.

In this last exercise, try putting your own name in the blanks where *love* should go. Are these words a good representation of how you act? All of us need to grow in love to become more like God. Ask Him to help you love like Him.

____________ is patient and kind. ____________ is not jealous, ____________ does not brag, and ____________ is not proud. ____________ is not rude, is not selfish, and does not become angry easily. ____________ does not remember wrongs done against [her]. ____________ takes no pleasure in evil, but rejoices over the truth. ____________ patiently accepts all things. ____________ always trusts, always hopes, and always continues strong. ____________ never ends.

Prayer Pointer

Jesus, thank You for always loving me. Help me love You and others in the same way.

A Roller Coaster Ride

If [a man] stumbles, he will not fall,
because the Lord holds his hand.

PSALM 37:24

Do you think roller coasters are awesome or awful? It seems crazy to step inside a metal car that shoots across a narrow track at insane angles and heights. What's the attraction? The thrill!

The slow *chink-chink-chink* climb up the first ridge, the dizzying height, the sound of release when the bottom drops out and your stomach is in your throat. It's intense, and your heart races! And even though you don't know what's coming next, you're smiling because it's super fun. You know the coaster will keep you on track and deliver you safely back.

Learning to trust God is a lot like stepping into a roller coaster car. Following Him and giving Him full control of your life can feel scary. But God will hold you firmly through all the twists and turns of life. When you realize every moment is under His control, you can enjoy the ride and lift up your hands in delight, knowing He'll deliver you safely to your destination.

Prayer Pointer

God, thank You for being by my side.
Please help me give You control.

The Men Who Saw God's Greatness

My dear children, you belong to God. . . . God's Spirit, who is in you, is greater than the devil, who is in the world.

1 JOHN 4:4

Moses sent twelve spies to look at the land God had promised to give His people. Each spy agreed that the land was amazing and filled with all the good things God had promised. But ten of the spies also said giants lived there! They didn't think God could handle giants.

But Joshua and Caleb, the other two spies, saw the situation quite differently. They remembered how God had taken care of His people, and they believed God would keep His goodness going. As a result, only Joshua and Caleb were allowed by God to enter the Promised Land (Numbers 13–14:9, 30).

Do you have any giants in your life? Not the tall-people kind, but situations that seem too big to handle? Turn to God, as Joshua and Caleb did, and think of how He's helped in the past. He is faithful to help you conquer your fears as He strengthens and guides you.

Prayer Pointer

Lord, nothing is too difficult for You to handle. You are my Protector and Provider!

Time Matters

There is a right time for everything.
Everything on earth has its special season.

ECCLESIASTES 3:1

God says we need to make the most of our time here on earth, spending it on what matters most. But life happens so fast, we don't always think about what we're doing with our time. So take a little time now to think about your time—and how well you're spending it.

1. When I come home from school, I typically _____________.
2. Whenever I have to wait in a doctor's office, in the car, wherever, I usually spend the time _____________.
3. The most important things that I can do in life are _____________.
4. The amount of time I spend each day doing the things I just listed above is _____________.
5. In light of what I believe is important, I could make better use of my time by doing _____________.

Prayer Pointer

God, please keep me from wasting time on what doesn't really matter. Help me use the time You've given me for good.

Building Blocks

You are being built into a place where God lives through the Spirit.

EPHESIANS 2:22

NOVEMBER 17

Imagine a big, beautiful house. Everything looks lovely, but when you look closer, you realize the walls are cracked and they're barely connected to the floor—or to each other!

You don't have to be a construction expert to know that a safe, strong house has to have a good foundation with walls and a roof that connect and hold everything up. Otherwise, the whole thing will fall in on itself!

Jesus tells us that He is the builder of His kingdom, and each of us is like a brick in that great kingdom. He's the foundation everything is built on, and His Spirit is the cement sticking us all together.

We weren't made to stand apart from God or other Christians. If we keep to ourselves, we leave a hole where our presence should be. But when we stay in friendship with God and His people, we can better understand His purpose for us. And we become part of a safe, strong fortress where others can clearly see God's love and glory.

PRAYER POINTER — *Glory*

Thank You, God, for making me a part of Your big plan and connecting me with Your people for Your glory.

Star Story

The heavens tell the glory of God. And the skies announce what His hands have made. Day after day they tell the story.

PSALM 19:1–2

Everyone loves to listen to a good story. We like hearing someone tell about another place and time. But it's not just the story itself that's important; the way the storyteller shares the tale brings it to life.

Did you know that the stars tell a story? It's true! The Bible tells us that day after day, night after night, they tell the story of God's glory and His creation. They don't speak out loud or use words we know or make any sound at all. But they have a message to tell, and they share it with the whole world. What's that message? It's simply this: something so grand and so wondrous, something so shining and perfect couldn't have just happened by accident. The universe was perfectly planned, created by the Great Creator. And if He can take care of all those stars, He can certainly take care of you.

Prayer Pointer

Lord, each night as I look up at the stars, help me to listen to their story—the story of You.

Serving One by One

"I am making myself ready to serve."

JOHN 17:19

If someone wanted to be famous today, what do you think she'd do? Run for a political office? Seek out the attention of large crowds? Or spend most of her time with just a few people?

Which of those tactics did Jesus use? The last one! Yes, Jesus wanted the whole world to hear about Him, but He didn't care about being famous. Instead of trying to get everyone to like Him, He chose to teach and train a handful of disciples. By living with them, teaching them, and showing them the power of God, Jesus changed their lives. When He returned to heaven, those men then taught others . . . who taught others . . . who taught others. Like wildfire, the Word of God spread all over the world.

You don't have to be famous to make a difference for Jesus. Pray and share God's love with those around you. Then wait for God to do what only He can—change lives.

Prayer Pointer

Lord, help me focus on doing Your work right where I am.

Out of the Box

Where God's love is, there is no fear, because God's perfect love takes away fear.

1 JOHN 4:18

Every day that you go to school, you follow the same routine. You know what to expect, and that's great—schedules and order make our world feel safer and easier to handle.

But God hasn't called us to feel comfortable all the time. Instead, He wants us to grow in our obedience and trust in His Spirit, and sometimes that means getting out of our comfort zone. That can feel scary, but remember: God can make you brave!

Consider the ideas below and pray about them, asking God if He'd like you to try them. Then ask for the power and bravery to obey!

- Invite someone new to sit with you and your friends at lunch.
- Look for the quiet person who rarely talks in class and strike up a conversation with her.
- In gym class, choose kids who are usually picked last to be on your team.
- Start a prayer club. Invite your class to meet and pray with you.

Prayer Pointer

Lord, please make me brave enough to go where You want me to go and tell others about You.

Great Grandparents

Gray hair is like a crown of honor.
You earn it by living a good life.

PROVERBS 16:31

NOVEMBER 21

Grandparents are great! It's fun to do all kinds of things together: sharing stories, shopping, cooking, fishing—and just hanging out. Grandparents are also great people to learn from. They know lots about life, mostly because they've been busy living it. The next time you have a day out or a phone call with your grandparents, try to find out more about them and their lives. Below are some questions you could ask (and be sure to add your own). You could even record your time together, like an interview. This would be fun to do with the older people at your church too!

- What's your favorite memory from when you were my age?
- What's the best/worst change in the world that you've seen?
- When did you decide to follow God?
- How have you seen God in your life?
- What was your favorite movie as a kid? And now?
- What kind of music did you like growing up? How about now?
- What one piece of advice would you give to me?

Prayer Pointer

Honor

Lord, thank You for blessing me with older, wiser people, like grandparents. Help me to see all that I can learn from them.

Brand-New Style

[The Lord] has covered me with a coat of goodness.

ISAIAH 61:10

Lie: I need to wear the latest brands and styles.

"Mom, I need a new backpack," Emma said.

"Why? We just got you a new backpack a month ago," her mom countered.

"Yeah, but I need the same backpack as the other girls."

"You mean the $100 kind?"

"Um, yeah," Emma huffed. "I don't want to be, like, a nerd or anything."

The Truth Is . . .

God says that true worth comes from your connections (John 15). Unfortunately, a lot of girls think that if they're connected to the popular kids, then they'll have a better life.

But girls were created for a far more important connection: one with God. When you know that God thinks you're awesome and stays by your side no matter what, well, suddenly the need for the latest fashions isn't so important. We don't have to build our self-esteem based on what other people think. Instead, we need to stand on the promise of God's love and show the world a better way to live.

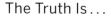

Prayer Pointer

Lord, help me believe You love me, and help me shut out the pressure to be like everyone else.

Loving the Least

Take care of the needs of those who are troubled. Then your light will shine in the darkness.

ISAIAH 58:10

Have you ever had a cold or the flu? People probably didn't want to get too close to you. Back in Jesus' day, the Jews didn't want to be around sick or disabled people either. They were afraid they might "catch" whatever those people had. So for those with long-lasting illnesses, like leprosy, life was miserable. Not only were they sick, but people avoided them and acted as if they were cursed.

When Jesus began His ministry, He didn't avoid the poor and sick; He touched and healed them. He never saw some people as better than others. They were all like lost sheep who needed Him, the Good Shepherd.

When you look at people, what do you see? Are you drawn more to those who look good and are popular? Do you avoid those who don't fit in? Ask Jesus to help you see His beauty in everyone you meet. Then ask Him to make you brave enough to love both the greatest and the least with all your heart.

Prayer Pointer

Lord, help me see the beauty and value in everyone You've made.

Patience Please

Show mercy to others; be kind, humble, gentle, and patient.

COLOSSIANS 3:12

Microwaves help us cook entire meals in minutes. Computers put information from all over the world right at our fingertips the second we need to know it. Fast-food chains, cell phones, cars—you name it—all promise to make whatever we want happen faster.

So how do we feel when what we want doesn't happen right away? We get mad, of course! We huff and stomp our feet and try to force our way, no matter how it affects others. In other words, we are being impatient, the opposite of being patient. What is being patient? It is learning to let God control the schedule, allowing Him time to work in our lives.

Read the following stories, looking for examples of patience and impatience:

"Mom, I need to go to the store right now," Madeline said.

"Honey, I'm making dinner," her mother replied.

"But I have to get those jeans before school tomorrow," Madeline argued.

"Have you saved enough money to buy them?" her mom asked.

"No! But can we just go now anyway, and I'll pay you back later?" Madeline pressed.

"Not right now, honey," came the final reply.

Madeline grunted angrily and stomped off. The whole family had been in the car for what seemed an eternity.

"Are we almost there?" Katelyn asked.

"Another hour," Dad answered.

A minute later Katelyn said, "What about now?"

"About the same," came the reply.

A few minutes passed, and Katelyn started to ask again, but something inside her said not to. She prayed instead, asking God to help her pass the time. Suddenly, she remembered a fun car game and asked her sister to play. The time flew by, and the family reached their destination.

Prayer Pointer

God, sometimes it's *so* difficult to wait for things I want. Help me remember all the blessings You've placed in my life while I wait patiently.

Trading Treasures

"Don't store treasures for yourselves here on earth. . . . Store your treasure in heaven."

MATTHEW 6:19–20

People spend years going to school to become a doctor. It takes a lot of money, hard work, and time, so it would make sense for doctors to work where they'll make the most money, right?

But some doctors don't. Instead, they go to places in poor countries where the people get no medical help, even though those doctors might never get a penny! Why would anyone do that? To live like Jesus.

Jesus left the wonders of heaven to come to earth and save His people. He felt compassion for all the people who were hurting and needed healing, both physically and spiritually. Jesus made Himself poor so that people could be made rich in God.

Whenever we help those who are hurting, we are showing Jesus' love to the world. When you sit beside someone who's lonely to cheer her up, or when you take food to the homeless, you are living like Jesus did. Your actions and love tell the world that Jesus cares for them, and you are building up riches that last—in heaven.

Honor

Prayer Pointer

Jesus, help me care about people the same way You do.

Caught by Pride

God is against the proud, but He gives grace to the humble.

JAMES 4:6

Hope's dad planned a fishing trip for her and her brothers. "Everybody pitch in so that we bring what we need," her dad said. The boys listened to their dad list what they needed, but Hope went into the garage, thinking she already knew what to do.

When they got to the lake, Hope realized she'd left her tackle box at home. But instead of asking her dad for help, she decided she'd figure it out on her own. After thirty minutes trying to find bait, she gave up. By then, her brothers had already landed two keeper-sized bass. Finally, Hope admitted that she needed help, and her dad was happy to give it.

- What do you call an attitude that says, *I don't need your help. I'm smart enough to do this on my own*?
- Read Philippians 2. What kind of attitude does God ask us to wear instead?
- Why do you think it's important to stay humble before God and others?

PRAYER POINTER Glory

God, I'm being prideful whenever I think I'm better than others or that I don't need Your help. I need You for everything!

Birds of a Feather

"Your heavenly Father feeds the birds. And you know that you are worth much more than the birds. You cannot add any time to your life by worrying about it."

MATTHEW 6:26–27

Everything seemed to be spinning out of control. Anna's father had gotten a great new job, but now they were moving. For Anna that meant leaving behind everything she knew and starting over in a new home, a new school, and even a new church. *What if I don't fit in?* she worried. *What if no one likes me?*

Changes—even good changes—can be hard. Jesus understands that. After all, He moved from heaven to earth. Talk about a big change! When you're facing changes, it's easy to let worries and what-ifs take over your thoughts. If that happens, stop and remember the birds. God knows each and every feather on each and every bird. He watches over them and cares for them. And you're much more important than birds to God. So just think of how much more God will care for you!

Prayer Pointer

Lord, when everything is changing, help me remember that You're watching over me—and that's one thing that will never change!

Write It Out

Always give thanks to God the Father for everything, in the name of our Lord Jesus Christ.

EPHESIANS 5:20

God wants us to thank Him for the good things, the not-so-good, and, yes, even the just plain yucky things. How can those not-so-good and even bad things be something to thank God for? Make a list of those things, and put your thankfulness ideas beside each bad thing.

Prayer Pointer

Lord, help me to see Your goodness at work in all things.

NOVEMBER 29

The People-Pleaser Pit

If I wanted to please men, I would not be a servant of Christ.

GALATIANS 1:10

Lie: I need everyone to like me.

Erika's stomach hurt because of stress. Jessica and some other girls wanted her to join them on the soccer team. But God had gifted her better at dance. *If I choose dance instead of soccer, all those girls are going to get mad,* Erika reasoned. *And I don't want to deal with that all year.*

The next day Erika decided to go out for the soccer team. "It's just easier that way," she said.

The Truth Is . . .

We really only need to please one person, and you won't find Him in your yearbook. And the great news is that God is already pleased with you.

God hasn't given you the impossible task of making everyone like you. But He *has* asked you to follow Him and do what He's called you to do. When you seek to please God instead of people, your joy in God will grow, no matter what others may do or say.

Prayer Pointer

Lord, I want to please You with all I say and do. Help me keep my focus on You and not my friends.

All Planned Out

A person may think up plans. But the Lord decides what He will do.

PROVERBS 16:9

Faith had it all planned out. This would be the absolute best day ever! She and her mom were going out to breakfast, just the two of them. Then they were going to pick up her best friend, Alison, and head for the mall. After some serious window shopping, they were going to see that new movie everyone was dying to see. It was going to be great!

And breakfast *was* great, but when they got to Alison's house, everything changed. Alison opened the door in tears. Her grandmother had gotten sick and had to go to the hospital. Alison really didn't feel like going to the mall or the movies, but Faith could see that her friend didn't want to be alone either. Faith was really disappointed. But as she comforted her friend, she could see that this was much more important than her plans for the mall.

When we have everything all planned out, it can be really frustrating when those plans change. But remember: God has a reason, and His plans are always better.

Prayer Pointer

gracie

Lord, when my plans get changed, help me to see how You're working through those changes.

Sparring Siblings

God can give you more blessings than you need.

2 CORINTHIANS 9:8

Jacob and Esau were twin brothers born to Isaac and Rebekah. Since their story is in the Bible, you might think they were a happy family. But you'd be wrong! Jacob and Esau were total opposites. Jacob lied to their father and tricked Isaac into giving him Esau's inheritance. Furious, Esau wanted to kill Jacob (Genesis 27). So much for family togetherness.

These two brothers let greed, lies, and anger separate them. But, over time, God showed that He loved them both and would take care of them. They forgave each other and acted like brothers again (Genesis 33).

Can you think of a friend or family member who has something you want but don't have? If so, tell God about it. Ask God to give it to you too, if it will bring Him glory. But if God doesn't, ask Him to make you content, and be thankful that He always provides everything you need. Be happy for your friend and grateful that God has you covered too.

Prayer Pointer

Lord, help me not be greedy or selfish. I trust You to take care of my needs.

Josiah, Who Repented

How can a young person live a pure life?
He can do it by obeying your word.

PSALM 119:9

King Josiah was crowned at age eight and worked hard to do what was right in God's sight. One day, while workers were repairing God's temple, they discovered the book of the Law. The high priest sent it to Josiah, and Josiah realized just how far God's people had gone from His ways. Josiah tore his robe and cried before God in repentance. Huldah, a prophetess, told Josiah that his tender heart toward God had pleased Him. Though the kingdom of Judah would be destroyed for its sin, Josiah would live in peace and not witness the destruction in his lifetime (2 Kings 22).

God takes sin very seriously because He's a perfect and holy God. Fortunately, we don't have to behave perfectly for God to love us. But we do need to walk in Josiah's footsteps. To know how to honor God, we must study His Word and apply it by obeying Him and repenting with a soft heart whenever we've wandered from the truth.

Prayer Pointer

Father, please create in me a heart that responds to what You say.

Home Helpers

You should do good deeds to be
an example in every way.

TITUS 2:7

Did you know that your parents aren't the only ones who have a job? You do too! You might not get a paycheck, but the character benefits of helping your family are priceless. How good of a helper are you? Take this quiz to find out.

1. Your mom just came home with a car full of groceries. You:
    a. hurry to your room where your mom won't find you.
    b. wait until she brings everything in so you can find the food you wanted.
    c. carry a couple of bags in so you can say you helped.
    d. help carry all the bags inside and put away the items.

2. Your dad is talking with a client on the phone at home. You:
    a. turn up the TV so you can hear it over your dad.
    b. keep running and playing in the same room even after he asks you to be quiet.
    c. keep tugging on his sleeve to get his attention.
    d. get your brothers and sisters to quietly leave the room so he can finish his business in peace.

3. Your sister is struggling with math, which is your best subject. You:
   a. make fun of her for not understanding.
   b. tell her she's on her own because you have homework too.
   c. get frustrated if she still doesn't understand after you explain it.
   d. patiently show her how to do the problem until she gets it.

4. Your aging relatives want your family to visit. You:
   a. ask to go to a friend's house instead.
   b. roll your eyes and moan.
   c. go, but keep your earphones in the whole time.
   d. go, hug them, listen, and answer their questions.

If you answered *D* for every question, congratulations! You're an expert family helper. If you answered *A*, *B*, or *C* for any of the above, ask yourself, "Who am I serving?" Then ask God to help you become a better helper.

Prayer Pointer

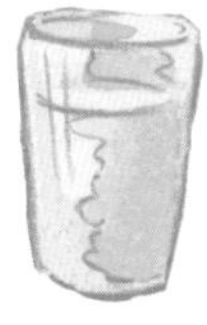

Thank You for my family, God. Help me to be a better helper for them.

Jilting Jealousy

"You must love each other as I have loved you."

JOHN 13:34

Scenario

Avery and Julia have been best friends for as long as Avery could remember. But ever since the new girl, Alyssa, showed up, everything seemed ruined!

"Did you have to invite Alyssa to spend the night with us? Now she thinks she's a part of our group, and she follows us around at school too!" Avery said to Julia.

"I thought you liked her," Julia answered, confused.

"She's nice, but I don't want her stealing your friendship away from me!" Avery snapped back, frustrated.

Julia thought for a moment and put her arm around Avery. "We will always be best friends. But can't we be friends with other people too?"

Solution

Making room for new friends when you already have good ones can be tricky. But Jesus showed us by His example that He was always welcoming new people to be a part of His group, God's family. There's always room for a new friend. In fact, good friendships give us strength and courage to befriend others and share God's love.

PRAYER POINTER — grace

Father, help me be open to new people and friends to help grow Your kingdom.

Making the Team

Some people did accept Him. They believed in Him. To them He gave the right to become children of God.

JOHN 1:12

DECEMBER 5

Andrea worked hard to make the soccer team. She ran every day after school and practiced dribbling and passing for hours in the backyard. On the day of the tryouts, she was a nervous wreck. Would she be good enough? She knew she'd done her best, but would it be enough to earn her a spot on the team?

When it comes to making the team, earning a good grade, or landing the lead in the school play, it all comes down to who's the best choice—which also means that some people aren't considered as good as others. And that can really sting.

But when it comes to God and making His team, there are no tryouts. You don't have to be better than someone else. You don't have to earn God's love; He already thinks you're amazing. You don't have to prove yourself to Him. Just be the person He created you to be. Believe in Jesus and obey Him—and you've got a spot on God's team!

PRAYER POINTER

Lord, I'm so glad I don't have to earn Your love. Thank You for making me a part of Your team.

DECEMBER 6

Turn to Listen

The slap of a friend can be trusted to help you.

PROVERBS 27:6

David had grown from being a simple shepherd boy to king of all Israel. Sadly, he took his eyes off the God he loved, and instead focused them on Bathsheba, a woman he wanted. Worst of all, she was already married to a soldier in David's army. David ordered Bathsheba's husband to be killed during battle, thinking, *Now I can have Bathsheba as my own wife.*

But Nathan, a man of God, came to David. Though it was risky, he told David that God knew what he'd done and was not pleased. David didn't get mad at Nathan. Instead, he was glad Nathan was brave enough to tell the truth and help him repent (2 Samuel 11–12).

Have you ever had a parent or friend tell you that you were doing something wrong? It's not easy to hear, is it? Yet God uses others to help guide us in the right direction. We just have to learn to listen so we can keep growing closer to God and to others around us.

Prayer Pointer

Lord, please help me listen to correction and turn away from doing wrong.

Lady in Waiting

Be strong and brave and wait for the Lord's help.

PSALM 27:14

DECEMBER 7

Sarah handled moving from home like a champ. She even trusted God to take care of her when her husband Abraham gave her some risky instructions. But waiting for a baby? That was tough. Years passed, and she still didn't have a baby. So she panicked and had her maidservant, Hagar, bear a child for her. But that wasn't God's answer.

While Sarah waited, she grew old—like gray-hair-and-rocking-chair old. But one day God sent a messenger to tell her she would have a baby! Her wrinkled face smiled, and then she laughed. *How could a woman my age have a baby?* she thought. But in less than a year, Sarah had baby Isaac (Genesis 21:1–7).

Sarah's story shows us the beauty of waiting on God. Worrying or trying to make things happen the way we want only frustrates us and keeps us from watching God work miracles. When we wait patiently for God to meet our needs, we learn to trust that He will keep His promises.

Prayer Pointer

Lord, help me to be patient and wait for You to lead me.

DECEMBER 8

Bigger Than Big

David said to Him, "You come to me using a sword, a large spear and a small spear. But I come to you in the name of the Lord of Heaven's armies."

1 SAMUEL 17:45

Goliath was bigger than big, huger than huge, the soldier of all soldiers. And David was definitely . . . *not.*

In fact, when David faced Goliath, he wasn't a soldier at all. David was only a shepherd boy. He was just out checking on his brothers. He wasn't even supposed to fight. But David saw that Goliath was a problem, and he also saw that no one else was willing to fix it. So David did what needed to be done. He went out to fight Goliath. But the thing is, he didn't go on his own.

David went in *the name of the Lord.*

He didn't have a shield or a spear, but he had God. And he knew that would be more than enough.

When we face a big problem—a Goliath of a problem—we need to remember who our God is. He's bigger than any problem, and God always fights for us.

Prayer Pointer

Hope

When my problems seem so big, Lord, help me remember that You are always bigger.

Clear the Path

DECEMBER 9

Let us run the race that is before us and never give up. We should remove from our lives anything that would get in the way.

HEBREWS 12:1

Kirsten stretched as she waited for her running coaches to finish clearing off the track. A storm had come through earlier and had left leaves and small branches scattered across the track. Though it was delaying the race, Kirsten was grateful for the coaches. She wanted to run her best race, and she didn't want anything tripping her up and making her fall.

Life is a lot like Kirsten's race. We want to live it the best that we can—in a way that pleases God. But sin can get in our way. It can trip us up and make us fall. So it's important to clear the track. Do certain friends tempt you to do wrong? Then it's time to find new friends. Are people who care about you pointing out songs or TV shows that may be a problem? Let them help you change your focus.

Run your very best race—and don't let sin trip you up!

gracie

Prayer Pointer

Lord, I want to make you proud of the race I run. Help me get rid of anything that might make me trip and fall.

Soft Spot

"I will put a new way to think inside you. I will take out the stubborn heart. . . . And I will give you an obedient heart of flesh."

EZEKIEL 36:26

The armadillo is pretty funny looking. Its back and shoulders are covered with bone and layers of tough skin that form a protective plate. These little creatures rely on that tough outer shell to protect their soft underside. One species even has flexible bands of skin that allow them to roll up in a ball and completely surround themselves with their armored skin.

Some people seem to wear armor like armadillos. If you come across kids who act really tough and are unwilling to let anyone be their friend, chances are they're trying to protect their feelings. They think if they shut out others, they won't get hurt. If someone is acting like an armadillo, don't stop trying to show them they're loved. God can use you to reach past their tough armor and help heal the hurts they feel inside.

Prayer Pointer

Lord, I don't need to shut out others with armor because You protect me. Help me love others who are too afraid to reach out.

Let It Snow

Take away my sin, and I will be clean. Wash me, and I will be whiter than snow.

PSALM 51:7

Last night, your yard looked brown and drab. But this morning, a miracle happened! Beautiful white snow blankets the ground, glistening and reflecting light back into bright blue skies. Here are some facts about snow you might not know:

- Snow isn't really white. It's clear! The way light reflects off it makes it appear white.
- Each snowflake is made up of approximately two hundred ice crystals and has six sides.
- Snow falls approximately three to four miles per hour from the sky.
- Billions of snowflakes fall in an average snowstorm.

So why do you think God gave us snow? Yes, it's perfect for making snowmen. But perhaps God wanted us to see a picture of His love in the snow. God says all of us carry sin in our hearts—dark, ugly sin. But when we admit our sin and ask God to forgive us, He washes us whiter than snow! Our lives then become clean and beautiful, reflecting God's light back into the world.

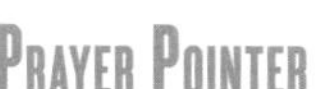

Jesus, thank You for forgiving me and making my heart whiter than snow!

Lunch Rules

When you talk, you should always be kind and wise. Then you will be able to answer everyone in the way you should.

COLOSSIANS 4:6

Everybody loves lunch, right? For some, it's a nice break from class and a time to catch up with friends. But for others, it can be the most stressful part of the day. The "Who will I sit with?" and "What will I say?" questions can get you so uptight that they ruin your appetite. But no need to stress. Just come prepared with these simple conversation tips, and lunchtime will go down easier than ice cream!

Unless your seat is assigned, it can be hard to know where to sit. If you're the first one there, stay toward the middle so you'll have people on all sides to chat with.

Once you've found some people to sit with, follow these guidelines:

Do

- Say hi to the people around you, making sure to mention their names.
- Think of a question to ask that will require them to answer, like "How's the food today?" or "Did anybody watch ____________ last night?"
- Listen for their answer, and ask another question about their answer that will get them to talk more. (For example, "What did you think of how it ended?")

- Volunteer some information about yourself, such as, "I went shopping yesterday" or "I won my soccer game last night." Wait to see if anyone asks you questions about it. If not, offer a few more details. Then change topics if no one seems interested.
- Keep the conversation clean and God-honoring.

Don't

- Talk with your mouth full.
- Gossip about other people.
- Look down at your plate, too afraid to make eye contact. Be brave!
- Keep talking about a topic no one else seems interested in.
- Talk over someone else.

Prayer Pointer

Lord, help me be bold when approaching new faces, and give me courage to make new friends.

Perfect for Him

Let us look only to Jesus. He is the one who began our faith, and He makes our faith perfect.

HEBREWS 12:2

Completely frustrated, Macie grabbed an eraser and started rubbing out her entire sketch.

Her mom noticed and asked, "What's wrong, honey?"

"I just can't get this sketch right," she said, tears starting to fall.

"It looks beautiful to me," her mom reassured.

"But I have to get it perfect. I guess I'm just not good enough to be in the art show."

Have you ever felt as if you had to be perfect? And that if you weren't perfect, people wouldn't like you as much? Did you ever worry that God might love you less if your faith wasn't perfect—if you messed up or had questions about Him? Well, the truth is, no one is perfect. And being perfect is something you never have to worry about with God. He loves you just as you are. He understands that you have questions and that you mess up sometimes. That's why He sent Jesus. Just keep trusting and obeying Him—even when you don't understand—and you'll be perfect for God!

Prayer Pointer

Lord, I want to do my best, but I'm so glad I don't have to be perfect for You.

It's Up to You

This is the day that the Lord has made.
Let us rejoice and be glad today!

PSALM 118:24

DECEMBER 14

Every day you have lots of choices to make. Which clothes should you wear? Which shoes work best with your outfit? Should you put your hair in a ponytail? Then there's breakfast to figure out—and you haven't even left the house yet!

But there's one good choice you can make every morning, even before you even get out of bed. Choose joy. Yep, joy. You see, our days are filled with lots of things—good things, bad things, exciting things, boring things, and thousands of other things in between. And you have to choose how you let those things affect you.

If you choose to focus on the bad, boring, and not-so-great, you'll be miserable. But, if instead, you choose to focus on the good, exciting, and amazing, you'll find something joyful on even the yuckiest of days. Things like how storm clouds can be beautiful and a hug from a friend can make you smile. So when you wake up in the morning, yawn and stretch—and choose joy. After all, it's your choice.

Prayer Pointer

gracie

Lord, I want to choose joy. Open my eyes to see all the joyful things You've placed in my life.

Crabby Habits

Wear God's armor so that you can fight against the devil's evil tricks.

EPHESIANS 6:11

Have you ever waded in the surf, searching for seashells, only to find one with a crab-like creature inside? If so, you've discovered a hermit crab. But did you know that hermit crabs don't grow their own shells? They borrow shells from sea snails. When the hermit crabs outgrow their shells, they *molt*, meaning they switch to larger shells. Until he finds a new shell, the soft hermit crab is vulnerable to predators.

Like hermit crabs, we're vulnerable to our enemy, Satan. But God has given us a "shell" to protect us too: the armor of God. (Read about it in Ephesians 6, where Paul described the belt of truth, breastplate of righteousness, sword of the Spirit, helmet of salvation, shield of faith, and shoes of peace.) As long as we're in the habit of covering ourselves with our armor and fighting the lies of the enemy with the truth of God's Word, we are protected and free to grow and encourage others to put on their special armor too.

Prayer Pointer

Jesus, thank You for giving us the armor of God to help protect us from harm.

Water Wonder

"If a person believes in me, rivers of living water will flow out from his heart."

JOHN 7:38

What would our world be like without water? No oceans, rivers, or lakes. No clouds or rain. Not even a swimming pool! Water also fills all living things. In fact, 50 to 65 percent of our bodies are made of water. Plants and animals are made mostly of water as well. Take away water, and you take away every living thing.

So, yeah, water is *really* important. And it's cool how God keeps it fresh and useful as it cycles from rain to streams to nourishing the earth, evaporating and condensing in clouds to start the cycle again.

Remember when Jesus spoke with a Samaritan woman at Jacob's well (John 4)? She was drawing well water, but Jesus offered her Living Water! He went on to explain that *He* is that Living Water. We need Jesus—even more than water—to fill our lives with His presence so we can grow and live and love the way we were meant to.

Prayer Pointer

Jesus, I need You more than water. Please fill me with Your Spirit so I can truly live.

Queen of Heart

God will make you rich in every way so that you can always give freely. And your giving through us will cause many to give thanks to God.

2 CORINTHIANS 9:11

Things were looking grim for Esther. Her parents were killed, and she was a Jew living in a country that didn't like Jews. But her cousin Mordecai rescued her, raised her as his own daughter, and taught her the ways of God.

When the king needed a new wife, he ordered all the young women to come to court so he could pick a queen. He chose Esther, and she was crowned queen of Persia!

Surrounded by servants and luxuries, Esther could've easily forgotten Mordecai and the other Jews. But she didn't. She risked her own life to save them from imminent death. (Read the whole story in the book of Esther.)

When you're elected to a special club or make a team that your friend didn't, do you stay true to your friendships? Esther's story reminds us that while God may grant us good things, those blessings shouldn't be used for selfish reasons. Use your gifts to love and serve others.

PRAYER POINTER

Lord, help me be humble when I succeed. Show me ways to honor You and bless others with my gifts.

Feeding Greed

DECEMBER 18

A greedy person causes trouble. But the one who trusts the Lord will succeed.

PROVERBS 28:25

My brothers and I normally get along pretty well. But some of my friends don't have it so easy. One friend said she and her sister fight all the time because they both always seem to want what the other person has.

You can see that kind of greedy competition in the story about two brothers named Jacob and Esau (Genesis 27). As the firstborn, Esau would get twice as much inheritance as Jacob would when their father died. But Jacob and his mother didn't like that idea. So they found a way to trick the father into giving Esau's inheritance blessing to Jacob instead. It made Esau so mad that Jacob had to leave home and break his family ties for a long time.

Greed—the kind of competition to get more for yourself—always hurts everyone. Instead of trying to think of all the ways to get what we want, we would do much better to ask God what He wants for us, and trust Him to give it at the right time.

PRAYER POINTER Hope

Lord, I want to serve You and others first, not myself. Help me see ways to be a blessing.

Thinking Power

We capture every thought and make it give up and obey Christ.

2 CORINTHIANS 10:5

What are you doing right now? Okay, reading. But you're also thinking. So think about this: every day, approximately seventy thousand thoughts go through your mind! That number isn't so big when you consider that your brain is made up of more than one hundred billion neurons—each connected by up to ten thousand synapses. Add to that a hundred thousand miles of blood vessels that bring oxygen and nutrients to each of those neurons. Just sitting there thinking, your brain produces enough energy to light up a light bulb. Wow!

With so much thinking going on, we need to make sure we're thinking right and true thoughts. Beautiful thoughts lead to beautiful actions, but ugly thoughts lead to—you guessed it—ugly actions. Learning God's Word and obeying it changes our way of thinking. Whenever wrong thoughts creep in, fight them with God's truth and make them line up with what God says. When we do, our actions will show that we love God with our hearts, souls, *and* minds!

Prayer Pointer

Lord, help me think about things that please You.

Taking Out the Garbage

DECEMBER 20

Put these things out of your life: anger, bad temper, doing or saying things to hurt others . . . evil words.

COLOSSIANS 3:8

Do you have a place where you stash stuff? You know, that stuff you should really just throw away but haven't gotten around to it yet (socks with holes, wadded-up paper, random gum wrappers). Maybe it's your school locker, the back of your closet, or under your bed. It's gross, right? Every once in a while, it feels good to clean out, clear out, and take out the garbage. Then we can use those spaces again.

Sometimes we need to do the same thing to our lives. When we decide to follow Jesus, we commit to taking out the junk: stuff like a short temper, lying, swearing, greed, and getting even. That's the stuff of our old, sinful lives. But Jesus gives us a new life—and there's no room for old ways. Ask Jesus to help you clear out the garbage, and enjoy that new, clean feeling!

Prayer Pointer

Jesus, I'm so thankful that You are making me into a new person. Help me clean out any of my old ways so I can be more like You.

Shine like the Son

Depend on the Lord. Trust Him, and He will take care of you. Then your goodness will shine like the sun.

PSALM 37:5–6

Honor was very upset. She and Amber had been assigned to work together on a history project, but Amber always seemed to have some sort of excuse for why she couldn't come to the library to help. Even on the days she did come, Amber mostly just flipped through the magazines while Honor searched for all the information.

Honor tried talking to her teacher about the problem, but the teacher just said they needed to learn to work things out themselves. In the end, Honor had to do most of the work herself. When the teacher had graded their project, and both Honor and Amber received an *A*. Honor couldn't help feeling frustrated and angry. It just wasn't fair.

Honor's right. That really wasn't fair. But in this world, we'll have to deal with lots of things that aren't fair. Sometimes the cheaters will win, and sometimes the people who choose to do wrong will get more glory than those who try to do right!

So what do we do? How do we handle it? Do we stomp our feet and throw a fit? No, we trust Jesus to somehow work everything out for our good.

Instead of getting upset, we work hard and try to do the right thing, even if the other person doesn't. And then we trust Jesus to

take care of the rest. When we choose to do what's right, no matter what others are doing, people will start to notice. Our integrity makes other people think. Who knows? Maybe when Amber realizes she needs to have better study habits to make good grades, she'll think back about the example Honor set during their project. When we do the right thing, our goodness will shine like the sun—and the Son.

Prayer Pointer

God, sometimes people who don't do what's right seem to win. Help me to trust that You'll always take care of me when I choose to do right.

Fear Not

When I am afraid, I will trust you.

PSALM 56:3

Arachnophobia is the fear of spiders. *Nyctophobia* is fear of the dark. *Glossophobia* is the fear of public speaking. And do you know what *arachibutyrophobia* is? It's the fear of peanut butter sticking to the roof of your mouth! You might laugh, but there's a big, fancy word for every fear—and everybody's afraid of something.

Even the heroes of the Bible were afraid at times. Moses was afraid of Pharaoh, Esther was afraid to go to the king, and all the disciples were afraid when Jesus was arrested. But God was with each and every one of them. He helped Moses face Pharaoh, He helped Esther save her people, and He gave the disciples the courage to come back to Him.

So whether you're afraid of spending the night away from home, standing up to a bully, or even opening the peanut butter jar, God will help you face your fears. It's His promise: "I am with you. Don't be afraid . . . . I will make you strong and will help you" (Isaiah 41:10).

Prayer Pointer

God, You are my Defender, my Protector, my Fortress and my Shield. I will trust You to help me when I'm afraid.

Step Up or Skip Out?

DECEMBER 23

I want to do the things that are good. But I do not do them. I do not do the good things that I want to do. I do the bad things that I do not want to do.

ROMANS 7:18–19

When your youth group leader asks for volunteers to clean up after the church dinner, you know you should volunteer . . . but you don't.

You know you should let your little brother have a turn with your new video game . . . but you don't.

Your mom's folding the laundry, and you know you should help . . . but you slip off to your room instead.

So many times we know the right thing to do, but we still don't do it. Why? Because we're human. It's a struggle to put aside our selfish wants and do what's best for others. God understands, and He doesn't leave us to struggle alone. He promises to help us do the right thing. So take a deep breath, say a little prayer, and go back and do the right thing! Stepping up when we don't feel like it makes us stronger, and it's a mark of real grown-up maturity.

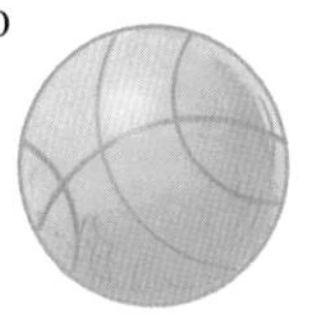

Prayer Pointer

Glory

Lord, help me to do what's right, even when it's hard!

Seeing Jesus

"You will help the blind to see."

ISAIAH 42:7

He was outside the city gate, probably begging for money, when he heard Jesus passing by. Immediately, the blind man called out, "Jesus, Son of David, please help me!" (Mark 10:47). Everyone around him tried to quiet him, but he just yelled louder. He wanted Jesus to hear him and heal him from the blindness he had suffered since he was born.

"What do you want?" Jesus asked him. The blind man wanted to see. So Jesus healed him! Everybody was excited—except the Pharisees. When the crowd took the man to the Pharisees, they accused him of lying. They even got his parents to come and explain how their son could have been born blind but could now see.

Filled with courage, the blind man told them plainly that Jesus was from God and that He was the One who healed him, even though it made the Pharisees angry. Then he worshipped Jesus! Now that's some serious truth-telling. May we be just as bold in telling people what a difference Jesus has made in our lives!

Prayer Pointer

Lord, help me see the truth of Your Word and share it with others.

Save the Best for First

The thing you should want most is God's kingdom and doing what God wants.

MATTHEW 6:33

You've probably heard the old saying, "Save the best for last." It's like a movie when they save the most exciting scene for the end, or a fireworks show when they save the biggest and best rockets for the big finale. Or it could be like a runner who saves her energy for that extra burst of speed at the finish line.

When it comes to movies, fireworks, or races, there's nothing wrong with saving the best for last. But it's wrong to save the best for last when it comes to God.

God doesn't want to be last on our list. He wants our first *and* our best. So when you pray, don't wait until you're so tired you can't even finish your prayer. And when it's time to give, don't give God whatever is left over after you buy everything you want. Give to God first—your money, your time, and your prayers. Because God wants us to save our best for Him first.

Prayer Pointer

Lord, I want to put You first in my life. Show me how I can do this better.

DECEMBER 26

Security Check

Lord God, you are my hope. I have
trusted you since I was young.

PSALM 71:5

Have you ever been through a security check at the airport? Scanners look over you and your things to make sure you're not carrying something you shouldn't. Well, this quiz isn't that kind of scanner. It's a test to see where you place your security—or confidence—in life. Are you carrying attitudes and ideas that you shouldn't, or are you able to freely walk through life being the person God made you to be?

1. When you look in the mirror, you:
   a. don't like what you see.
   b. do like what you see.

2. When you are at church, you:
   a. watch everybody else to see what they're wearing and if your clothes fit in.
   b. greet everyone with love and concentrate on learning about God together.

3. When an adult asks you a question about yourself, you:
   a. tend to look down and only give short or one-word answers.
   b. look them in the eye and answer honestly and thoroughly.

4. When your pastor says, "God loves you," you:
    a. think it applies to everyone else except you.
    b. feel grateful and love God back.

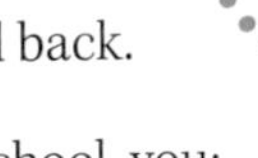

5. When you see a new girl at school, you:
    a. avoid talking to her because she might not like you.
    b. go over and talk to her so she'll feel better about the new school.

If you answered mostly *A*s, then you're carrying extra baggage that you can throw away. God wants you to feel good about yourself and what you have to offer the world. Always remember that God lives inside you and will help you be the person He created you to be. If you answered mostly *B*s, you've passed with flying colors. You understand that God not only loves you, He likes you—a fact that makes you beautifully confident in Him.

Prayer Pointer

God, help me to see that all those wonderful promises in Your Word aren't just for other people—they're for me too!

Talk About Ants

Go watch the ants, you lazy person.
Watch what they do and be wise.

PROVERBS 6:6

If you could talk to an ant, what would you say? Would you ask it what it's up to, or tell it to build its colony somewhere else? Unfortunately, you don't have the special *pheromones* (body chemicals) that ants have. These unseen but very powerful chemicals help ants "talk" to each other. Messages like "I've found food" or "Attack the intruder" can spread rapidly throughout the colony. Then the ants all work together to achieve their goal.

Learning to communicate well is important for humans too. The look on your face, the tone of your voice, and the words you say all communicate what you're thinking and feeling. If you want to pull people together for a common goal, you have to learn how to speak so they'll understand—and how to treat them so they'll want to join you. Talk to others in a way that shows they're important to you. Look in their eyes, be encouraging, and listen carefully. By supporting and learning from one another, your group of friends will grow stronger, as will your power to do good.

Prayer Pointer

Lord, thank You for using something as small as an ant to show me a better way to live.

Write It Out

The Lord is good. His love continues forever.

2 CHRONICLES 5:13

God is so good, and He loves us so much. He blesses us zillions of times every day as proof of His love—with things like sunrises, wildflowers, families, and best friends. Make a list of all the ways you see God, His goodness, and His love. And don't stop here when you run out of room. Can you list fifty blessings, a hundred, or more?

Prayer Pointer

Lord, Your love is all around me. Thank You for helping me see it!

Better Sweet

Your promises are so sweet to me.
They are like honey to my mouth!

PSALM 119:103

Chocolate. Just the word brings to mind sweet thoughts of delicious candy and cookies. All over the world, almost everyone loves the curious, dark delight. But where does it come from?

Believe it or not, chocolate grows on trees in large, ridged pods that grow directly out of the trunk of the *Theobroma cacao* tree. People harvest these pods and remove the seeds inside them—little beans that taste absolutely horrible right out of the pod. Workers process and dry the beans. Then they are sent to factories that grind them and combine them with a lot of sugar to create that wonderful chocolate taste you love!

Did you know that people can be like the chocolate bean? By themselves, they aren't always very pleasant to be around and may make you want to leave them alone. But instead, try praying for them. God is able to change any heart so that others can taste and see how good He is.

Prayer Pointer

Father, help me pray for others and share with them the sweetness of Your friendship.

Take It Down a Notch

Your beauty should come from within you—
the beauty of a gentle and quiet spirit. . . .
[That] is worth very much to God.

1 PETER 3:4

Some people just naturally seem to have a quiet spirit. Nothing appears to make them angry or upset. But others of us aren't wired that way. When things don't go according to our plan, we can explode in frustration or anger. So how can Jesus want *all* of us to have a gentle and quiet spirit? It's because Jesus isn't asking us to change our personalities. He just wants us to let His Spirit rule over them!

A gentle and quiet spirit is someone who has learned to obey God by loving Him and others, no matter how talkative or quiet he or she is naturally. God will help all of us live in a way that honors Him. We just need to ask Him to show us where our spirit is getting too loud (telling God what we're going to do) and help us "take it down a notch" (choosing to obey God's Spirit instead).

Prayer Pointer

Lord, please create in me the gentle and quiet spirit that is worth so much to You.

DECEMBER 31

Do What You Can Do

"This woman did the only thing she could do for me. She poured perfume on my body. She did this before I die to prepare me for burial."

MARK 14:8

J*esus has done so many amazing things,* the woman thought. *He has stilled storms. He has healed the blind and the sick, and He has raised people from the dead. He has even taken away my sins. What can I possibly do for Him?*

What that long ago woman did was break open a bottle of perfume and pour it over Him. She couldn't stop the Pharisees from hating Him, and she couldn't stop Him from going to the cross. But she could love Him and worship Him. So she did what she could do.

The Lord has done so much for us too. He's loved us, cared for us, and taken away our sins. What can we do for Him? We can love Him, and we can worship Him. We can praise Him for who He is and for all that He has done. So be brave, and go and do what you can do! God's going to love it.

PRAYER POINTER — gracie

Lord, I want to live my life praising You. Thank You for all You do for me, each and every day.

Brave Verses

Be strong. Let us fight bravely for our people and for the cities of our God. The Lord will do what he decides is right.

2 SAMUEL 10:12

All you who put your hope in the Lord be strong and brave.

PSALM 31:24

She is strong and is respected by the people. She looks forward to the future with joy.

PROVERBS 31:25

Watch, stand fast in the faith, be brave, be strong.

1 CORINTHIANS 16:13 NKJV

Finally, be strong in the Lord and in his great power. 11 Wear the full armor of God. Wear God's armor so that you can fight against the devil's evil tricks.

EPHESIANS 6:10–11

Brave Girls is a brand from Tommy Nelson

that strives to pour the love and truth of God's Word into the lives of young girls, equipping them with the knowledge they need to grow into young women who are confident in Christ.

BRAVE GIRLS BIBLE STORIES

Learn the Bible alongside the Brave Girls, who are just like you! Each devotion begins with an introduction from a Brave Girl, dives into a story about a brave (or not-so-brave) woman of the Bible, and closes with some insight from the Brave Girl character.

BRAVE GIRLS DEVOTIONALS: BETTER THAN PERFECT, FAITHFUL FRIENDS, AND BEAUTIFUL YOU

The Brave Girls are back! These three 90-day devotionals let readers learn more about the lives of the Brave Girls and how they tackle important issues like being a good friend, knowing God loves you no matter what, and loving yourself just as God made you.

BRAVE GIRLS BIBLE

This beautifully illustrated, two-color, expanded-content ICB study Bible features characters from the Brave Girls brand who are eager to teach readers about the Word of God and how they can apply the Bible to their everyday lives.